THE HISTORY MAKERS

THE HISTORY MAKERS

ADVENTURES IN NEW ZEALAND BIOGRAPHY

VAUGHAN YARWOOD

RANDOM HOUSE
NEW ZEALAND

To Theo and Elaïs

National Library of New Zealand Cataloguing-in-Publication Data

Yarwood, Vaughan.
The history makers: adventures in New Zealand biography/Vaughan Yarwood.
Includes bibliographical references.
ISBN 1-86941-541-8
1. New Zealand—Biography. I. Title.
920.093—dc 21

A RANDOM HOUSE BOOK
published by
Random House New Zealand
18 Poland Road, Glenfield, Auckland, New Zealand
www.randomhouse.co.nz

First published 2002

ISBN 1 86941 541 8

Design and production: Kate Greenaway
Cover illustrations: refer to credits on p.254
Cover design: Matthew Trbuhovic
Printed in China

Contents

Introduction

That quintessential historian Edward Gibbon conceived of history as a record of events suffused by what might be called the wonder of people. My favourite American historian, Daniel Boorstin, subscribes to much the same thing. In the introduction to a collection of his own work, he declared: 'Wary of dogmas, ideologies and other skeleton keys to human experience, I have focused on people and their mysteries, not forgetting that the historian himself is part of the story.'

I find it a congenial approach. Narrative drive, human mystery and a sense of connectedness, after all, are at the heart of vital history writing.

The ten biographical essays in this book attempt to engage with the past through the lives and enthusiasms of a diverse group of New Zealanders. The interests and endeavours of these men and women range from aviation to politics, from ecology to religious ministry. Some were active in the colonial era while others are vigorously alive today. Several devoted themselves to a single goal or an overriding ambition; others applied their energies to a range of pursuits over a lifetime. One way or another all have left their mark and collectively they demonstrate that interesting people have this in common: the gift for turning their lives into stories.

The book's subtitle, 'Adventures in New Zealand Biography', points to a distinguishing feature of the essays: they are records of very personal forays into the country's past. Whether trapped by a raging storm at Guthrie-Smith's Tutira station in Hawke's Bay or soaring over Waitohi in a microlight piloted by a descendant of Richard Pearse, I have sought a meeting with these individuals on their own terms (or, at least, on their home turf).

Often a physical journey has been at the core of the experience, as when I trekked to Tengboche monastery in the Himalayas while tracing the footsteps of Edmund Hillary. At other times, as with poet James K. Baxter, the journey has essentially been an inward one, following a path through self-doubt to renewal.

Seven of the essays first appeared in *New Zealand Geographic*, to which have been added three new pieces — on Jean Batten, Suzanne Aubert and James K. Baxter — written specifically for the book.

My intention was not to assemble a definitive list of notable New Zealanders, but rather to offer a stimulating sampler from the spectrum of human experience. The varied origins and subjects of the pieces lend the collection a sense of accidental grouping. In giving them a shared space, I wanted to evoke the attachment to place, the significance of the particular and the atmosphere of intimacy and random collision which pervade snapshot albums.

I also wanted to suggest ways in which the past can be inhabited, or at least fashioned into something more substantial, more enlightening, than mere rumour or a skein of irredeemably remote events.

Though the essays incorporate recent scholarship, and in some cases present the findings of new research, I have resisted the temptation to insert footnotes where none originally appeared. To signal the provisional and time-bound nature of biography itself, I have noted the writing dates of the individual pieces.

In this context it should be said that, although a great deal of care has been taken to verify facts and correct the errors of earlier writers, objective truth has at times proved elusive. I alluded to this in a short postscript to the original essay on Felix von Luckner and, as it is somewhat salutary, I will risk repeating it.

This is what I wrote:

> The higher a person is elevated toward the heroic, the more slippery and unstable the base of facts seems to become. With the passing of time, exploits are amplified into legend. Contradictions multiply and kaleidoscope.
>
> So it was with Count von Luckner, a naval adventurer who flamboyantly rebelled against grey conformity; a salty colossus whose every gesture appeared to be a magnification of common life.

For some events we have only von Luckner's highly coloured retelling. For others we have the accounts of historical witnesses or chroniclers such as the American broadcaster and writer Lowell Thomas.

Every detail surrounding the Count, it seems, is open to alternatives. It is as though we are watching a movie with all the out-takes edited in. Among them . . .

His ship, the *Seeadler*, had one 1500 horsepower engine. It had two 500 horsepower engines. Two 1200 horsepower engines. It weighed 1571 tons. It weighed 2000 tons. 5000 tons. He destroyed seventeen Allied ships. Fourteen ships. Fifteen.

The *Seeadler* itself was wrecked by a tidal wave. By heavy seas when at anchor. When careened.

A shot was fired across the bow of the scow on which he escaped, said the Count and a host of others. It was fired across the scow's stern, due to an obstructing anchor on the pursuing vessel, says a diary kept against regulations, and concealed in the butt-trap of a gunner's rifle.

Von Luckner claimed, via Lowell Thomas's biography, to have escaped from Motuihe by setting fire to a barracks and slipping away in the ensuing confusion. Other accounts have endlessly repeated the story, yet soldiers on Motuihe made no mention of such a fire. After his recapture, von Luckner said he had devised several untried escape plans, among them torching a building, but that the end of the war stopped any being put into practice.

Finally, at the age of 84 the Count died. He died again the following year. He died in Sweden, the homeland of his wife. He died in Hamburg, Germany.

He lives on in New Zealand.

I first learned of the swashbuckling and piratical von Luckner on a childhood visit to Motuihe Island in the Hauraki Gulf where he had been for a time imprisoned. This and the fact that New Zealand took him to heart persuaded me to make room for him in these pages.

Likewise, I have shown an unfashionable interest in the doings of George Grey, a towering, Tolstoyan figure who has become a whipping-boy for all manner of discontent with the country's colonial past.

Other, less whimsically chosen, subjects have often produced satisfying coincidences. For instance, the earliest biographical essay here — a 1993 piece on palaeontologist Joan Wiffen — mentioned Arthur Conan Doyle's novel *The Lost World*, a high-voltage yarn about the imagined discovery of living dinosaurs in a remote corner of South America. Shortly after *New*

Zealand Geographic ran the piece, I heard that the BBC intended filming a version of Doyle's book in Rotorua, not far from the valley in the Urewera ranges where Wiffen first found evidence of dinosaurs in New Zealand.

A remarkably resourceful and energetic fieldworker, Wiffen followed the career path of Amy Hodgson, a self-taught botanist who was also active in Hawke's Bay. Like Wiffen, Hodgson fitted in her interest around the demands of raising a family and running a household, winning respect for her discoveries (she specialised in liverworts) through hard toil and dedication.

Such echoes and symmetries are the very stuff of history. They also hint at the richness of New Zealand's past. In biographical terms, a myriad doors are yet to be opened — as *The Dictionary of New Zealand Biography* has proved. The final chapter of this book, which deals with the ongoing dictionary project, is intended to suggest, in the manner of an infinitely extending hall of mirrors, the endless possibilities, the abundant affirmations of life, generated by 'people and their mysteries'.

Needless to say, over the years during which these essays were written I have received help and encouragement from a great many people. In particular, I would like to thank John Gully for his unstinting support in Nepal and the Asia 2000 Foundation for making available a grant towards the trip. Claudia Orange and her colleagues at *The Dictionary of New Zealand Biography* were patient and helpful beyond the call of duty. The Sisters of Compassion at Jerusalem and Island Bay were warm-hearted hosts and willingly made available the archives of the Home of Compassion. Gordon Ogilvie, Richard Pearse's biographer, generously shared the fruits of his research and checked the finished article, while Richard Warne Pearse, Jeffrey Pearse and Evan Gardner helped illuminate the life of their extraordinary forebear. Joan Wiffen and her team took time out from busy lives to introduce me to their palaeontological work in the remote Te Hoe valley. Donald Kerr, printed collections librarian at Auckland City Libraries, made available original manuscripts and willingly shared his knowledge of George Grey. Station manager Steve Reiri and his partner Margaret greatly increased the pleasure of my stay at Tutira, while Gretchen Absolom kindly gave me unrestricted access to the papers, books and photographic plates of Herbert Guthrie-Smith. My thanks also to Roger Hickin and Jennifer Barrer for sharing their recollections of James K. Baxter and helpfully commenting on the finished typescript, and to Jacquie Sturm for permission to reproduce extracts from Baxter's poetry. I must also acknowledge the unflagging support of *New Zealand Geographic* editor Kennedy Warne, who continues to greet story suggestions with unwarranted enthusiasm. Jane Connor at Random House was from the start a champion of *The History Makers* and following her departure Tom Beran has skilfully guided the book through to completion. Finally, I must record my debt to all those writers whose research I have drawn on. Their most significant works are listed at the end of this book.

The Governor's Island: A Life of George Grey

It was late on a calm autumn evening in 1885 when, at the end of its 50-kilometre run, the weekly steamer from Auckland parted company with the red-sailed fishing boats drifting lazily homeward and cleared the headland of Kawau Island.

At the rail as the steamer nudged into Momona Bay was Englishman James Froude, the close friend and biographer of Thomas Carlyle and himself a hugely popular historian and essayist. Fresh from the heated mud of Rotorua, and on the last leg of an antipodean tour in the company of his son and a friend, the well-travelled writer carried letters of introduction to governors and cabinet ministers. He needed none. As the most celebrated intellectual to visit New Zealand in the second half of the nineteenth century, Froude found every door open. He was followed by crowds, feted by the powerful, and lionised by the press.

Yet Froude had forsaken visiting Dunedin and Christchurch, the seat of government and the Southern Alps, Lake Manapouri and Lake Wakatipu, to be here in this remote, deeply wooded inlet; to spend time in the company of someone he considered the most interesting person in the country — a man who was leading a 'Robinson Crusoe kind of existence' on a solitary island in the Hauraki Gulf.

As Froude scoured the approaching jetty, his eyes found what they were searching for. Standing at the end of the pier, framed by his imposing two-storeyed house and parklike grounds, was a frail, white-haired man of 73 — Sir George Grey.

The fourteen years since their meeting in London had visibly aged this singular man, a former governor of three nations and New Zealand premier, a man who, more than anyone, had stamped his mark on the colony and moulded its destiny. His piercing blue eyes had lost some of their colour, his once-elastic gait had stiffened, and his movements were hesitant. Yet Froude, himself a lean 66-year-old, was to find Grey's voice clear still, his mind agile and his memory sharp.

Alongside Grey stood William Aldis, professor of mathematics at Auckland University College, and his wife. They were just two among an endless stream of distinguished guests who over the years had been moved to seek out Grey's company on this island retreat.

'From Ohinemutu and its tourists, from the Auckland Club and its politicians, we had passed into an atmosphere of intellect, culture, science, and the mellow experience of statesmanship,' Froude was later to write.

Entering George Grey's kauri-lined drawing room, he discovered a veritable treasure-house. The walls were hung with oil paintings and steel engravings. Greenstone mere formed decorative patterns with Aboriginal

boomerangs and assegais and shields from Africa. Cabinets of curiosities stood beside loaded bookcases and tables stacked with London quarterlies and weeklies only a month or two old. Froude was impressed: 'Every important movement in domestic, foreign, or colonial politics could be studied as exhaustively at Kawau as in the reading-room at the Athenæum.'

That first night, perhaps in deference to his new guest's literary interests, Grey produced some of the jewels in his rambling collection: a fourteenth-century French illuminated manuscript, a twelfth-century Greek volume of the four gospels presumed to be from Mount Athos, early editions of Geoffrey Chaucer and William Blake, biblical texts in Maori by Colenso and Yate.

The next morning Froude swam and then dined on homemade bread, cream and mullet, 'silvery as salmon and almost as good', that he had earlier seen Grey's men haul from the bay with a seine-net.

He then took in the surrounding gardens, temperate as any in southern Italy and perfumed with orange blossom, citron and stephanotis. Scattered informally about the grounds were rare flowering shrubs from South America and Japan. In Grey's earthly paradise grew magnolias, Brazilian palms and Indian rhododendrons, the coral tree and the Moreton Bay fig. On the shore stood massive pohutukawa, their lower boughs encrusted with oysters, while further up the valley and on the flanking hillsides a bewildering variety of exotics flourished alongside native kauri and rata. There were Indian deodars, oaks and elms from England, South African silver firs, red gums, wattles and blue jacarandas from across the Tasman, Mediterranean oleanders and walnut, Fijian spider lilies, bamboos and bougainvillea.

Surveying the groves of laurel and bay in the grounds, the pines 80 and 100 feet high and the immense stand of cedars, Froude was struck by their collective beauty. 'No landscape gardener could have spread his plantations with better art than Sir George,' he wrote.

As to the catalogue of animals that had made a home there, it almost defied belief. Indian peacocks strutted across the well-tended lawns while Chinese pheasants, emu, turkeys, guinea fowl and Californian quail went about their business. Rosella parakeets flashed in the greenery and kookaburras added a discordant note from the treetops. Less obvious were the larger and more wary creatures — the wild hogs and elk, the Cape sheep, antelopes and wapiti, the kangaroos, possums and wallabies. Though his zebras, imported at great expense, had died shortly after arriving, monkeys thrived, taking a special interest in the fruit of the Chilean wine palm that grew near Sir George's house.

Kawau impressed itself on Froude as a tranquil province of learning and refinement, an idyllic kingdom created by a towering statesman now in his sunset years, a well-loved patriarch surrounded by servants — gardeners, shepherds, household help — and one who had earned a degree of loyalty uncommon in the fiercely democratic colony.

The Aldises soon returned to Auckland, and Froude's son and their companion headed inland with the keepers to shoot wallaby — a thing hateful to Sir George, but necessary to hold the island's vigorous marsupial population in check. Froude seized on the chance to take the air with his host, discussing Carlyle, whom Grey had known in England, and mulling over the plight of the Boers in South Africa. Grey had 25 years earlier been governor of the Cape Colony and had come to admire the hardy and independent Dutch farmers. Like Froude, he deplored their poor treatment at the hands of the British.

Froude the historian, who distrusted universal suffrage for its tendency to encourage what today would be called the 'dumbing down' of politics, must have objected to Grey's passionate determination to help create a truly egalitarian society. But in other ways — in their love of nature, their attachment to the British Empire, their Anglo-Irish ancestry and their strong Christian faith — they found much common ground.

In advanced age, as in his prime, Grey was buoyed by an unshakeable faith in Providence and by a simple evangelical piety. He said grace before all meals and held a Sunday service for staff in his wood-panelled drawing room. His religion was that of a man to whom duty was the highest good. He radiated the calm of a person no longer plunged into the fray of things, yet often had pressing matters to attend to — and, as ever, when persuasion failed, he usually won arguments by thorough preparation, by a mastery of detail his opponent had ignored.

So, while Grey pored over his facts, Froude was left to occupy himself — by hooking sharks, sketching or exploring the library. Froude, with the help of Grey's boatmen, was perhaps most successful on the water. Once the three of them caught and clubbed 29 sharks in two hours. 'Their livers are full of oil, and our afternoon's sport was worth three or four pounds to the men,' wrote Froude. 'But it was not a beautiful operation, and a single experience was enough.'

That was not the case with the visit itself, which he was to remember as one of the most interesting times in his life. In the 1886 account of his travels, *Oceana* — a runaway bestseller, with 75,000 copies sold in six months

— Froude devoted one adulatory chapter and two of the volume's nine illustrations to Kawau and Sir George.

Yet life on Kawau, regulated though it was by the soothing rhythms of nature, by the weekly arrival of mail and official despatches, and by urbane conversation and uplifting pursuits, was not entirely what it seemed.

Froude had come in the twilight of the life of one of New Zealand's most remarkable, and perhaps most impenetrable, nineteenth-century figures. Soldier, humanitarian, administrator, explorer, champion of the poor, favourite of Queen Victoria and longtime friend of the Maori — a person who, more than any, could be said to have been the architect of the nation — Grey had reached the bitter end of his political career: an outcast, beached by history. Stubborn, energetic, audacious, wilful and often a brilliantly effective leader, he had worn himself out in unflagging service on behalf of the country and his beloved monarch.

Changing times demanded different hands at the helm, people more used to constraint and less animated by an uncompromising idealism. Grey — who had once, famously, told the commander of British Imperial troops in New Zealand that he regarded Colonial Office orders as no more than 'general indications of a line of policy to be pursued' — was now out of step and out of favour. 'A rogue elephant in the political jungle,' one biographer called him. Seven years had passed since he had been forced to resign as premier and now, a mere opposition MP, he had little public influence and no followers.

Distanced from his estranged wife for quarter of a century, and separated now also from his niece and her family of nine children who had long coloured his days, he lingered on at Kawau with a remnant of his former staff and in a house now fallen silent.

Dogged by ill health and visited often by moods of black depression, he was not long to remain in paradise. The books that Froude so admired had already been gifted to the citizens of Auckland, and the following year would be crated up and shipped to their new home in the Auckland City Library.

Within two years Grey would sell Kawau and follow his books to the city. Then a curtain would fall over the clipped lawns and unkempt wild places, over stately architecture and the riotous excess of exotic species.

The life of the man described as one of the greatest figures in the colonial history of Empire began on a tragic note. Eight days before his birth on 14 April 1812, in Lisbon, his father, a British army officer, was killed at the

storming of Badajoz.

Early on, Grey showed a trademark impatience with the discipline and confinement of school life and with a classical syllabus he felt was railroading him towards university learning and a cloistered profession. He rebelled, and entered the Royal Military Academy at Sandhurst. At eighteen, he graduated and went to serve in Ireland.

His job there was to collect tithes from a resentful and suffering population, at the point of a sword if necessary. The experience affected Grey profoundly. Instead of being a stepping stone to a military career, it awakened in him a lifelong desire to serve common humanity. 'I saw enough there to give a bias to my mind for ever as to the necessity for change and reform,' he wrote. 'It was really from a desire to find relief for that misery that I went to Australia. In all my walks on deck, on my first voyage, my mind was filled with the thought of what misery there was in the world.'

With Royal Geographical Society support, he had engineered British government backing for an expedition to north-western Australia, where he hoped to find a sizeable river system and so encourage settlement in the vast open interior. There, freed from Old World ills and injustices, the downtrodden poor could be given a new life.

Grey set out from England in 1837 as the Victorian age dawned — his ship, the sloop HMS *Beagle,* had lain provisioned and ready at Plymouth the day Victoria came to the throne. The hard-working *Beagle* had just the previous year returned from Darwin's ground-breaking five-year voyage, and Grey, who later befriended Darwin, used the naturalist's cabin on the first leg of his own journey of discovery.

The expedition, ill-conceived and poorly equipped, was not a success, but it highlighted Grey's leadership qualities. One incident threw these into relief. Less than two weeks into their trek, and away from the main party, he and two others were ambushed by Aborigines. Grey fired shots into the air, to no effect. Advancing, he was struck almost simultaneously by three spears, one wounding him badly in the leg.

'As I fell, I heard the savage yells of the native's delight and triumph,' wrote Grey of the incident. 'These recalled me to myself, and, roused by momentary rage and indignation, I made a strong effort . . . The spear was wrenched from my wound, and my haversack drawn closely over it, that neither my own party nor the natives might see it, and I advanced again steadily to the rock.'

Grey shot his attacker dead, and suddenly the fight was over. In stunned silence, the Aborigines withdrew. He had saved the others, but at the cost of killing, for the first and only time in his life, a fellow human. 'I already felt deeply the death of him I had been compelled to shoot,' Grey recorded in his journal. 'And I believe that when a fellow-creature falls by one's hand . . . it is impossible not to sincerely regret the force of so cruel a necessity.'

For another month, in the heat of Western Australia, Grey pressed on with his party, taking laudanum to dull the pain of a wound that was to trouble him all his life. It was to no avail and, to avoid killing himself through lack of proper treatment, he was forced to call off the expedition.

Neither in this nor in a second attempt months later did he discover a suitable river. But his report, notable for its descriptions of wildlife and of the life and language of the Aborigines, and especially for its discussion of colonisation and the treatment of indigenous peoples, alerted the Colonial Office to his abilities.

In 1840, after a spell as resident magistrate at Albany near Perth, and when still just 28 years old, he was appointed governor of a bankrupt South Australia. He set about fixing the troubled colony with an audacity and confidence that even now seems scarcely credible. By cutting spending, discouraging land speculation and helping farmers, he brought stability and, little by little, prosperity. His measures were tough and, to begin with, unpopular — 'Dismal Jimmy' Allen's *Southern Star* newspaper carried on every issue the line from Shakespeare's *Richard III*: 'Think upon *GREY* and let thy soul despair' — but they worked. Wheat farming and the discovery of lead and copper quickly brought economic success to the temperately managed young colony.

Lord John Russell summed up the gratitude felt towards Grey by both the settlers and the Colonial Office: 'In giving him the government of South Australia I gave him as difficult a problem in Colonial Government as could be committed to any man . . . he has solved the problem with a degree of energy and success which I could hardly have expected from any man.'

In June 1845, while riding near Adelaide with his stepbrother, Grey was waylaid by a messenger and handed a despatch from England. The situation across the Tasman had got away from Robert FitzRoy, the former captain of the *Beagle* on Darwin's voyage and now the Crown's representative in New Zealand. Grey was to be appointed lieutenant governor of the colony in his place. Grasping the moment, he wound up his official business in Australia and, gathering up what money he could from Adelaide's treasury, sailed for Auckland.

On arrival, Grey found everything in confusion. Poor FitzRoy, out of favour with settlers and missionaries alike, had an empty till and no policy worth talking about. War flared here and there through the country, with militant Maori becoming more confident with each success and less willing to talk peace with Pakeha newcomers, whom they still outnumbered by more than ten to one.

Reluctant, as always, to rely on second-hand reports and the advice of others, Grey left town to parlay directly with Maori. He reassured them that their lands were safe, but declared he would not tolerate neutrality among the chiefs. They must choose where they stood: with Britain or with the rebels.

Returning to Auckland, he then led troops and friendly Maori north to lay siege to Kawiti's formidable pa, Ruapekapeka — the 'bat's nest'. After weeks of hacking tracks and hauling artillery through dense and rugged country, they bombarded the pa and ousted its wily defender. Though the British proclaimed it a great victory, the battle did little to subdue disgruntled Maori. Instead, by not confiscating land, by fair dealings in his government land purchases and by an instinctive empathy (he never resurrected the irksome flagstaff at Kororareka), Grey won the support and friendship of the chiefs through diplomacy.

This first posting in New Zealand was, in many ways, the high-water mark of his career, and the many taonga given to him throughout his life bore witness to his mana among Maori. When at the end of his governorship in 1853 he left for England, the Otaki chiefs expressed their sorrow: 'Forget us not; keep us in mind frequently. Look back upon us, and in kindness remember us.' 'Friend, do not persist in going hence,' said Rotorua Maori. 'Turn and reside amongst us.'

The autumn morning I set out for Kawau — just a few weeks more advanced in the season than Froude had been — the weather is crisp and clear. It is not yet eight, but even from Sandspit wharf the island, nine kilometres out, is sharply defined against the pewter plate of the sea. The ferry's only other passenger is Rita Duytshoff, a Department of Conservation officer on her way to Mansion House, Grey's former home. As the elegant residence swings into view around the point, wedding-cake white amid the trees, Rita gathers her things together. Manager of the DoC-administered historic building for eighteen years, she has spent more time in the house as Grey knew it than anyone — Grey included.

We step ashore to a scene that would not have been unfamiliar to Grey, though east of the old wharf the sea has chewed back the beach five paces, and his mighty Kaffirboom tree, said to have been the largest in the world until reduced to a stump by Cyclone Bola, is just a mass of thorny regrowth.

I draw attention to what is the most obvious change since Grey's time — the ornate two-storeyed veil of a verandah, added by Eliza Thomson in 1888, the year she bought the island from him. Should it not have been removed during the extensive and otherwise accurate restoration of the building in the late 1970s? I cannot help the feeling, whenever I chance on a photograph of the house dating from Grey's tenure, that there is the soul of the man made solid. Honest, forthright, haughty even, but with a dignity shorn of ornament.

'No,' says Rita with all the finality her Dutch accent can muster. 'With the verandah gone the building would look like an institution.'

Exactly what Grey himself became, I manage not to say.

Rita unlocks the house and heads upstairs to polish and clean in the warren of rooms, leaving me to drift through the governor's life at my leisure. I think of George Herbert's phrase: 'A Box, where sweets compacted ly.' The previous day a television crew, here to film a short travel item, had been cursed by poor weather. Today motes lift serenely in the sun.

I enter the drawing room, so admired by Froude and now fitted out with bequest furniture and collected period oddments, yet still redolent of Grey. Most of his furniture, made by his workers from local kauri, has long gone. But the four honeyed kauri pillars, pit-sawn on the island and sent to England for turning, still stand as they did when Grey was forced to prop the sagging ceiling 120 years ago. At the far end of the room a Bible lies open on the

carved davenport where he corresponded with luminaries from the worlds of science and the arts, with explorers, politicians and men of the cloth.

Grey bought Kawau for £3700 in 1862, fourteen months after he had returned from a seven-year stint as governor of Cape Colony in South Africa. Despite a record tarnished by wilfulness and disobedience — he persisted, for example, in attempting to reunite independent territories in South Africa, against clear Colonial Office policy, and upset the War Office by keeping the German Legion there on full pay — Grey had asked to be sent back to New Zealand. On the strength of his early successes, it was agreed, and he was given a second crack at the job, especially at the task of bridging the deepening rift between Maori and Pakeha.

In his absence overseas, however, the office of governor had lost much of the autocratic power and freedom of action on which Grey thrived, and New Zealand was virtually self-governing. Moreover, the settlers, now three times more numerous, had developed a relentless desire for land, and Maori were in no mood to give it up. Unable to work his old magic, Grey embarked on what was to become an often-compromised, 30-year rearguard action in defence of democracy, equality and racial harmony.

He also made some questionable judgements which undermined his principles, such as authorising the confiscation of over a million hectares of

Maori land in 1864 to help pay for the war in the Waikato. Such actions have left historians wondering at his true motivations.

Perhaps as a distraction from what he saw as the unprincipled infighting of colonial politics, Grey threw himself enthusiastically into constructing his island retreat. Kawau's first industry, copper mining, had recently foundered, and he spared no expense in turning the old mine manager's cottage and adjoining assay house into a suitable residence. The original building was extended and a new wing added in the Colonial Georgian style by the versatile Frederick Thatcher. An architect best known for the buildings of Bishop Selwyn in Auckland and Old St Paul's in Wellington, Thatcher was also a cleric — he often took the Sunday service when at Kawau — and sometime secretary to Grey.

Ironically, the oldest part of the house suffered most at the hands of later owners, and needed rebuilding entirely during the restoration work. Not that anyone would notice straight off — authenticity extends to the replica waxed kauri panelling in the morning room, stained with ox blood in the nineteenth-century manner.

The morning room itself was the province of Annie Matthews, Grey's niece and adopted daughter who, even after her marriage to his estate manager, acted as his companion and hostess at Kawau. Grey, childless since the death of his five-month-old son in Australia in 1841, had separated from his wife Eliza two years before buying Kawau. The circumstances are unclear, and Grey remained mute on the subject all his life, but it seems that while the pair were returning to South Africa from England Grey discovered his wife engaged in some indiscretion, and immediately asked the ship's captain to turn to the nearest port, Rio de Janeiro, where she disembarked.

It was the sort of decisiveness that worked well enough for Grey in the field and, who knows, perhaps it was in their best interests. Eliza, pinned like a colonial brooch to the fringes of Empire, had grown impatient with life so far from the heart of London society. More than that, she had had a serious nervous breakdown while in South Africa, and Grey's own health had been battered by the strain of the job there. So she went back to her friends in London, and Grey got on with his solitary, often emotionally bruising, career.

Upstairs is one of the focal points of Mansion House, the room — more likely one of several rooms — that housed Grey's library. Not the first collection of books on Kawau — miners had earlier got up a subscription library — nevertheless it dwarfed in size and reach what those autodidacts put together, containing some 15,000 volumes dating back to the tenth century. Over one bookcase, Grey had inscribed the words: 'Learn from the Past. Use well the Present. Improve the Future.'

James Grey, a journalist who visited the island in 1878, reported it to be the finest private collection in the colony. 'A visitor to Kawau could spend quite a month in the library, and by the end of that time he would find that he had not exhausted all the objects of interest and curiosity which it contained.' Among his discoveries were letters by John Milton and a stack of recent correspondence from the missionary–explorer David Livingstone.

He might also have mentioned George Grey's own labours with the pen. A lifelong lover of languages, he collected material wherever he went, in some cases leaving the only record of languages that are now dead. He put together vocabularies of the Guanches (the first inhabitants of the Canary Islands), of Mauritius and of the Aboriginal dialects of south-western Australia.

When Grey first set foot in New Zealand he realised that to govern effectively he needed fluency in Maori, so in his few spare hours he set about learning the unwritten language. His aim was to listen sympathetically to stories of Maori suffering, and 'even if I could not assist them, to give them a kind reply, couched in such terms as should leave no doubt on their minds that I clearly understood and felt for them'.

He soon struck an obstacle. Maori chiefs often alluded to mythology and wove proverbs and poem fragments into their speeches, the meaning of which was largely lost on outsiders. To better understand what was being said, Grey began collecting traditional poems and legends, proverbs and myths wherever he went. Three years after his arrival, Government House in Auckland burned down and everything was destroyed. It was a bitter blow. Grey lost not only the narratives but, as he told the naturalist Richard Owen: 'All my plate, china, linen, wine, and the most valuable of my books, collections of curiosities, objects of natural history, native songs of different countries which I have been many years collecting, these have all now vanished in the flames.' Undaunted, Grey began again.

Recording an incident late the following year, Grey's private secretary described his method of accumulating his material during a journey through the roadless interior of the North Island. It was the summer of 1849, and they were making their way along the Thames River towards Rotorua when heavy rain barred their progress at Te Aroha. Taking advantage of delays caused by the swollen river, the governor, who travelled in a common shooting jacket, a Jim Crow hat and worn trousers, 'amused himself all day in his tent surrounded by natives, learning their songs, proverbs and ceremonies'.

At length, having reached the hot lakes, the party paddled out to Mokoia Island. Grey was delayed at the landing-place by a strong wind, and an old Maori began to tell him a story. At the very place where they now sat, he said, Hinemoa had rested after swimming from the shore. Under the branches of a pohutukawa Grey then took down, word for word, the lovely legend of Hinemoa, who 'rose up in the water as beautiful as the white heron and stepped upon the edge of the bath as graceful as the shy white crane'.

After a labour of eight years he had the stories that appeared in his classic 1855 book, *Polynesian Mythology, and Ancient Traditional History of the New Zealand Race*, first published in Maori the previous year. There, in one volume, were the legends of Maui, of Rupe's ascent into heaven, the adventures of Rata, Kae's theft of the whale, the curse of Manaia and many other stories, recorded with an empathy which makes *Polynesian Mythology* richly rewarding even today.

Grey admired Maori from the start, writing to his friend Sir Samuel Davenport in 1846: 'They are splendid warriors, very eloquent, very sensible of praise, very proud . . . and they have shown at times as much devotion to me as if I was one of their most highly prized chiefs. Indeed they have won all my feelings and sympathies in their favour by their conduct to me.'

Such was the mana among them of the man they called 'Kawana Kerei' — in the case of the Waikato, long after he had ceased to be 'Governor Grey' — that he was invited to attend tribal assemblies throughout the country and in return pressed chiefs to visit him in Auckland. When Government House was destroyed, a Maori work gang offered to rebuild it without charge. It was even rumoured that he had contrived the escape in 1864 of Maori captured in the battle of Rangiriri and held briefly on Kawau near the old smelting-house. Grey, however, blamed the government for the break-out. In a fiery memorandum to the premier, he claimed that no captured chief would have broken his word if he had been generously treated.

'He certainly managed to endear himself in a wonderful way to a population with whom it was his duty to be fighting,' wrote English novelist Anthony Trollope of Grey, whom he met six years later.

Yet Grey was not without guile. In his first governorship he had ended warfare in the lower North Island by the simple expedient of kidnapping the ostensibly neutral chief Te Rauparaha while he slept — a legally indefensible but effective act of political cunning which his Maori opponents would have appreciated. Later, he encouraged the ageing chief Te Rangihaeata to open up his roadless lands by the seemingly innocent gift of a pony and trap.

Even the well-attested strength of his public oratory revealed his manipulative skills, as the anonymous 'Phiz' reported in 1892 of a speech by Grey about poverty: 'He, the speaker, is for the moment himself a shivering, starving outcast, creeping foodless and homeless along the cruel wall of some great London dock, creeping through the bitter frost or driving sleet. It chills you to the bone to look at him! . . . So we weep — weep at the pitiable lot which is not, but might have been ours . . . and to do Sir George justice he weeps a little with us — except when perhaps he smiles a little at his power and our weakness.'

If Grey responded warmly to Maori, and to the public platform, his love of children knew no bounds. After the marriage of his niece Annie to Seymour Thorne George in 1872, Grey had a new nursery wing built, and he was eventually to indulge three grand-nieces and six grand-nephews. One of them, Zoe, recalled having chocolate in bed with Grey and, along with her brother Sydney, being entranced by his stories, especially of big game hunting in South Africa with Prince Alfred. The only tale he would not tell was how he came by the terrible leg wound with 'a hole you could put your hand in'.

Whenever Grey descended into one of his 'vampire moods' — the fits of ill temper, mostly at imagined wrongs, that visited him increasingly in his 70s — the children would be sent up to him in the knowledge that their innocent high spirits would invariably pull him out of his dejection.

Grey's visitors were ignorant of such stratagems. Close friends and distinguished guests such as Froude had the use of a spacious upper bedroom next to his, sharing a spectacular view of the bay, and they seemed to spend their time on the island in a trancelike contentment.

A distant relative, William Grey — later the Earl of Stamford — recorded a typical day at Kawau in 1887: '6.45 am: cup of tea. Exercise on the beautiful breezy promontory hard by — wooded sides, grassy top with scattered trees. A little theological reading. Godet on Romans at present; 9 am: Breakfast. Walk about ground with Sir George Grey. A little light reading and writing, study of NZ political history; 1 pm: Dinner. Walk and talk with Sir George; 5pm: Cup of tea. A little more reading and walking; 7 pm: Tea. Walk up and down the jetty with Sir George. Somewhat profound discussions; 9.30 pm: Bedfordshire [Grey's word for a hot drink prior to bed].'

To sample this cracking pace for myself, I abandon Rita to her work and step out into the afternoon light. The wind soughs in the pines. Birds chatter. I am the only one in the valley, the small party that arrived by the late ferry having set off on foot up the old Coach Road towards the copper mine. I decide to retrace Grey's circuit, which wound up through the trees towards Momona Point, then round to Lady's Bay. He was fond of showing it to his guests — it was, said Froude, 'his special pleasure'.

A track of sorts begins on the wooded slopes to the west of the house. Beyond a picket fence lie the bones of an old, well-made track reached by a gate which is jammed shut by undergrowth. Pine resin scents the air and dry needles spill down the bank. A taut spiderweb spans the path. Here and there are the massive trunks of fallen trees, lodged at the base of others which tower up 30 or more metres.

These are survivors, mostly, from plantings by Grey. He was an early champion of conifers, advocating sequoia as a kauri replacement and writing with Auckland nurseryman David Hay *The Pine Tree in New Zealand*, which predicted a great future here for radiata.

Out near the point, a clearing reveals the deep waters leading in to the Mansion House jetty. Way below, a yacht on its motor slices a path across the bays beyond, and up into Bon Accord Harbour.

'In the course of our progress we could not help reflecting how bountiful nature had been to this gem of the Southern Pacific,' wrote James Grey, who had accompanied his attentive host along this same path in 1879.

Turning south from the point, I startle a wallaby, which thumps off unseen through the scrub and saplings. Like the pines, it is another legacy of the governor, who introduced at least five species of the marsupial, four of which can still be found on the island.

A little further on, past a luxuriant patch of agapanthus, is a small wooden hut. On the lip of sandstone cliffs 25 metres above the heaving sea, it stands where Grey is said to have had a lookout — a rustic shelter where he came to brood, to scan the horizon for ships from the city, or just to feel the knock of the wind.

Here too are the remains of a coastal pa, all but obliterated by time and the bulldozer road pushed through in the 1980s — its deep defensive perimeter trench a reminder of volatile days before the discovery of manganese, then copper, turned European eyes towards the island.

Not far off, Martello Rock squats in the water above its pencil of reef, a tempting target for every passing gunner until Grey put a stop to their practice. Taking the visible lid off Martello with cannon balls would, he reasoned, make getting to his door by sea that much more dangerous.

Lady's Bay, when I get down to it, is something of a shock. Great chunks of golden cliff have cleaved off along its length, falling to the beach and taking big pines with them. The erosion has gathered pace since I was last here eight, maybe nine, years ago, and it is hard not to blame the pines which have spread naturally from shelter-belts, plantations and ornamental plantings, ousting karo, pohutukawa and other natives.

But then, in a way, the fast-growing exotics symbolise what Grey was all about on the island. True, he bought Kawau as a bolt-hole from the pressures of public life. Equally, he bought it because a temperate island would best serve his interest in acclimatising plants and animals.

Kawau was not his first choice, though. His interest in the culture and traditions of the Maori had prompted him to look for a place with mana, saturated in the history of the people he loved, and he had originally tried for Kapiti Island, near Wellington. Kapiti, however, was considered too sacred to be sold, and he had no more success with Papaitonga in Lake Waiwiri, now known as Lake Papaitonga, near Levin. Eventually he settled for Rakino Island in the Hauraki Gulf, before hearing that Kawau, a larger and more suitable island some 30 kilometres away, was available.

Grey had by then bought Rakino, which he continued to farm. His niece even moved there briefly when she married — before the old man's loneliness drew her back to Kawau.

He lost no time in turning Kawau into a zoological park, importing animals largely from his former postings, Australia and South Africa, and separating the various breeds on smaller outlying islands to avoid interbreeding.

The plants, chosen for their economic potential, were more widely sourced. Grey grew Mediterranean carob and stone pine, arrowroot from the West Indies, coffee and liquorice. He and his nine gardeners experimented with hemp from Mauritius, Sri Lankan cinnamon, cork oak, camphor and mulberries, medicinal aloe and the castor-oil plant.

With acacia trees in mind, he once told fellow parliamentarians: 'My idea is to prepare what I call prospective industries. You might have these trees growing perhaps thirty years, and be of very little use; but the time will come when people will feel the want of the materials, and then instead

of having useless shrubs you will have something growing which will give wealth to the country.'

'Grey's role in introducing plants into New Zealand is not widely known,' Department of Conservation historic resources officer Robert Brassey told me before my visit. An archaeologist by training, he had just released a 20 mm-thick report on Grey's Kawau Island gardens. A meticulous labour of research, the report includes a checklist of plants known to have been trialled there by Grey. Incomplete, it runs to more than 30 pages. Fold-out maps show trees that Brassey and his team have identified as being planted by Grey. 'There is a lot more surviving in the garden from his time there than we had expected,' he said.

From Kawau, Grey distributed plants and seeds widely, sending them as far away as the Bell settlement on Raoul [Sunday] Island in the Kermadecs. To help speed propagation, he invited nurserymen to take cuttings, which they then sold to the public. One of his more successful efforts was the isolation of the New Zealand grapefruit, which he called 'poorman's orange' for its heavy fruiting, and which became widely grown throughout the northern North Island. The first budwood was given to nurseryman Edward Morrison, who won a gold medal for best citrus novelty at the 1890 Brisbane Citrus Exhibition with poorman oranges 'five inches in diameter, with skins no thicker than a penny'. In 1883, the *Thames Advertiser* reported that the first olive oil pressed in this country had come from Grey's five-hectare olive plantation.

Grey also helped enrich public gardens, gifting plants to Wellington Botanic Gardens, Auckland Domain, Albert Park and elsewhere.

The return walk from Lady's Bay, back down the Coach Road to Mansion House, is tranquil. Hereabouts taro, planted by early Maori, still grows wild and here too arum lilies were cut for the Wellington market in the early 1900s. John Buchanan, a naturalist who catalogued the island's flora in the 1870s, was taken by these same exotic plantings, framed by banks of native trees. He wrote: '. . . the extreme beauty of the landscape . . . is very pleasing. There is seen to great advantage that scientific combination of nature and art, which is ever the aim of the landscape gardener.'

Near the house, the path crosses a flat sward punctuated by phoenix palms. Though the scene looks to be a part of Grey's original design, I know better, thanks to Brassey. The palms date from the late 1950s and 60s. When Grey moved here, the central avenue was lined with some nineteen buildings, including a stable, an assay house and old miners' cottages retained by Grey to house workers and guests — and to satisfy the period vogue for injecting landscapes with a sense of history.

Grey needed those cottages, and more he had built elsewhere on the island. At his most active, he employed some 25 helpers — gardeners, kitchen staff, shepherd, governess, dairyman, farm manager, housekeeper. One who left a record of life under Grey was his factotum, Thomas Osborne. Carpenter, boatman and handyman, Osborne was even pressed into service on occasion to 'do the Butler business'.

The pages of his diaries are full of arrivals and departures, of the comings and goings of schooners, cutters, ketches and steamships. Of daily routines — sharking, curing 'waleaby' skins, prayers in the drawing room. And of unusual breaks in routine. The entry for Tuesday, 18 March 1884 reads: 'The Maori king, his two sons, Rewi, and Daughter and three other chiefs come to see Sir George Grey. A busy night.' In April 1884 a Japanese warship arrives. 'A number out fishing, shooting,' notes Osborne in his big plain hand. Mostly, though, it is the weather that occupies him. 'Fine.' 'Very stormy.' 'Wet and miserable.' 'Moderate.' 'Fine.' Every entry in the hand-ruled notebooks prefaced by whatever meteorological phenomenon the gods have thrown down.

Then comes a change of focus. 26 November 1886: 'Among the Books but getting along slowly . . . A dirty looking night blow hard wind East.'

Grey is making good his promise to gift his library to the people of Auckland. Osborne's packing is supervised by Grey's old friend, Professor Aldis.

In 1861, Grey had donated an equally impressive collection of manuscripts and early printings to Cape Town. Perhaps, as he languished on the back benches, he felt the time had come for this long-awaited grand gesture.

Osborne's diary charts the progress. 10 December: 'We pack History and Sciences to day.' 17 December: 'Book packing working at the Bibles.' It was a slow business. By April the following year, Osborne was announcing, between observations on wind and sun, that he had just finished packing case 52 — a full month after the library housing the collection was opened.

Sorting through his vast accumulated correspondence, now part of Auckland City Library's George Grey Collection, was even more troublesome. There were boxes of it. Grey was proud of this part of the collection. 'As I have lived in an age of discovery and movement,' he said, 'to do this was to preserve a record of the history of the world at a most interesting period, written in all the confidence of friendship by the men who made the history.'

The remark smacks of conceit, but sitting one day in the air-conditioned chill of the Auckland Central Library's heritage floor, I have to admit Grey was right. There before me is a spread of letters — originals — that Grey

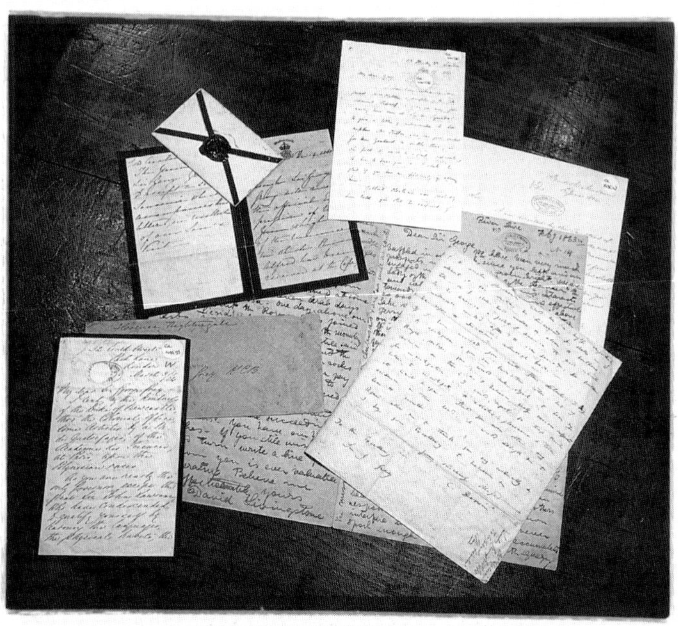

had at one time or another got in the mail.

A sheaf of pages in David Livingstone's generously rounded script dated February 1863. 'We have been very much baffled in our work since you left and our prospects are far from bright,' says the doctor, who is engaged in transporting the steamer *The Lady of the Lake* past Murchison's cataracts in the hope of doing 'something effectual toward stopping a stream of 20,000 slaves from the Lake regions . . .'

Geologist Charles Lyell, a year earlier: 'I am coming out with a volume on the "geological evidence of the antiquity of Man" & shall treat of many subjects we talked over together.'

Charles Darwin suggests that Grey might profitably examine limestone caves for evidence of contemporaries of *Dinornis*, and 'erratic boulders' for clues about climate change.

Florence Nightingale telling Grey: 'If a child's brain is forced, whose father's brain has been free, the child dies.'

Then there are the letters of appreciation — hundreds of them — from horticultural and geological societies, museums, botanical gardens, libraries, friends and acquaintances. Philip Sclater of the London Zoological Society thanks Grey for young lions, zebra, snakes, springboks, ostriches. Henry Ellis of the British Museum is pleased to have received sea leopard skulls, albatross eggs, various birds, the skin of a Maori rat.

Facts and artefacts. Grey stalked them tirelessly — in tribal language, on medieval parchment, across the plains of Africa. Such things, he told the New Zealand Society, 'may serve to fill up links . . . to the true clue to some mystery of nature, or to establish some truth which may prove of the greatest usefulness to the human race'.

By 1894, Grey must have felt at the end of his own usefulness in New Zealand. Holed up with his niece in Parnell after the sale of Kawau, and almost friendless — his growing inability to admit past mistakes got him into arguments at Auckland's Northern Club, or got him ignored — he longed to be gone. Intending only to travel to southern New Zealand, Grey, now a frail 82, arrived in Wellington to find a steamer, the *Gothic*, about to leave for England. On impulse, he took it.

Once there, he was reconciled to the Colonial Office against which he had wrestled for the best part of half a century. He became a Privy Councillor. He was even reconciled to his wife, through the intervention, it was said, of Queen Victoria. It was a sad, superficial affair. After 37 years of bitter separation, neither could muster much enthusiasm. Less than two years later, on 26 September 1898, Grey died. He was buried in St Paul's Cathedral, where he lies in the company of Nelson and the Duke of Wellington, having outlasted Eliza by two weeks.

It is hard to fathom Grey at this distance. He has recruited admiring biographers and suffered at the hands of revisionist historians, becoming in turn either a saint or an oily-tongued scoundrel. Even his own memory began playing tricks. He fabricated or omitted. At Grey's London fireside, journalist James Milne took down the much-embroidered story of this scarred veteran. How his quick support of Lord Elphinstone during the Indian Mutiny had averted disaster. How, when framing New Zealand's constitution, he had gone up into the mountains as the prophets had done, camping on Ruapehu 'in a little gypsy tent' and drawing inspiration from the snow-capped solitude. How, in his every dealing with the Colonial Office or colonial parliaments, Grey had been right and the city-bound bureaucrats or grasping politicians wrong.

Stretching my legs in the direction of Two House Bay while waiting for the ferry, I think over Grey's acts of friendship with Maori in this place. King Tawhiao, at Grey's suggestion, entering into a solemn pact here that bound them both to keep away from the alcohol that threatened Tawhiao with disgrace. The old chief Eruera Patuone, who settled north of the island to keep an eye on his friend, paddling across to see Grey once more before departing from this world. Patuone pressing into Grey's hands a walking stick set with one of his teeth — a token to remember him by.

On the eastern point, before following the track down into Two House Bay, I stop to look back. In the late afternoon sun Mansion House is brightly illuminated, as though played on by a torch through scalloped cloud. Around it, dark and majestic, stand the towering trees.

'What we have in this world is like so much stage property lent to us to play our parts with,' Grey had written. 'Lent to us to see what good we do with that entrusted to us.' Grey had gladly given it all away. In the end, it is not the rare books, the fiery despatches or the bitter enmities that burn brightest in the memory, but a few stories of friendship. These, and the lengthening shadows of the trees.

June 1998

Kawau Island

Te Kawau-tu-maro, island of the motionless shag, might better have been called Motumuru, for the small spotted shark prized by early Maori — and known today as lemon fish — which was plentiful in the sheltered local waters.

From the 1720s on, intermittent clashes over these fishing grounds occurred between the local Kawerau and the Murutuahu tribes, which were prominent in the southern Hauraki Gulf. In the 1820s, both iwi came under attack from northern Nga Puhi armed with muskets, and the area was abandoned for a decade.

When the missionary Samuel Marsden, one of the first Pakeha to set foot on Kawau, landed in 1820, one of his party reported finding no one there. The locals had gone, abandoning the island, the muru and their thirteen or more headland pas.

In 1840 an Aberdeen company bought Kawau from the island's Maori owners to farm it, but the discovery of manganese prompted a change of tack. New Zealand's first underground mine was quickly sunk, and export of manganese to Australia and England began.

The discovery of copper ore in 1844 lent new vigour to the enterprise and resulted in the country's first large-scale industry. Miners from Cornwall, a county with a long history of working the green veins, settled in neat purpose-built houses in the flat and fertile valley of Momona Bay. A mine manager's two-roomed wooden cottage, soon replaced by a larger one of red brick, was erected near the beach, not far from that of the company surgeon.

Mining on the island was not without its difficulties. For one thing, the workings were coastal and prone to flooding. A steam engine, possibly the country's first, was installed to keep the seawater at bay. Its sandstone engine-house, partially restored in recent years, remains a prominent landmark.

Then there was the unforeseen danger of the ore overheating in the holds of wooden cargo ships. To overcome this, Welsh smelters were brought in from Swansea, and for a year almost no ore was dug while all hands built a brick smelting works — now reduced to a ruin — in nearby Bon Accord harbour.

At the industry's height there were some 300 miners and smelters, together with their families, on Kawau, and 200 or more Maori labourers and woodcutters. A complex method of burning off the sulphur from the ore was tried, but proved expensive. A German metallurgist by the name of Beeger set things right by doing away with the initial smelting process entirely, instead setting fire to ore — five or six tonnes at a time — mixed with firewood, in the open air. The heaps were left to smoulder for months on end before being refined in the furnaces. The waste or slag, three-quarters iron, was pressed into service as ship ballast. It also found its way to Momona Bay, where it can still be seen forming the piers for the wharf, said to be the country's oldest still in use.

Though profitable for a time, with 1200 tonnes of copper exported in 1846 alone, the business was far from wholesome. Families living near the smelting house had to contend with Beeger's endlessly smouldering bonfires, whose noxious vapours stripped nearby trees of every green leaf, while those housed in Miners Bay endured the incessant thumping of the mine engines, which laboured night and day to drain the workings.

The rough island life, not surprisingly, had limited appeal. According to one observer: 'The people living on Kawau were rather a queer mixture — runaway sailors, old soldiers, tradesmen of nearly all descriptions were to be met with and then they were of such a nomadic character that steadiness or fixity was not to be expected.'

Conditions for the miners were made more difficult with the onset of competition. Unbelievably, an unscrupulous rival company gained the rights to adjacent 'land' below high tide — even securing control of the original company's wharf — and set about undermining its business in a rather literal fashion.

Only in 1848, after the intervention of George Grey, the colony's recently appointed governor, was the complex legal wrangling ended in favour of the first company. By then it was too late. Reckless mining by the newcomers had allowed the sea to break into the shafts, some up to 50 metres deep, and both mines were flooded. The miners left soon after, and most of the island's buildings, its school and library, cottages and chapel, fell silent.

In 1862, after an attempt to reopen the mines had failed, Grey himself bought Kawau as a restful antidote to his hectic political career and an ideal setting for his experiments in acclimatising new plants — many of which still thrive.

Grey owned the island for 25 years, at one time employing a staff of two dozen, including nine gardeners. He often entertained eminent visitors and frequently opened his house and grounds to the public.

Failing health forced Grey to sell in 1888, and a succession of owners tried to make a living by subdividing the island and by running Mansion House as a guesthouse. During the 1920s and 30s, Lawford Reeves and his family coaxed the languishing property into something of a revival, holding dances and parties and putting in tennis courts, bowling greens, an eleven-hole golf course — even, in the remodelled kitchen, a three-metre-long stove, a showpiece from Dunedin's South Seas Exhibition.

At this time, Kawau became a popular destination for weekend excursions from Auckland, with up to 1000 visitors at a time spending the day on the island. What must have been Mansion House's grandest occasion came in January 1929, when the entire New Zealand Division of the Royal Navy dropped anchor in Bon Accord harbour. Families and friends arrived on ferries, which rode at anchor alongside the launches and yachts of holidaymakers.

The fleet commodore and his officers stepped ashore as the *Dunedin*'s band struck up under the coral trees and sailors in white paraded on the drive beneath flapping flags. With more than 3000 people disporting themselves by the sparkling waters of the bay, it would have been a sight to gladden the heart of the old governor himself.

By the late 1940s, however, hard times had again fallen on the property. A new commercial owner was busy felling trees for the Auckland timber market and further subdividing what remained of Grey's land. In 1948 Mona Gordon reported bitterly: 'Old Kawau is but a shadow of its former self, its drooping spirits uncheered since the departure of its creator by crowds of holidaymakers, its gardens ransacked, its charm largely evaporated with the passing of the tall figure from among the pines he had grown from seed to maturity.'

Its spirits drooped even further when a later owner, keen to see the land and house maintained as a historic property, sold it to the government in 1967.

Unaccountably, for the next ten years it was leased to a brewery, which added an ungainly conference room, swimming pool and public bar while committing hideous architectural atrocities inside the house.

The venture failed to turn a profit, and in October 1979, after painstaking restoration by the Hauraki Gulf Maritime Park Board, Mansion House was opened to the public as a National Trust property.

With 60 private jetties and a permanent population of around 80 — no more than in George Grey's day — Kawau itself remains a roadless haven for those seeking solitude. 'The visitor . . . can only wish that a settled population may never be found within its shores, and that its peace and beauty may always remain undisturbed,' wrote naturalist John Buchanan after visiting Kawau in 1876. More than 100 years on, that wish looks close to having been granted.

Illustrations

New Zealand's 'Terrible Lizards': The Dinosaur Discoveries of Joan Wiffen

The valley, cloaked in a mantle of mist, lies silent. The sky above, scoured to a dull metallic zinc, is empty. In the high tops of the conifers, a flapping umbrella of blackness jabs the air and is gone. Run-off soaks the land, giving it a shop-soiled second-day-of-creation look.

Suddenly, river-bank ferns quiver as a squat, horn-studded animal breaks cover, beads of light playing across its armoured skin. Nostrils twitch as it scents danger. A dismembered carcass the size of a bull — an allosaur — is drifting downstream towards the lagoon, its toothy meat-eating jaws gaping hungrily, even in death.

The ankylosaur watches the carcass until it is out of sight, then turns its tank-like body and is lost once more in the dense foliage . . .

Twenty years ago, such a scenario in New Zealand would be unthinkable. Now, thanks largely to the work of amateur palaeontologist Joan Wiffen and a handful of helpers, dinosaurs have begun to reclaim even this island vestige of Gondwana.

To date, all the evidence has come from one place: the Mangahouanga stream bed, deep in the Urewera ranges — a lush site that in the depths of winter looks uncannily as though lifted from the pages of Arthur Conan Doyle's *The Lost World*.

Wiffen, 71 this year, and recently recovered from a knock-out dose of influenza, leans against a tree to catch her breath. With ash-grey hair and slender frame, she is an unlikely ground-breaker. But her steady eyes and lively speech reveal an active, inquiring mind.

As a child, she had wandered over the bare hills of Hawke's Bay, running her hands across shells embedded in the rough limestone outcrops, trying to piece together a reason for them lying so far from the sea.

Later, as an adult, she took to gem prospecting in Australia with her husband, Pont, but soon grew disillusioned with the greed and addiction that gemstones often fostered. Then, at a roadside shop in Queensland, Wiffen bought a 50-cent fossil, a trilobite, and the course of her life suddenly and irrevocably changed.

With her children, Chris and Judith, she and Pont made a pilgrimage to all the fossil grounds they could find in New Zealand, gathering ammonites from Kawhia, belemnites and plant remains from Port Waikato, crabs and fossil teeth from Oaro, a nautiloid from the West Coast . . . Then came the discovery of fossils much nearer home — in the Te Hoe valley — and all the wearisome journeying was at an end. It proved to be a fulfilment of all their dreams.

Every step of the steep winding valley track has been worn into memory over the years that she, her late husband and friends backpacked out more than 100 tonnes of fossil-bearing rock.

An aluminium ladder — one of the many scavenged pieces of equipment that help lubricate this shoestring enterprise — extends down the cliff face to the river bed. Hefting a rock-cutting saw, I follow Trevor Crabtree, a fellow enthusiast, down to what he calls 'mosasaur beach'.

We ford the icy stream with the aid of cable and guide wires, and soon the hills resound with the throaty snarl of the converted chainsaw as Trevor attacks a split boulder. These mossy concretions, each a grey pearl of calcareous sandstone surrounding a nucleus of organic matter such as wood or bone, litter the stream bed like geological giftwrap.

The technique of slabbing fossils for removal, perfected over many summers, involves cutting two rectangles around the exposed fossil — the inner one to prevent specimen damage — then 'springing' the rock, cracking it open by hammering rhythmically along the outer blade cuts.

Hauled by car to rock-strewn backyards in Napier, 100 kilometres away over logging track and twisting highway, the bones are then liberated by further sawing, drilling and immersion in glacial acetic acid to eat away the encasing rock.

'Acid is a wonderful tool, but very expensive and destructive,' says Wiffen.

The acid attack must be interrupted periodically while newly exposed bone is coated in protective resin. Delicate final work is often done with an air scribe, a miniature jackhammer which blows dust away with a jet of compressed air.

Crabtree shows me the partly freed head and jaws of a primitive snapper-like fish, which looks to be hewn by a modern Michelangelo from a slab of rock. It has taken a week of twelve-hour days to get this far, he says, but the effort has been well worth it. The reward is an impressive specimen of a large Late Cretaceous fish.

To get an idea of the effort needed, imagine this: a neighbour gets hold of the chicken bones from your last dinner — bones that for some reason you badly want — and heaves them into your newly poured concrete drive. It so happens that you can't get to the drive for a few months. Then, when you do, you find it broken into beachball-sized pieces and jumbled every which way. Still want those bones?

Joan Wiffen's band of amateurs do. And their dogged perseverance has won them over recent years a gradually lengthening roll-call of dinosaurs, beginning with the epoch-making discovery in 1975 of what proved to be a tailbone from a four-metre-long, half-tonne carnivorous dinosaur. Then came astounding evidence of a nine-metre allosaur — effectively an economy version of *Tyrannosaurus rex*, though by human standards there was nothing economical about its formidable teeth and claws.

In 1988, an ankylosaur, a low-slung armoured beast the size of a Volkswagen Beetle, was identified, followed by a three- to four-metre-long, two-legged plant-eater: a hypsilophodont — the gazelle of the dinosaur world.

Comparison with modern animals is apt. Palaeontologists stress the usefulness of seeing dinosaurs as creatures of flesh and blood rather than of fevered nightmare. Alien though they may seem to us, dinosaurs went about their daily lives in ways that are strikingly similar to those of animals today.

The excitement caused by the more recent New Zealand dinosaur finds stemmed in part from the witness they give to a viable ancient ecosystem comprising both predators and prey. Prior to that, the country's sole carnivorous dinosaur was thought to have eked out its life scavenging among shellfish and seaweed on the shore — a most unlikely existence for such a creature.

The discovery in the Te Hoe valley of plant remains, two insects (a cockroach and a leaf-eating beetle) and a freshwater turtle added further detail to the emerging picture of life in Cretaceous New Zealand.

In 1986, Crabtree stumbled on an unusual bone while rummaging through the rock hoard in his yard. The delicate, layered bone looked to be that of a bird. Painstaking cleaning and consultation with overseas authorities showed it to be something more astounding: the lower wing bone of a pterosaur, a flying reptile with a span of some four metres. Months later, Wiffen found additional proof that this pelican-like creature once flew in New Zealand skies when she uncovered part of the shoulderblade of a juvenile.

But be advised: pterosaurs are not dinosaurs. Neither are ichthyosaurs, those primitive reptiles resembling dolphins, nor elasmosaurs, the long-necked plesiosaurs associated by many with the monster of Loch Ness. As a simple guide for party conversation: if it flew, swam, had the splayed legs of a crocodile or did not live between 230 million and 65 million years ago, it was not a dinosaur.

The discovery of dinosaurs in New Zealand was made more likely by finds of marine reptile fossils. As Joan Wiffen tells it, she was hunched with her family over a geological map one day in the early 1970s when they came across the words: 'In the Te Hoe Valley the beds are partly brackish water, and contain reptilian remains . . .' Though in small print among the gaudy pinks, mauves and yellows of the map, the gloss was for them a buzzing neon of enticement.

The note, it turned out, dated from an oil company survey in the 1950s which had not been followed up. The Wiffens found the spot, at the end of a little-used dirt road, and struck pay dirt: the stream-bed rocks fairly bristled with fish scales, sharks' teeth, ancient squid-like creatures called belemnites and teeth from the first-known southern hemisphere sawfish.

The first fossil bones discovered by Joan and Pont were identified as plesiosaur vertebrae. Later, in 1978, a complete skull was exhumed. A New Zealand first, it is one of only a dozen complete elasmosaur skulls in the world.

Plesiosaurs have proved to be the most numerous inhabitants of the valley graveyard, with the remains of very young offspring as well as large 10-metre adults being found. Bones, including complete skulls, from another marine reptile, the mosasaur, have also been found at Mangahouanga, though in smaller numbers. Mosasaurs, which plundered the world's oceans relentlessly for 35 million years, a mere fraction of the plesiosaurs' 120-million-year spree, succumbed to the worldwide extinctions that ended the reign of the dinosaurs on land 65 million years ago — now thought to

have been caused by climate change following a massive meteor strike.

The existence of such marine remains 80 kilometres inland and at an altitude of 1000 metres is readily explained. The Mangahouanga reptiles lived in what palaeontologists and geologists call the Cretaceous Period, which, along with the Triassic and the Jurassic, make up the Mesozoic Era: the age of the dinosaurs. At that time, the site lay on the coast of a very different New Zealand. A nearby river, loaded with silt and debris from the surrounding hills, fed into a protected estuary or lagoon, enriching the coastal waters. It must have been a salubrious location with plentiful food, because the plesiosaurs and mosasaurs bred there for an almost incomprehensible span of time. As these reptiles died, their bones sank into the mud of the lagoon, to become entombed in coastal sediment.

Dinosaur remains were also borne by the river into the shallow waters of the bay, as sheep carcasses from Hawke's Bay farms sometimes are today. It is likely that the bodies would have been badly mauled and dismembered by scavengers, both on land and in the water, defeating the hope of ever assembling complete skeletons from the valley.

In this, the site differs from the world's prime Cretaceous fossil grounds, many of which were once great inland seas — Mongolia's Gobi Desert, for example, and Australia's outback, the prairies of Montana and Wyoming and the badlands of Alberta. They were like vast dinner plates, gradually accumulating the debris of the ages.

By comparison, inland Hawke's Bay has a tortured geological history, having been raised and lowered, tilted, folded and torn over the past 80 million years to form the present rugged terrain. Today, the fossil-bearing rocks have been brought once more to the surface, where an ongoing process of natural violence, from earthquake and tropical storm to flash flood and erosion, reveals and often also reclaims them.

In 1985, as a result of a cyclonic storm that one local geographer called 'the biggest regional upheaval in 20,000 years', the Mangahouanga rose nine metres, and kilometre-long tracts of forest were cleaved from its banks. Wiffen and her team lost promising fossils that were awaiting recovery, and for months access was closed while culverts were repaired.

But the landslips also brought fresh material to the stream bed. Indeed, the renewal process occurs every time a flood rips rocks from the geological anticline and scatters them among the river's deep pools. There, 30-degree summer sunshine and stubborn winter frosts often crack the concretions to reveal strange new forms of life from the underworld.

It was in just such circumstances, after Cyclone Bola in 1988, that one of the most spectacular finds, a New Zealand ankylosaur, was made. Ankylosaurs, 'stiff lizards', were the combat tanks of the dinosaur world. With broad, blunt heads and short legs, they relied on bony armour set into leathery skin for defence. They compensated for weak teeth and stubby claws with powerful tails, often ending in clubs, a blow from which would have been crippling.

Garages in the suburbs of Napier and a pair of huts at the Te Hoe roadhead are piled high with enigmatic fossils awaiting classification. Any one of them could provide clues to equally impressive animals. The huts themselves are outposts of civilisation fourteen kilometres from the nearest telephone and reticulated power, and perhaps 45 kilometres from the nearest sealed public road. A sign on one reads 'Hawke's Bay Palaeontology Group'. A few metres away stands what is possibly the country's most remote flushing toilet. Crabtree confesses to sometimes making the gruelling journey from Napier just to savour the tranquillity. And to ponder better ways of parting stone from bone in the valley below.

In the early 1970s, explosives were used to break up large, unwieldy boulders, but potential damage to vulnerable fossils, and the advent of rock saws, prompted a change. Even tungsten-tipped electric drills, acid baths and air scribes blunt enthusiasm in time, however. Now Crabtree is toying with the idea of using sonic vibrations. The technique is used in hospitals to break down gallstones, he says. And, being made of calcite, gallstones are not unlike the calcareous concretions that litter the stream. He has his eyes on a Scandinavian device which could, with modification, bring a new refinement to palaeontology — an otherwise low-tech discipline. As one wag noted, the most revolutionary advance in fossil hunting of recent years has been the advent of the self-sealing plastic bag.

It may come as a surprise to those raised on images such as the towering *Diplodocus* in London's Museum of Natural History — to those of us 'haunted with the heads colossal in death', as English poet Peter Redgrove has it — that New Zealand's dinosaur catalogue is being assembled from scraps: a broken toe bone or pelvic fragment here, a wingbone the size of a teaspoon there. Yet that is all we antipodeans are likely to get. No complete skeletons and, unfortunately, little likelihood of identifying the genus, or in some cases even the family, to which individual specimens belong.

In this, however, New Zealanders are less alone than they might imagine. Few articulated museum showpieces anywhere have been retrieved whole, most being composites of several animals. Despite its resonant place in the popular imagination, for example, only four complete skulls of *Tyrannosaurus rex* have been unearthed.

For many newly discovered species, the anatomy is pieced together only after much trial and error. A reconstruction in 1853 of the first dinosaur found, *Iguanodon*, pictured something like a mythical griffin, minus the wings. It was fitted out with a curious blunt nose horn, now known to be one of its thumb spikes. A 1940 *Iguanodon* model located the thumb spikes correctly, but had the beast take what is today thought to be an uncharacteristically kangaroo-like posture.

Even the printed guide to New Zealand's first exhibition of dinosaurs, held at the Auckland Museum in 1987, misrepresented the long-dead. Its cover carried a photograph of a distinctively crested hadrosaur from China called *Tsintaosaurus*. The unicorn-like appendage was thought to be unique among dinosaurs until palaeontologists realised the horn consisted of a nasal bone that in life lay flat along the snout.

Canterbury Museum staff experienced the difficulties of postulating probable forms when the museum purchased the country's only complete dinosaur skeleton, a four-metre-high replica of an *Allosaurus* found in Utah. On opening the consignment's two wooden crates, curator Margaret Bradshaw found a bewildering collection of bones with neither labels nor plans for assembly. Finally, she resorted to the technique used by palaeontologists the world over: clear a space on the floor, lay out the bones, then connect the leg bone to the thigh bone . . .

Of course, the entire enterprise would be impossible without the ability to draw on comparative material held overseas. From the beginning, Wiffen and her co-workers have relied on palaeontologists in Australia and elsewhere. Even so, some fossil fragments have a frustratingly fugitive identity. The New Zealand pterosaur, for example, is not known at family, genus or species level. That is akin to being able to identify a domestic cat only as a member of the order *Carnivora*.

Added to the frustration of dealing with mere slivers of bone are the delays in the identification process itself. For the best results, casts must be made of the fragile and irreplaceable bones for mailing to overseas experts. Casting is itself a difficult art to master, as even a brief glance around Wiffen's workbench and reject box testifies. Then there is the inevitable nailbiting before a verdict is reached.

To help identify the hypsilophodont, Wiffen tried to get a cast of the toe bone of an Argentinian specimen. The process took eighteen months, and when the cast arrived she found there were few similarities. A problem facing researchers worldwide, she says, is the difficulty of matching the same type of dinosaur from the same period.

Nevertheless, the astonishing speed with which dinosaur knowledge is accumulating worldwide encourages Wiffen to believe many gaps in the jigsaw of the Late Cretaceous will one day be filled. More than half of the

350 known dinosaur types have been discovered within the past decade, with a new one being described on average every seven weeks. These include the discovery, in the foothills of the Andes, of *Euraptor*, the oldest dinosaur ever found, and believed to have lived 225 million years ago.

Wiffen hopes more bones from New Zealand's ankylosaur, of which little is known, will one day be discovered, enabling a link to be made with other southern hemisphere ankylosaurs. It is possible. Palaeontologists estimate that less than one per cent of the dinosaur species that walked the earth have so far been identified. Yet the picture of life on what was once the great supercontinent of Gondwana has already clarified surprisingly in recent years.

Ankylosaur fossils have been retrieved from Late Cretaceous sediments on James Ross Island in Antarctica, and a small plant-eater similar to *Hypsilophodon* has been found in the region. Indeed, Antarctica and New Zealand are among the last places on earth to yield dinosaurs. Wiffen takes the ankylosaur finds in Antarctica, Australia and New Zealand as evidence for a southern land route by which the armoured dinosaurs, and the meat-eaters which preyed on them, spread across Gondwana before the component landmasses separated 80 million years ago.

When dinosaurs were discovered in New Zealand, they were assumed to have arrived from Australia because, it was argued, the path by which the southern beech forests had spread (via Antarctica) would have been too cold for the lumbering cold-blooded leviathans. A more respectful view of dinosaurs, taking account of the discovery of vast trackways which prove

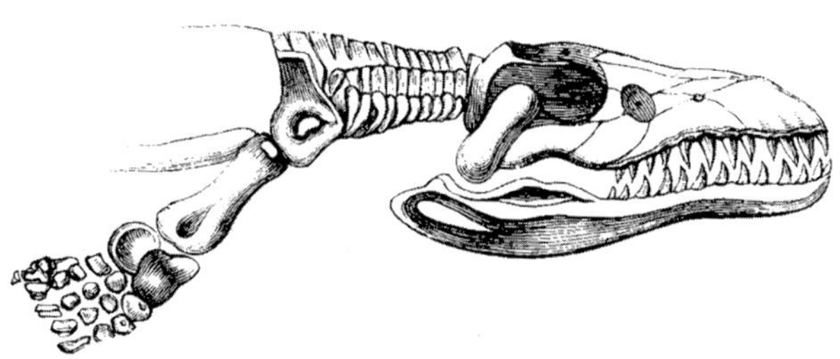

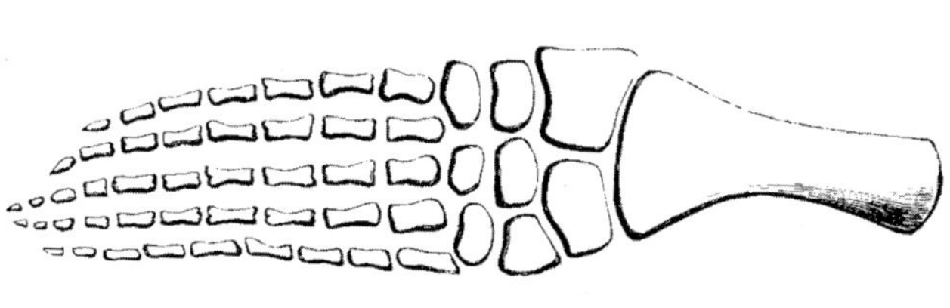

that migration took them to cold climates, suggests many species may have been warm-blooded and able to endure the southern route.

For much of the Mesozoic, Queensland Museum's Ralph Molnar pictures a polar environment throughout what is now Australasia, supporting specialised dinosaurs able to endure the bleak, five-month Antarctic night. He puts Hawke's Bay on a list of polar sites that includes Alaska, Spitsbergen and Victoria's Dinosaur Cove.

The presence of dinosaurs for 15 million years in post-separation New Zealand, prior to the great extinction 65 million years ago, prompts tantalising questions. Did these animals remain in a state of 'suspended evolution' in the isolated haven in which they found themselves? Or did they evolve in unique ways, as did much of the country's later bird life?

And speaking of bird life, says Wiffen, where did the moa fit in? Did their evolution from proto-birds — relatives of the great carnosaurs — happen in Gondwana? Or did it occur elsewhere, and the moa, along with other ratites, move into Gondwana later? 'From the end of the Cretaceous to recent times is one big hole in our knowledge. Although there are a few bird fossils as old as the Palaeocene — penguins, especially — the first mammals, whales, make their appearance in the record 20 to 30 million years ago. There are no moa records beyond 2 million years ago.'

It is difficult for us, living in a world where mammals rule the global roost, to imagine what the age of dinosaurs was like. Yet, as University of Auckland associate professor of geology Jack Grant-Mackie comments: 'For close to 200 million years there was nothing on land bigger than a turkey that was not a dinosaur.'

Slowly, outdated notions of dinosaurs as tail-dragging, walnut-brained heavyweights are being replaced by a picture of a diverse and highly adaptable group of animals. Recent research indicates that some dinosaurs were warm-blooded while others, such as *Tyrannosaurus*, may have had different metabolisms at different stages of their life cycle. It has been suggested that one tree-browsing giant, *Barosaurus*, may have had as many as eight separate hearts to get blood to its head — a lofty twelve metres above the ground.

Contrary to popular belief, many dinosaurs nurtured their offspring and protected them in the manner of today's herding animals. Nests made by hypsilophodonts have been found in Montana, for example, suggesting they bred in vast rookeries as today's seabirds do, and that the young remained in the area after hatching.

And, if palaeontologists like American Jack Horner are to be believed, life in the Mesozoic was far from being a theatre of blood. The fearsome horns of many herbivores like *Triceratops*, he argues, were used mainly for establishing dominance within herds and for attracting a mate, rather than for fighting pitched battles. And — heresy — *Tyrannosaurus rex* was primarily a scavenger. When it did take on living prey, it picked sick stragglers rather than healthy adults.

Furthermore, dinosaurs were just getting into their stride when disaster overtook them. Admittedly, some lines, such as the towering five-storey-high *Brachiosaurus*, had been discontinued early on, but throughout the Cretaceous there lived an enormous number of dinosaur species, from extravagantly crested pachycephalosaurs to lethal pack-hunting velociraptors. Elegant creatures, they were equipped with brain-to-body ratios greater than present-day reptiles, and had sophisticated physiologies and behaviours.

Grant-Mackie believes it is only a matter of time before new dinosaur grounds are discovered in New Zealand. And, because New Zealand has few suitable deposits of land origin, those finds will probably be made in marine sediments. Besides, the country's largest land deposits are coal-bearing sequences which, owing to their acidic nature, seldom preserve bones. On the other hand, New Zealand has Mesozoic marine rock totalling perhaps 25 kilometres in thickness which may conceal entirely new species, he says.

The country is certainly not without ancient sites. We already have our own Jurassic Park in Southland's Curio Bay — a fossilised forest 170 million years old. No dinosaur remains have yet been found there, though it is probable dinosaurs trod its wooded corridors back in the time when it was still part of Gondwana. Other possible sites include North Canterbury's Waipara Gorge, a location that has yielded marine reptiles, shellfish and wood and leaf fossils.

'The prime reason dinosaurs were found in Te Hoe is that people invested time in the search,' says Grant-Mackie. 'The ones who find them are the ones who turn over the most rocks.'

Despite his interest as a palaeontologist in New Zealand's dinosaur past, Grant-Mackie admits that the field is likely to be left to amateurs for the foreseeable future. It is, he says, a criticism of the funding of science in New Zealand that neither university nor government scientists are able to undertake such activities. The lack of direct commercial spin-off is a major factor. It has been estimated that for salaried scientists to shoulder the work of Wiffen's group the cost would be up to $1 million a year.

The problem is not confined to this country. Surprisingly, a mere 50 or so professionals worldwide are hunting dinosaurs full time — fewer people than worked on *Jurassic Park*, the film based on their findings. And the palaeontologists' combined annual budget is minute by comparison.

The New Zealand amateurs plugging away with their worn air scribes are even less well resourced. The Mangahouanga group is almost entirely self-funded. Grants totalling around $600 over 20 years, along with the occasional small donation, have been put towards the purchase of hard-to-get reference books and equipment for everyday toil at the fossil face. Travel to scientific meetings — essential for keeping up with the latest palaeontological thought — 'is determined by the state of my piggy bank', says Wiffen ruefully.

All the important finds have been deposited with the Institute of Geological and Nuclear Sciences, Lower Hutt, for permanent curation in a national fossil collection. But recognition of the discoveries has been slow. Wiffen's first dinosaur find was officially announced by Ralph Molnar at the fifth Gondwana symposium in Wellington, in 1980. 'The reaction was a thunderous silence and a general lack of interest or understanding of the geological significance of dinosaurs in New Zealand,' Wiffen recalled in her 1991 book *Valley of the Dragons*.

Now, as an increasing number of exhibitions including animated reconstructions tour the country, and as more people are exposed to film and television entertainment based, however inaccurately, on dinosaur life, interest is being aroused in the indigenous species.

But the classified orthodoxy of museum galleries reveals little about the serendipity needed to prise evidence from the unyielding rock. Mangahouanga, the country's only known burial site, does not give up its treasure readily. Twenty years of hard labour have resulted in fewer than a dozen identified dinosaur fossils.

The rugged Hawke's Bay hill country, once a hideout of the Maori warrior and prophet Te Kooti, and now the preserve of hardy hunters and trampers, has flung an almost impenetrable cloak around its past. Yet perhaps intimations of that past have been leaking from the rocks for longer than we acknowledge.

Within bellowing distance of the dinosaur valley is a place called Maungataniwha — 'mountain of the dragons'. The area round about, for all its remoteness, has a history of Maori settlement. Visible from the palaeontologists' huts are the forested hills where once Maori had their gardens and pigeon troughs.

Could the early peoples of Aotearoa have seen the fossils and recognised them for what they were — evidence of awesome other-worldly creatures? The importance of dragons in Chinese culture, after all, has been influenced by that country's dinosaur fossils, some of which are even now used in 'dragon' potions. In Maori mythology, taniwha were creatures with astounding powers, able to travel through earth and water. Come to think of it, that is just what Wiffen's stonelike menagerie has done, lying down in soft coastal mud, only to rise again amid the violence of electrical storm and flash flood.

Crabtree, a possum hunter and deerstalker from way back, covered a lot of territory in his gun-carrying days. He and other members of the Hawke's Bay group have hauled out vertebrate fossils from sites that read like palaeontological battle honours: Waiau River, Camp, Looney and Half-hour creeks, Te Hoe valley.

'Over the years, we've extended the fossil area from four kilometres of

stream bed to 20 kilometres square,' he says as we stop on our journey out of Mangahouanga to survey the sharply folded land. 'We have also had reports from goat cullers and deerstalkers about fossils seen in the rugged outback gullies. One bloke grabbed a rock and cut his hand open on a row of teeth,' says Crabtree cryptically. He nods at the distant rain-shrouded hills. 'The teeth are still out there, somewhere.'

As evening begins to fall, we head for the sealed road with its active ribbon of lights. Behind us, in the brooding hills, unnumbered taniwha sleep on. One day, their time will come.

September 1993

Illustrations

Dinomania: Celebrating nature's 'special effects'

Ever since New Year's Eve 1853, when Richard Owen was feted with a seven-course banquet in the half-finished reconstruction of *Iguanodon*, dinosaurs have been the toast of science and a magnet for marketeers the world over.

Owen, a comparative anatomist, and the first person to recognise dinosaurs as a distinct group of animals, coined the name, which in Greek means 'terrible lizard'. He did not have much to go on with *Iguanodon*, however, and the full-size model built by sculptor Benjamin Hawkins under Owen's direction to decorate Crystal Palace Park in England quickly came to look outdated.

In identifying dinosaurs, he built on the work of two predecessors: Gideon Mantell, a doctor who had become obsessed by *Iguanodon* after being handed fossil teeth plucked from quarry stone by his wife, Mary Ann; and the eccentric clergyman and geologist William Buckland, the first to describe and name an individual dinosaur, *Megalosaurus*.

European finds were soon eclipsed by discoveries in the United States, which cast doubts on the anatomical accuracy of Owen's elephantine creations. In what became a bizarre 'bones rush', two bitter rivals, palaeontologists Edward Cope and Othniel Marsh, scoured North America for dinosaur remains. Between them, they named nearly 130 dinosaur species.

Even wealthy industrialist Andrew Carnegie got caught up in the fever, funding a scientific expedition to Wyoming which dug up, among other things, *Diplodocus carnegiei*. Plaster casts of the enormous beast were made and shipped around the world to great public acclaim, one finding a home in the foyer of the Museum of Natural History in London.

With these discoveries, it was as though a door had suddenly been flung open on a vast and outrageously different past. A past so long in its unfolding that constellations had changed shape in the heavens and the earth's continents had drawn together and parted in a stately square dance of plate tectonics. A past ample enough for nature to throw any old possibility together and see what happened — gigantism, baroque armour, the gift of flight.

Through the work of the early scientists and popularisers, dinosaurs got a grip on the human imagination that they have never relinquished. In 1914, for example, the cartoon *Gertie the Dinosaur* was filmed. Then came other monster pictures, with increasingly realistic animal protagonists, culminating in Steven Spielberg's big-budget thriller *Jurassic Park*.

The success of *Jurassic Park* could have been predicted in Owen's day. After all, his 30-tonne ferro-cement dinosaur replicas were set on an artificial island in Exhibition Park as one of the commercial operation's main attractions. The circumstance, dinosaurs as theme park drawcards, is not unlike that of Spielberg's film storyline.

The paying public, it seems, is hungry for whatever it can get in the way of 'Godzillas with fangs'. Now the offerings have broadened to include everything from dinosaur T-shirts and lunchboxes to bubble gum, postage stamps and slippers that roar like T-rex when you walk. Inevitably, in this era of the microchip, a CD-Rom computer disk is available with dinosaur articles, photographs, sound effects and a blood-curdling video sequence called 'The Hunt'. There are also any number of robotic dinosaur displays, roaring at children and winking menacingly at adults in big cities the world over.

Oddly, and in an echo of Owen's 1853 publicity feast, the biggest maker of robotic dinosaurs started down that road after lending a *Triceratops* as a backdrop to a patron's banquet at the Los Angeles County Museum of Natural History. Lending 'live' dinosaurs to museums proved a hit for the company, with attendance for client institutions jumping by up to fifteen times the rate for normal exhibits.

Even dinosaur droppings are likely to excite public attention these days, with a collection of 23 lumps of fossilised excrement selling at auction in London recently for $8500, more than ten times the expected price. A nest of rock-hard dinosaur eggs sold the same day for more than $120,000.

Like cats in ancient Egypt, dinosaurs have walked into our lives and hearts and have refused to budge. One explanation is that people need their familiar human boundaries tweaked a little. They want to get close to something so big, so old and so mean that it sends a *frisson* down the spine.

Dinosaurs also have that one essential ingredient to immortality: mystery. Because so many questions are unanswered — it is doubtful, for instance, whether we can ever know the colour of their skin — they will continue to awaken a sense of wonder, that faculty which more than anything keeps us young . . . and queuing at the box office.

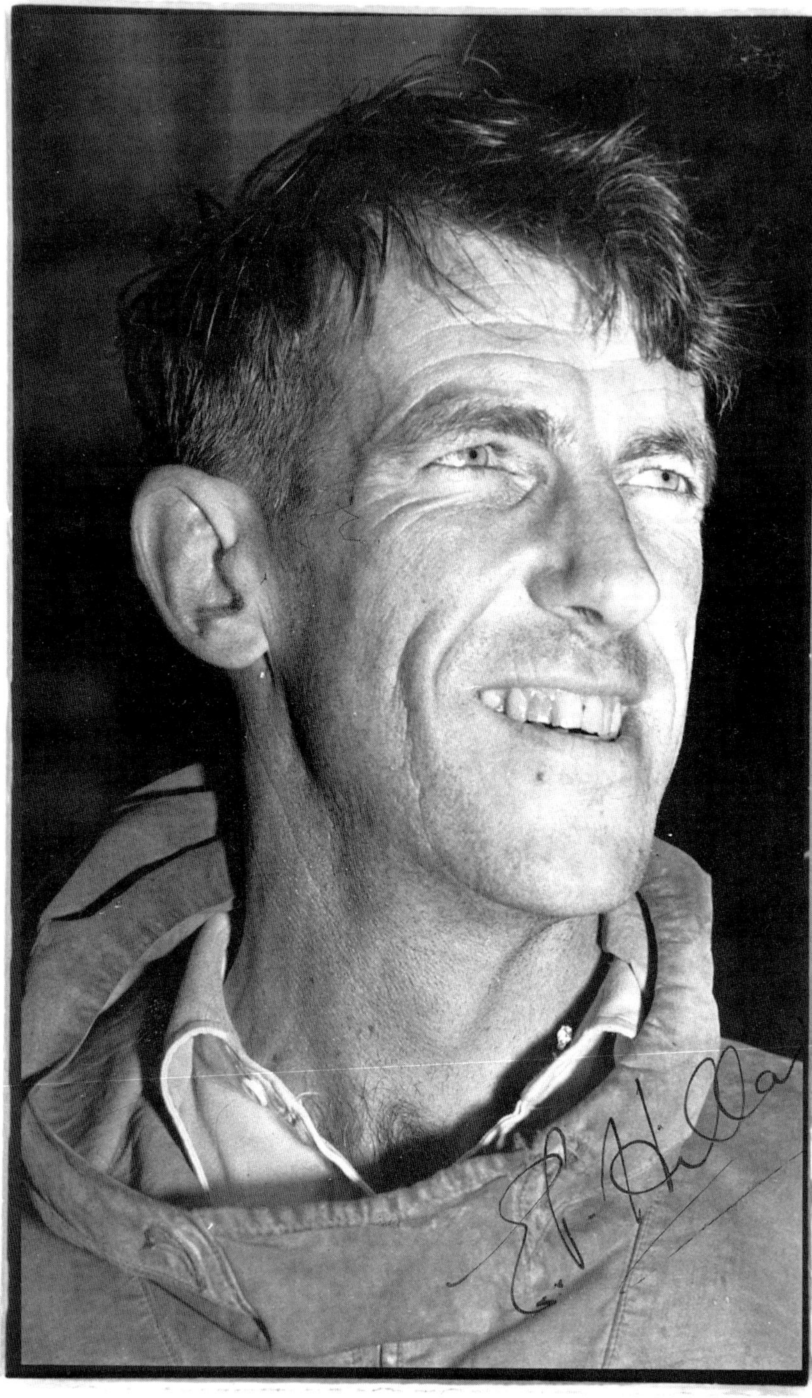

Burra-sahib: The legacy of Sir Edmund Hillary

Steam rises from the pit as crumbling earth is spaded out, uncovering the muslin-wrapped food and hot river stones. The porters in their checked shirts and bright nylon jackets bunch closer to examine the haul as it is prised from the ground.

The New Zealanders have seen it all before. But they too watch intently as, one after the other, carrots, potatoes and tender meat are opened to the crisp mountain air.

John Gully, director of the Nelson-based trekking company Everest Expeditions, grins. It's his gig, and he is enjoying every minute of it. So are the 30 or more teenagers and parent helpers he has gathered from the length and breadth of New Zealand and shepherded all the way here to this remote corner of north-eastern Nepal to partake in what is an extreme version of cultural 'Outward Bound'.

Beyond the courtyard of the Panorama Lodge, the natural basin of Namche Bazar— chief town and trade hub of the Sherpas — dips a hundred metres or more, curving and tilting in the manner of a Greek amphitheatre, orienting its bald terraces and sturdy stone buildings toward an unprotected lip of land. Over that lip, everything plunges 500 metres to the twisting bed of the Bhote Koshi river, then on the far side climbs with equal abruptness 1800 metres to towering peaks of rock.

Namche Bazar itself lies at 3440 metres above sea level and is circled by mountains. They rear up from massive buttresses of chiselled stone — snow-laden, haughty and indifferent. Seductive, yet unapproachable as Judgement Day.

Not 30 kilometres from this very terrace looms the most unapproachable, the most seductive of them all. Called Chomolungma by the Tibetans and Sagarmatha (Mother of the Universe) by the Sherpas, the world knows it simply as Mount Everest. Apex of the earth.

It is Everest that brings me to Nepal. Or, rather, I am drawn here by the first man to break Everest's spell of invincibility by the feat of hauling himself up onto its frozen, wind-blasted summit, then getting back down to tell the tale. Ed Hillary. Sir Edmund. One-time beekeeper of Papakura, Auckland. Adventurer, explorer, writer, humanitarian. Friend of the Sherpas. The man they call 'Burra-sahib' — big in heart.

A member of John Hunt's British expedition, Hillary reached the summit

on 29 May 1953, in company with Sherpa Tenzing Norgay, sending ripples of patriotic pride out across the Commonwealth and through the world. The achievement was a fitting gift for the new queen's coronation and one which was to bind for ever the name of Hillary with the mountain that has come to symbolise the ultimate in endeavour.

Hillary first arrived in the Himalayas in 1951, and in spirit he has never left. During early climbs there, and over the months of preparation for the Everest summit attempt, he developed an abiding respect for the Sherpas. 'Few of us had failed to learn something from the character and temperament of the men themselves, their hardiness and their cheerfulness; their vigour and loyalty; and their freedom from our civilised curse of self-pity,' Hillary wrote.

As friendships deepened, he has found reason to return time and again to the Sherpas' homeland, Solu Khumbu: to build schools and clinics, to lay water pipes, build airstrips and cart out rubbish. To climb.

There are poignant personal connections too with the rugged Solu Khumbu. Here, in 1975, he confronted the aftermath of an aircraft crash that took the lives of his first wife, Louise, and their sixteen-year-old daughter, Belinda. And here, late in life, he has been forced to come to terms with increasingly severe bouts of altitude sickness which threaten to end his mountain visits.

Despite such physical discomforts, Hillary, now in his 81st year, still throws himself into campaigning and fund-raising on behalf of the Sherpas. These days, other footsteps have joined his, and younger backs help shoulder the load, further strengthening the bonds between the Sherpa people and generations of New Zealanders. But no matter how many new hands appear on the scene, throughout the rugged valleys and lofty villages of Solu Khumbu the work and the name of Hillary endure, a fitting tribute to one of the greatest of our adventurers.

At the world's highest hangi, the Kiwis are carving the meat and dishing up vegetables. John Gully's guests — village elders, an army man, the chief park warden — are warming themselves at a woodburner in the lodge's dining hall. But Gully's thoughts are elsewhere. The mountaineer-turned-friendship-ambassador is holding forth to me on the plight of the Nepalese lowland porters. Uneducated and with few prospects, the $5 a day wage for hefting tourist gear up the winding trails is, says Gully, the only hard currency they are likely to see.

'They often get treated like scum. Tour parties load them down, trying to save an extra 20 rupees a day,' he says. As he and his offsiders coax the reluctant porters through the dining-hall door and to the tables, he explains how his approach differs.

'It's like back home. You look after your people.'

Gully should know. He is a veteran of several Everest expeditions, including the 1988 New Zealand–Czechoslovakian attempt on the difficult south-west face, the 1989 New Zealand–Sherpa expedition and the 1990 international expedition.

The porters take a while to grasp the notion that not only are they being invited to eat indoors, but they are to be served by the New Zealanders. Waited on by their employers. The food arrives and, after an awkward silence, their reserve breaks. They tuck in.

Sherap Jangbu and his wife, Lhakpa, owners of the lodge and longtime friends of Gully, oversee proceedings with hospitable warmth. Sherap has made a two-day journey on foot from another village, covering the ground in a single day, to be back in time for the hangi. It has become something of an institution in these parts, as have the Kiwi and local songs that match and mingle in the crowded, low-roofed dining hall when the plates have been cleared.

Later, I slope off to bed, climbing the narrow stairs to the gompa — the lodge's devotional chamber. With accommodation stretched by Gully's big group, I was billeted in this fragrantly scented room on arrival — the first Westerner, said Gully, to do so — and I have called it home ever since. Each night after removing my boots, I have swung back the heavy door and entered, crossing the room's worn boards to doss down on one of the cushioned benches.

I liked the room on sight, with its richly ornate cabinetwork, its elaborate figurines and brightly polished bowls. When the candles are lit, flames flicker and dance across the 110 glass-fronted cubby-holes, each of which cradles a book of sacred Buddhist writings. As I lie awake on the bench, my gaze loses itself among the room's details. Hillary later tells me that one of the most encouraging signs among the Sherpas — a people facing enormous challenges — is the way they have tenaciously clung to their cultural and spiritual links.

From down below the shouts and laughter of the porters cut the air. Emboldened by food and friendship, they have taken to dancing and singing in the courtyard. Tomorrow, Good Friday, we will turn for home.

I have been here less than three weeks, but in that time I have come to understand the devotion to the place of people like Gully, and Hillary before him. It is impossible to spend a day in Solu Khumbu without being overwhelmed by the sheer physicality of the landscape, and to detect something of the special qualities it has forged in the Sherpas.

Like most visitors, I had the first intimations of grandeur thrust at me before I had even set foot in the place. For close to an hour during the flight from Kathmandu, I had watched razorbacks and ever-deepening gorges slide under the wings as we left behind the cultivated lowlands with their houses scattered like spilt salt across the landscape and climbed delicately towards the Khumbu. The nearest road succumbs to the inevitable and calls a halt some six days' walk short of Lukla, our destination and the major gateway to the Sherpa homeland.

In the early 1950s Kathmandu itself was thoroughly isolated, with no airport or road connections to the outside world. Travellers fortunate enough to get an entry permit were forced to walk in through steep hill country, and the few cars on Kathmandu's streets had arrived the same way, carried along the narrow tracks by gangs of porters.

As the Twin Otter aircraft touched down at Lukla on the rag of cleared ground that passes for a hillside airstrip, nervous passengers around me burst into applause. The meagre ramp of a runway, inclined at fifteen degrees, is an early warning of the difficulties this mountainous terrain imposes on people trying to get about.

Built by Hillary so that he could get in building materials for Sherpa schools and for a proposed hospital at Khunde, the airstrip opened the floodgates for tourism. For a time, Hillary fretted that the human deluge would swamp or corrupt Sherpa culture. But after a little uncertainty the Sherpas adapted, learning to charge for food and accommodation, and taking modest precautions to deter theft.

At Lukla I met my two young Sherpa guides, Kami and Kanchha, whose broad, boyish grins and easy good humour went a long way towards explaining Hillary's lingering attachment to the place. They were to help pack in my excessive Western clobber to Namche Bazar, where Gully and his party were resting. I was also scheduled to rest up in Namche.

The importance of acclimatisation at heights above 2500 metres had been drilled into me before leaving Auckland. Failure to adapt gradually to altitude can cause a potentially lethal condition known as acute mountain sickness (AMS). It is triggered when the body succumbs to the effects of low air pressure at high altitude. Only half as much oxygen is absorbed at the altitude of Everest base camp as at sea level, and only a third as much at the summit.

At its most benign, AMS causes headaches, dizziness and sleeplessness. At its worst, it can cause the lungs to fill with fluid and the brain to swell. When it strikes, the only solution is immediate rest and, if things deteriorate, to get down to a lower altitude fast. Despite widespread publicity about AMS, Westerners are still regularly evacuated from the mountains in bad shape. Some die. On Everest itself, even more die. Since Hillary and Tenzing planted themselves on the summit in 1953, 982 others have reached the top of the 8850-metre mountain and 168 have died on its slopes. The odds aren't good: about one in six.

Equipped with that sober statistic, I followed my lively Sherpas through the beautiful foothills. It was a Mary Poppins moment. On the hillsides rhododendrons were breaking into colour, and in the neatly tended fields crops of potato and buckwheat were starting to show. The rock-studded path wound through villages of rectangular stone houses and beside water-powered prayer wheels. Often we came across painted or carved mani stones bearing Buddhist invocations and posts draped with seasons-old prayer flags which fluttered in the light breeze, releasing their faded petitions to heaven. The paths were alive with porters and cattle, laden with goods for distant settlements — everything from bottled water and tins of kerosene to hewn timber and corrugated iron.

The imprints of Ed Hillary hereabouts are not hard to find. Mahendrajyoti, a school near Lukla, carries a sign above one of its modest buildings: 'Sir Admund Hillari, Block A, 1965.' Another notice testifies that, 20 years later, Block C was added. As we walked, Kami pointed to low buildings on the far side of a field overlooking the icy, boulder-choked Dudh Koshi river, whose waters drive headlong from the Everest massif. They belong to Chaurikharka, another school supported by Hillary.

The schools had their beginnings in a conversation which took place in October 1960 around a smoky fire in a barren, windy tract of land beside the Tolam Bau glacier. *World Book Encyclopedia* had earlier agreed to sponsor a ten-month study on the effects of high altitude and low temperatures on human performance, bringing Hillary and others to the Khumbu. They had dutifully hunkered down in what was dubbed the 'Silver Hut' at 5800 metres for a prolonged stay undergoing various scientific tests.

Part-way through the study, while sitting around the fire, Hillary asked his Sherpa friends what they felt would most help their village. A clinic? Improvements to their farms? The answer, reported Hillary, was unequivocal: 'knowledge for our children'.

With financial help from the expedition sponsor, Hillary and some of his mates returned the next year and put up a prefabricated aluminium building, the material having been flown in from Kathmandu to a hazardous makeshift airstrip in the Mingbo valley. It was the first schoolhouse to be built in Khumjung, and the region's first aid project.

A teacher was recruited from the expatriate Sherpa community in Darjeeling, and over the following year glowing reports reached Hillary of the fine work being wrought among the children of Khumjung. Along with the heart-warming comments came petitions from neighbouring villages for similar schools.

Hillary responded with characteristic speed, and the building programme began in earnest with the Himalayan Schoolhouse Expedition of 1963, which involved 200 porters in a sixteen-day marathon journey to pack in everything from window joinery to cumbersome rolls of alkathene irrigation pipe.

The main motivation behind the expedition was Hillary's deep respect and affection for the Sherpas, but he candidly admits to a more political reason: the inroads being made by Chinese communist propaganda and money to the north. 'I . . . felt the Sherpas should at least have some opportunity to see that Western society had its virtues and its opportunities for growth and freedom.'

This time, Hillary managed to raise money not only from the publishers of *World Book Encyclopedia*, whose staff dug deep into their own pockets for the expedition, but also from Chicago-based Sears Roebuck, whose camping equipment Hillary helped design.

Fund-raising is one of the least glamorous but most vital ingredients in any volunteer aid project, and here Ed Hillary's personal qualities proved invaluable. Close friend Mike Gill quotes a *World Book* executive's revealing first encounter with 'this guy Hillary who'd climbed Everest and got a knighthood for it'. The Americans knew Hillary would not work for nothing, and would probably be packing a whole gang of lawyers and accountants, but they figured they could tough it out.

'Then in comes this tall guy, by himself, with his hair all over the place and carrying an old briefcase held together with string. Well, that threw us right from the start. And then when . . . we asked how much he would like for himself he says: "Well, on an expedition we usually don't take any money for ourselves." We didn't know whether he meant it. For a bit we thought he might just be the coolest cat we'd ever met. Then, we began to feel sorry for him. We felt we had to help this guy — force him to take the money. Up till then I'd never been able to understand why he hadn't made a million bucks out of Everest.'

Well planned though it was, the schoolhouse project did hit snags. One of the biggest was in Namche Bazar. A request to take over the government-funded school in the town — which at the time had a reputation for deceit and banditry — was subverted by local politics, and by the resident teacher's attempt to make off with money earmarked for school supplies.

Hillary proved no dupe, and the ruse failed, but division in the community slowed attempts to bring education within reach of all Sherpa

children. Nevertheless, Hillary persevered, in 1964 setting up a charitable foundation, the Himalayan Trust, to raise funds and oversee building projects in the Khumbu. Almost 40 years later, a total of 30 schools have been established, and the trust has had an impact on twice that number.

Recognising that teachers at the primary schools lacked training, the trust decided in 1997 to start a one-month teacher training programme in the winter off-season. 'We expected about 40 teachers, but 160 turned up,' Hillary told me. 'At the moment, the number is closer to 200.'

John Gully is another veteran climber who has taken up the education challenge. Just days before I arrived in the village of Phakding, his group handed over to the local school more than a thousand books they had brought out from New Zealand. As a form of loss insurance, the wily Gully had taken care to distribute carbon copies of the book list to the mayor, the local lama and the village committee.

After an early breakfast of porridge and toast at Phakding's Namaste Lodge, I stepped outside to get the measure of the day. The pine-clad hills smoked with mist. Here and there magnolias put out creamy white flowers among the red stains of rhododendrons. Crows fussed and flapped about. At my feet, icy water foamed and spat, making noisy work of getting past the river boulders. I could not recall having felt more in love with the sheer act of standing somewhere. Of surrendering to the simple pleasure of stepping out purposefully into a landscape.

The Khumbu lies just outside the tropics, so when the midday sun gets a good angle of attack on the crepuscular gorges, temperatures can soar. With that in mind, I secured an extra bottle of 'Hill Sweet' mineral water and set off with my guides Kami and Kanchha.

Beyond Phakding, the Dudh Koshi river grows more assertive and the swing-bridges, with their arcing wires and festoons of prayer flags, develop into true feats of structural engineering. As we approached one, the air came alive with the dull thud of a chopper labouring in thin air up toward Everest base camp. The sound fired medivac images in my head, and grim anecdotes about death by AMS. Less than a week before I arrived, two climbers had been killed in icefalls and a German visitor suffering from AMS and vomiting blood had been airlifted out. At this altitude, most helicopter flights are evacuations.

Such intimations of mortality were soon swept aside, however, when we came across yet another reminder of the energetic Admund Hillari: the entrance to Sagarmatha National Park. The idea of a national park which incorporated Everest and the valley systems settled by the Sherpas had been kicked around for some time when a United Nations forestry worker got talking to Hillary in Kathmandu. The Khumbu was park-sized, said the UN man, and, being familiar with New Zealand's mountain parks, he thought New Zealand had the necessary expertise to oversee the job.

'He said someone would need to inspire them, so I went to the New Zealand government,' Hillary told me. 'I must have given them a good line because they went ahead with it.'

Following talks with local leaders, New Zealand project managers arrived in the Khumbu in 1975 under a bilateral aid agreement, and for the next six years they helped shape the amenities and policies for this rugged land of deep gorges and glacial valleys, home to 3500 Sherpas and around 500 Tibetan refugees and Nepalese officials, soldiers and labourers. In 1976, Sagarmatha was gazetted as Nepal's third national park. Three years later it was declared a World Heritage site.

The New Zealand government's handiwork includes a visitor centre and three park lodges at Namche as well as a tree nursery in Teshinga — all now funded by Hillary's trust. The government also trained Sherpas as wardens.

Seated at a small wooden desk in a sparsely furnished office, Sagarmatha National Park's chief warden, Nima Wanchu Sherpa, confided with me that the job was not without its problems. For one thing, he said, it was poorly paid. He was a graduate of New Zealand's Lincoln College and held a MSc from the United States, but here he was earning less than Sherpas working for the trekking companies in Kathmandu. Of his 38-strong staff, only two were Sherpas — that in itself told the story.

Deforestation was another worry. In the 400 years since the Sherpas came here from the north, 50 percent of the forest has been cut. At high altitude it is slow to recover. In Jorsale, just within the park boundary, a 35-year-old blue pine stands 24 metres tall. At Namche Bazar, 600 metres higher, a tree of that age reaches a mere sixteen metres. It is doubtful whether the slow-growing rhododendron forests will ever recover.

Recent legislation limits locals to collecting dry firewood for their own use in the park. It cannot be sold to visitors, who must bring in alternative fuels. But the law has to be policed. Sometimes villagers are driven to cut green wood, said Nima, in which case he must impose a fine.

An experimental tree-planting has been made at park headquarters, funded by the trust. Encouraged by this move, villagers have replanted the hill behind Namche. The trees look healthy, though, like all plants here, they are in no hurry to get bigger.

Not far beyond Jorsale, a spectacular swing-bridge makes a final crossing of the Dudh Koshi. The river's blue glacial melt-water courses through the boulder-choked gorge 80 metres or more beneath the bridge's wooden planks. After waiting for a couple of yak trains — which tend to get right-of-way on the flimsy structure — we crossed and followed the zigzagging dirt track up the wall of the gorge.

An hour and a half later we reached the maze of paths and rock-walled corrals that mark the lower fringe of Namche Bazar. Twenty years ago there were one or two shops and three lodges here. Now more than 40 lodges and a warren of shops line its crowded thoroughfares and cramped terraces, with new ones added every year.

Across the Khumbu as a whole, fifteen to 20 new lodges are built every trekking season to cater for the 15,000 or more tourists who beat a path to this tranquil corner of the world. Who can blame the locals for seizing a business chance? Growing crops and herding livestock have never been easy in Namche. Early on, the town made its mark as a commercial centre, lying on the trade route between Tibet and India. When the trade dried up, mountaineering, then trekking, stepped into the breach, and the Sherpas welcomed both with open arms.

Indeed, mountaineering had exerted its influence on the Sherpas long before the first climbers set foot on the stony paths that thread between the villages. With Nepal closed to the outside world until the early 1950s, the first British expeditions were forced to sidestep the Khumbu entirely and attempt climbs from the Tibetan side. The man responsible for throwing Sherpas into the equation was Scottish physician Alexander Kellas, who had had first-hand experience of their abilities at high altitude. With a good many emigrant Sherpas working in Darjeeling when the first British Everest expedition set out from there in 1921, it was natural that they should be hired in large numbers as load-bearers and helpers — a practice that continues to this day.

In 1933, a seventeen-year-old Sherpa by the name of Tenzing Norgay emigrated to Darjeeling to take advantage of just such an opportunity. His moment of glory was to come 20 years later when he stood beside Hillary on the world's highest peak.

As Kami, Kanchha and I climbed the winding path to the Panorama Lodge, we looked down at clusters of colour-co-ordinated tents pitched on scraps of dusty terrace. This was the climbing season, and the brightly equipped mountaineers had almost succeeded in turning Namche into a giant Ludo board.

At the Panorama, bad news awaited us. Though he had not mentioned it to me, Kami's mother was dying of stomach cancer. Dave Austin, the doctor with Gully's group, did not expect her to live more than a week. He had done what he could to ease her pain.

The illness left Kami's father, Nima Dorje, not only grief-stricken but in financial difficulties. Searching for a cure for his wife over the past months had eaten through his meagre savings. Unable to read or write, he had no prospect of becoming a sirdar — head Sherpa on an expedition or trek. It was a cruel twist of fate for the talented 49-year-old, a man who had climbed five times with Everest legend Reinhold Messner. It was heart-rending to realise what few resources the poorest of these isolated people had to draw on when tragedy struck. Just resilience and an indomitable courage.

Not all news on the medical front was grim. Austin had worked something of a travelling clinic on his way to Namche, attending to fourteen Sherpas in Phakding alone. As the head of Whangarei Hospital's intensive care unit, he was well used to seeing the results of whatever life could throw at the human body. And having served time on a Whitbread yacht, on ski fields and dive trips, he had developed into something of an adventure specialist.

Austin had with him a formidable kit of pharmaceuticals and equipment, including a portable device for fighting AMS by artificially increasing atmospheric pressure. A veteran of Gully's 1992 Youth to Everest expedition, he knew what to expect in the Khumbu, and before leaving New Zealand had approached more than 30 drug companies for medical donations.

'They all gave,' he said. 'It was magnificent.'

When Austin made the short climb up to the hospital at Khunde, which stands on a narrow plateau above Namche, I went with him. The doctor in charge, Canadian Jim Litch, was glad of the donated medicines. He and his staff treat around 9000 patients a year — 250 of them Westerners.

The squat, stone-walled hospital and a nearby school are further reminders of Hillary's impulse to build things in the Khumbu. Doing something about education had been his first response to Sherpa needs, and attending to their health was a close second.

Just two days' walk from Khunde, during the 1963 Schoolhouse Expedition, Hillary and his climbing mates encountered their first large-scale medical challenge: smallpox. Powerless to help a widow's dying daughter, and realising the contagion was spreading quickly, they resolved on a vaccination programme. Hillary arranged for an airdrop of vaccine, and soon foreigners and Sherpas alike were administering the life-saving doses to hundreds of people at a time in the nearby villages.

Eventually, it became clear how the smallpox had arrived. A Sherpa employed by an American Everest expedition had become infected in Kathmandu and, though brought low by fever, had doggedly persevered — as only Sherpas can — unknowingly carrying the deadly disease into the heart of the Khumbu.

Being of necessity frugal, many villagers declined to burn the clothes of their dead relatives, instead trusting to a hard scrub in running water. To make matters worse, the Sherpas, who normally cremated bodies, were seized by the notion that the smallpox would be borne aloft by the smoke to infect others. So, after death, many smallpox victims were committed to the rivers. Although Hillary's team had been vaccinated within the previous twelve months, they put themselves forward for a new dose. To their surprise, every one of them reacted positively to it, developing fever, swollen glands and aching arms.

When I came across that information, it did nothing for my own sense of invulnerability. For reasons best known to the world of science, Nepal is a haven for pernicious diseases. In Auckland, my travel medicine specialist had furnished a long list of recommended vaccines, including hepatitis A, diphtheria, tetanus, typhoid and polio, each of which I was duly subjected to. She also passed on the helpful information that smallpox has now been eradicated.

About his own encounter with the disease, Hillary later wrote: 'Of all the programmes we carried out on the expedition — schools, waterworks, medical clinics, and the like — the one most widely appreciated was undoubtedly the vaccination, and this hadn't been part of my original plans.'

Those words were penned in 1964, the year Hillary built Khunde hospital. It was also the year he and others bought a tract of pasture and terraced potato fields in the small village of Lukla on behalf of the Nepalese government, and turned it into a landing-strip. By making the seventeen-day porter trek from Kathmandu redundant, the Lukla strip soon became Nepal's busiest mountain airfield and the gateway to Everest.

Pinned in Namche by a scheduled rest day, I decided to find out more about the effect of tourism on the Sherpa way of life.

Sherap, the Panorama Lodge's genial host, recalled the time 40 years ago when the outside world was little more than a rumour. He remembers as a boy seeing his first handful of cooked rice and tasting its puffy sweetness. In those days, buckwheat and potatoes were the staples, and rice was reserved for feasts. It came from the Terrai, the fertile lowland plain of southern Nepal, ten days away.

In the early 1970s, Sherap served as cook boy on various Everest expeditions. He had embarked on the classic Sherpa career path, from cook boy to cook, then sherpa and finally sirdar. Then, in 1975, even as New Zealanders were helping turn the Khumbu into a park, trekkers began appearing on the trails in promising numbers, and Sherap switched vocations.

All Sherpas hereabouts now have some connection with trekking. Once, they were farmers or traders. Sherap's father had been a trader, travelling four times a year over the 6150-metre Nangpa La Pass into Tibet as far as Lhasa. Large numbers of Tibetan refugees have since made the reverse journey, settling as far away as Kathmandu and northern India. Some 200 of them live in Namche Bazar.

Was there enough for everyone — Tibetans included — to make a living from trekking, I asked Sherap.

'I hope so,' he said.

I found Ang Phurba Sherpa, the town's former mayor, in one of Namche's labyrinthine alleys, behind the counter of the Potala Mountaineering Shop. The shelves were laden with packaged and bottled goods laboriously brought here on the backs of porters. Across the dusty, flagstoned lane stood the Everest Book Store, its sign offering phone, fax and e-mail services. It is one of the ironies of modern life that satellite dishes now bring the world to the Khumbu, a place so physically isolated that it has not seen a wheelbarrow, let alone a car.

Ang Phurba began his eighteen-year stint as mayor in 1973, when Namche was a very different place. In the early days, expeditions with 1500 porters passed through here. Now, he told me, expeditions had shrunk in size to perhaps ten members and 100 porters. But the number of expeditions has rocketed: in 2001, 51 separate groups were signed up to besiege Everest from both the Tibetan and Nepali sides — 26 of them, sharing seventeen permits, at base camp alone.

'People have good jobs now,' Ang told me, 'but it is difficult to protect our culture. Our children leave the villages and go to boarding school in Kathmandu or India. Of our eight- and nine-year-olds, 60 percent have left — a lot of them sponsored.' Ang's own children are scattered: a daughter and two sons live locally, but two daughters are in the United States and another son is in Kathmandu, along with two grandchildren.

At the Khangri Money Exchange, Dorje Lama Sherpa was worried about another pressing matter: the environment. Until recently he headed the Sagarmatha Pollution Control Committee, set up in 1991. A big problem, said Dorje, was the difficulty of removing glass and other litter. During their

1990 expedition, New Zealanders Rob Hall and Gary Ball oversaw the removal of five tonnes of rubbish from base camp. That was a start, and other commercial operators have since smartened up their act. In 1998, shopkeepers, lodge owners and the expeditions themselves stopped packing in glass beer bottles.

The previous evening, I had struck up a conversation with someone at my elbow as we leaned on a rail watching the last gilding of sunlight wash from a high peak. He introduced himself as Roger Drake, from Grand Canyon National Park, specialist in back-country toilets; a man who had been to Everest to put a public amenity somewhere on the north side.

Drake acquainted me with the fact that one in six children here died before the age of five. A lot of that mortality had to do with sanitation. He was finding out just how much by, among other things, running faecal coliform tests. In Drake's view, there was no easy answer to tourist pressure. The locals knew how to work a composting toilet, he said. The problem was too many toilets and not enough fields to put the waste on.

By the 1990s, the route in had become so well used that it was known as the 'Kleenex trail', and discarded waste in the glacial valleys had begun accumulating in unmanageable quantities as the number of commercial climbs grew. In 1991, 21 climbers had reached the summit almost simultaneously, and on one day in 1993 some 40 people stood at the top of the world. The trend toward guiding novices up Everest for a fee stirred Hillary into a rare public comment. Such operators were, he said, 'engendering disrespect for the mountain'.

Respect was a natural concept for Hillary to fall back on. It characterised his half-century-long relationship with the Sherpas. Respect for them and their fragile, unforgiving landscape, for their culture and their religious beliefs.

Not a convert to Buddhism himself, Hillary the gruff, craggy mountaineer is nevertheless attuned to the spiritual impulse. Indeed, he looks back on his 1977 jetboat expedition up the Ganges as one of the most rewarding he has undertaken precisely because it combined adventure with spirituality. On that occasion, Hillary and his team — which included his son Peter — journeyed from the river's mouth in the Bay of Bengal 2575 kilometres to its source high in the Himalayas.

Of a ceremonial blessing *en route*, Hillary wrote: 'We were transported into another world, a world of religious fervour, of deafening sound, of the importance of Mother Ganga, and the surprising acceptance of our journey as a sacred pilgrimage . . . I think for a brief space of time, we almost became Hindu in our thoughts. We were completely absorbed into the beliefs and the history and the understanding of the people of Mother Ganga.'

Hillary has done what he can to preserve the spirituality that lay at the very core of Sherpa life. The Himalayan Trust has helped build the Salleri Monastery and restore others that had fallen into disrepair. In the course of his work, Hillary also developed a warm friendship with the abbott of Tengboche Monastery, the vital spring of Buddhism in Nepal. The monastery, perched on a jutting spur of land high up the valley toward base camp, presides over some of the most imposing scenery on earth.

It was to Tengboche that Kami, Kanchha and I bent our steps early one morning.

Our way, as we left Namche, was made aromatic by braziers of burning juniper balanced on steps and courtyard walls about the houses. The crisp mountain air was invigorating, and electric with promise. It offered up the detail of even distant objects with crystal clarity. This was true Everest country. Hillary country.

As we walked I fell to thinking about what it was that instilled in people the vocation, the compulsion, to climb. George Leigh Mallory, the dashing English climber of the 1920s whose every action — including reading Shakespeare aloud at high altitude — lent a romantic sheen to the enterprise, famously answered, 'Because it is there', when asked why he persisted in attempting Everest.

No one since Mallory has said it better. Hillary himself confessed to having always had a sense of adventure, but one that was undirected, inchoate, until at sixteen he went with a school party to Mount Ruapehu. 'Ten days of skiing and scrambling about sold me on snow and mountains and all the rest of it. That trip got me going,' he told me. 'Then, as I developed, it became more important. Mountains and the people of the mountains became *the* interest of my life.'

Climber Jon Krakauer has written about what he calls the 'culture of ascent'. An idealised and uncorrupted community of souls. Competitive, yes. But sharing a concern not just with getting to the top, but with how it is done. The hard way. 'I quickly came to understand,' wrote Krakauer of his own experience, 'that climbing Everest was primarily about enduring pain.'

On his epic ascent Hillary had used bottled oxygen — 'English air' — but few aluminium ladders or fixed ropes, scores of which now clutter Everest.

In May 1978 Messner got up without even bottles, making what some purists hailed as the first true ascent.

In the spring of 1999 climber Babu Chiri Sherpa went one better, spending 20 hours without oxygen on the summit. Before leaving Namche, I had noticed on the bakehouse door a poster announcing that the local hero was now attempting a sixteen-hour 'speed expedition'. Undoubtedly, he was already somewhere in the vast landscape up ahead, making his antlike preparations.

My first view of Everest — Peak XV, the 'Third Pole' — was not something I was prepared for. Rounding a bend, I was stopped in my tracks by a breath-taking panorama of sharply hewn summits, a gallery of icy pinnacles towering above forested foothills. Out on a distant ridge, insignificant against its overwhelming backdrop, lay the speck that was Tengboche Monastery. High above, from behind the shoulder of a neighbouring peak, reared the blunt cone of Everest, trailing a plume of ice crystals.

It was humbling to think of the rangy 33-year-old from Papakura and his main man, Tenzing, up there, tenaciously hauling themselves into the jetstream amid ice and rock. Not knowing what to expect. Eight kilometres high, and climbing. Fighting exhaustion, they overcame the last hurdle, a twelve-metre-high wall of smooth rock — known ever after as the Hillary Step — and clawed their way to the summit.

'A few whacks of the ice-axe, a few cautious steps, and Tenzing and I were on top,' Hillary wrote. It was 11.30 am.

Anglo-Saxon that he is, Hillary held out his arm to shake hands, but that gesture fell short for the excited Tenzing. Filled with emotion, he threw his arms about Hillary and, four-square on the roof of the world, the two men hugged each other.

Hillary snapped a picture of Tenzing holding aloft an ice-axe strung with flags: Indian, Nepalese, United Nations, the Union Jack. He had not remembered to pack the New Zealand flag. Nor did he think to pose for a photograph himself. Such things, like the knighthood that came soon after, meant little. Instead, he took shots down the major ridges as proof of the climb.

Tenzing dug a hole in the snow and placed in it some biscuits, a piece of chocolate and a few sweets. Beside this offering Hillary buried a white crucifix on behalf of expedition leader John Hunt. They nibbled mintcake. Hillary glanced at his watch. 11.45. Time to move.

Earlier that day, in the grey light of dawn, they had looked out from the

small ledge they called Camp Nine and seen, 5000 metres down, the old monastery of Tengboche. 'To Hillary, perhaps, it does not mean much,' Tenzing later wrote in *Man of Everest*. 'To a man from the West it is only a far, strange place in a far, strange country.' But in truth for Hillary it did mean, or at least came to mean, a great deal.

Tengboche was the site of the victorious British Expedition's first base camp, and in the years that followed the climbers who passed this way availed themselves of the monastery's hospitality and sought the blessing of the abbot. When, in 1989, news came through that the old monastery had burned to the ground, Hillary (then New Zealand High Commissioner in India) travelled the world raising money to rebuild it.

Cresting the ridge at Tengboche after a steep climb, we arrived on the flattened knoll occupied by the monastery buildings. To the west rose Khumbi Yul Lha, the sacred mountain. To the east, the haughty precipices of Kangtega and the beautiful Ama Dablam. North-east, at the head of the valley, lay the massive wall between Nuptse and Lhotse, which all but curtains off the final act — Everest. The scale and grandeur of these mountains seems to create a sort of spiritual parallax, blanking out mundane worries and pulling down new perspectives on life.

A fine place, then, to replant the flower of Buddhism uprooted from Tibet by years of Chinese persecution.

The monastery has an unlikely ally in Michael Schmitz, a German architect who has logged 30 years in Nepal, planning new towns in the south and rebuilding schools in the wake of the devastating 1985 earthquake. Schmitz now devotes seven months a year to the monastery, overseeing the building of accommodation blocks and stone walls, and conducting daily tours. 'If this monastery dies, everything is lost. It is the heart of Sherpa culture,' he told me, counting the donations after a well-patronised tour. It was a good take — the equivalent of US$50. Enough, in this remote region, to buy half a bag of cement.

Before crawling into my tent, which had been pitched on a narrow tongue of land, I took in the view. I was higher than Mount Cook, and all around me brutal rock rose heavenward. There were bodies entombed in this landscape. I thought again of the 168 climbers, New Zealander Rob Hall among them, still on the slopes of Everest. Even now, the mountain's blunt peak was releasing a long ribbon of ice, stripped from it by gale-force winds — testimony to the raw power unleashed here. Just last year, Tengboche had been battered by 180 km/h winds.

I learned that Babu Chiri Sherpa had achieved his speed ascent, taking just under seventeen hours. Less than a year later, the 35-year-old climber, veteran of ten ascents, fell to his death while taking photographs.

That's how it goes in this place. Death and beauty. The thorn with the rose. And both writ large.

'The Sherpas' finest traits have been developed in their battle against their tough environment,' Hillary once said. 'The last thing I would wish to do is to remove them from battle completely; better to put some sharper weapons into the Sherpas' hands.'

The next morning I met the spiritual leader of the Sherpas, the 63-year-old abbot of Tengboche — Ngawang Tenzin Jangpo. As he draped round my neck the white prayer scarf I had presented to him, all of Hillary's work seemed to resurface. A rope across rock. A hand outstretched. It was through acts, not words, that Hillary worked. Like the best of friends.

It had been a cold night in the tent. One of the coldest I had known. Now light was throwing ice and rock into relief, brightening paths and passes. I shouldered a bag and looked for Kami and Kanchha.

Time to move.

September 2001

Illustrations

Flower of the Sky: Jean Batten

Some time on 25 November 1980, as former Heathrow air traffic controller Judith Chisholm worked the controls of her single-engined Cessna Turbo Centurion above the endlessly unfolding Tasman, her eyes fixed on the distant curving horizon, a voice came to her. It was the voice of Jean Batten.

Fresh from breaking the long-standing England–Australia solo speed record set by Batten 44 years earlier, Chisholm was mid-ocean, en route to Auckland to challenge the aviator's celebrated England–New Zealand record when she heard the voice, unmistakable and 'rather plummy': 'Hello, Judith, you look tiny down there.'

It was one of those surreal moments in aviation history. The newcomer, the protégé watched over by a heroine of 1930s flight, a poster girl of the machine age. One of the Immortals. Craning her neck, Chisholm could see the Boeing 747 high above, contrailing through the blue vault of sky; could picture Jean Batten, whom she had met in Sydney, scrutinising her progress from the Boeing's flight deck.

The 71-year-old air veteran had hitched a ride on a Qantas flight in order to be at Mangere when the young flyer landed.

With this convergence, the two women were bridging time as much as ocean. Chisholm had not even been born when, in vulnerable piston-engined aircraft, Batten set her long-distance records. With little more than a watch and compass to guide her, the New Zealander had performed near-

miraculous feats of navigation and endurance. In four short, exhilarating years she had blazed a meteoric trail through the world's press, garnering undreamt-of fame and recognition for her exploits.

The tributes were quick in coming: the Britannia and the Segrave trophies, the Johnston Memorial Air Navigation Trophy, the Challenge and the Harmon International trophies. The Coupe de Sibour. Medals. Decorations.

And how the old benchmarks fell. In 1934, the England–Australia woman's record. In 1935, the first return flight to England by a woman and the world record for a flight from England to Brazil. The following year, the fastest flight from England to New Zealand, the first direct flight from England to Auckland, fastest trans-Tasman flight. In 1937, the Australia-England solo record . . .

They were the achievements of a complex and driven woman, much courted yet never married; a woman who became the channel for the frustrated ambitions of a domineering mother. One who, although desperate for fame and adulation, invariably shrank from it into a guarded, private world.

It could have been very different.

Born Jane Gardner Batten on 15 September 1909, Jean was the daughter of a Rotorua dentist and a socialite mother with a fondness for the stage — both of them second-generation New Zealanders. In childhood she proved herself to be an accomplished musician, an enthusiastic swimmer and a talented dancer, but unexpectedly, at the height of her musical promise, she folded the lid of her piano for good and took up flying.

It is easy to see in the grain of Batten's life the controlling influence of her mother, Ellen. A strong, independent-minded woman, after marriage Ellen had thrown herself into small-town committee work, dabbled with the easel and engaged in amateur theatrical work. Mounted on her white mare and wearing a feathered hat, she was a common sight on the streets of Edwardian Rotorua.

Later photographs show Ellen as tall and strikingly attractive, with a haughty bearing and a taut, controlled smile. Even as a mature woman with a string of achievements to her name, Jean often gave the impression of being in the lee of her formidable mother — sheltered yet stifled, overprotected. In a state of permanent surrender.

Jean's father, Fred, was also good-looking in a robust, clean-cut way. A keen rugby player, he was also a skilled boxer and prize-winning rower. Through her childhood, he developed something more — a reputation as a womaniser. This, together with Ellen's increasing dissatisfaction with her own life, put fatal strain on the marriage.

When the split came, there was never any doubt where Jean's loyalty lay. A sickly child, she had needed special care from birth and the attentions of her mother seem to have cemented between them a life-long bond.

The expression of that bond was in flight.

Soon after Jean was born, Ellen pinned to the wall above the mantelpiece newspaper clippings of Louis Blériot and his aircraft. Just weeks earlier, the French aviator had become the first person to cross the English Channel by air, taking 37 minutes to achieve the feat and claim the *Daily Mail*'s £1000 prize.

In his approach the disorganised Blériot showed a proclivity to improvisation typical of pioneers. Lifting off from France in poor visibility and with no compass, he soon became lost. Chancing on several fishing boats, he guessed the way to Dover and once there followed the coast until he saw someone waving a flag. He then crash-landed.

The girl in the cot beneath his photograph would grow up to do things differently.

Jean Batten came into the world just as the foundations of heavier-than-air flight were being laid. Six years earlier, the Wright brothers had made the world's first powered controlled flight by aeroplane. Closer to home, Richard Pearse had been experimenting with a home-made flying machine in Upper Waitohi, near Dunedin. In 1906 Alberto Santos-Dumont made the first official flight in Europe. In 1910 Baroness Raymonde de Laroche became the first woman to gain a pilot's licence.

Then, in 1914, the First World War unleashed a fevered race to design high-performance aircraft and to train the hundreds of pilots needed to fly them. Dedicated factories sprang up across Europe and the United States to satisfy the demands of the new industry.

At war's end, hundreds of unwanted aircraft came cheaply onto the market, spurring recreational flying. Former military pilots at home in the new medium found work as barnstormers, entertaining crowds with aerial stunts and flying demonstrations. Air shows, festivals, exhibitions, prizes and race trophies stirred public enthusiasm, new distance and endurance records were set and, with the start of experimental airmail deliveries, aviation began to insinuate itself into the civilian mainstream.

Meanwhile, Jean Batten got on with her childhood, shifting to Auckland with her family at the age of four and living with them in a succession of rented houses. She was enrolled at a private school, Melmerley College, but when Fred sailed for France with the New Zealand Expeditionary Force in 1917 Ellen was forced to find a less expensive school. Life quickly became a downward spiral of cost-cutting and ever more shabby accommodation.

Nevertheless, in those years Ellen found the means to stock her daughter's bookcase with biographies of action heroes: Drake, Stanley, Cook and Columbus. Florence Nightingale. Joan of Arc. She also took her daughter to Kohimarama Beach, where the Walsh brothers had formed the country's first flying school to train pilots for the Royal Flying Corps.

Batten later claimed it was this experience of seeing aeroplanes on the harbour that first filled her with the desire to fly: 'The little seaplane would skim across the water throwing up a curtain of spray and rise like a seabird up into the blue sky. At such moments as I watched spellbound and the plane turned to fly back and circle the bay with the sunlight glistening on its silver wings, I experienced such a surge of exhilaration that I felt quite sick with longing to be up there in it.'

Her parents' marriage didn't long survive Fred's return from the war, though in later life Batten was to cloak her childhood years with warming tales of family bliss. Ellen left her husband, taking Jean with her. She enrolled her daughter in exclusive Ladies College in Remuera, and the institution set about refining Jean's speech and polishing her deportment and society manners. It also instilled in her an unappealing yet unshakeable obsession with status and wealth.

Jean learned the piano and studied ballet under a former dancer in Diaghilev's company who styled herself Madame Valerie. Jean was a determined if somewhat withdrawn student with a flashy and rather superficial keyboard style. After some clumsiness, however, she revealed an aptitude for dance — sufficient for Madame Valerie to choose her as soloist at the school's annual public performance.

It was to be the same, years later, with flight: awkward, anti-social, stubbornly persistent, then solo.

In May 1927 Jean's attention was wrenched from the provincial boards to the world stage by the achievement of young American aviator Charles Lindbergh. That month, flying a Ryan single-engined monoplane romantically christened *The Spirit of St Louis*, Lindbergh made the first non-stop solo crossing of the Atlantic from New York to Paris, covering the 5600 kilometres in 33.5 hours. He was an instant hero and the toast of aero clubs everywhere. His flight rekindled the excitement Jean had felt at Kohimarama and awakened in the seventeen-year-old a desire to take to the skies on some long distance odyssey of her own.

There was no shortage of fresh achievements to fuel the dream. The following year an unassuming Australian, Bert Hinkler, made the first solo flight from England to Australia, taking just over two weeks to complete the epic journey in a lumbering Avro Avian biplane.

Three months later, another Australian was in the news. With long-time associate Charles Ulm and two Americans, Charles Kingsford-Smith flew his none-too-quick Fokker trimotor, *Southern Cross*, from the United States across the Pacific to Australia. The men took off from San Francisco on 31 May 1928 and made the journey in three stages — the longest, from Honolulu to Suva, took a numbing 35 hours — battling a series of violent storms to arrive in Australia on 9 June. It was another world first and one of aviation's epic flights.

In September, Kingsford-Smith and his crew became the first to cross the Tasman, and the conquerors of isolation were given rousing welcomes throughout New Zealand. Fred Batten took Jean to a reception in Auckland where she met the aviation legend and excitedly announced her intention to learn to fly. The news was taken as a joke, but it had the instant backing of Ellen, who, relishing secretive rebellion, turned the notion into a fully fledged conspiracy.

The following year, while on holiday in Australia with her daughter, Ellen arranged a short flight for her with Kingsford-Smith in his 'Old Bus', *Southern Cross*. It worked the same magic. On her return to Auckland, Jean told Fred that she intended to quit ballet and music and become a professional pilot. More than that, she wanted to emulate Kingsford-Smith and blaze new air routes. To become the first person to fly from England to New Zealand, to prove that women were up to the challenge.

It could have been Ellen talking.

Fred took a dim view of such plans, provoking Ellen and Jean to new heights of deception and frosting the relationship with his daughter. On the pretext of taking up study at the Royal College of Music in London, Jean sold her piano and in early 1930 bought one-way liner tickets to England for her and Ellen.

For both women it was to be the beginning of a life-long exile.

North London's Stag Lane aerodrome in the early 1930s was home to the de Havilland Aircraft Company and to the London Aeroplane Club, one of the country's biggest commercial flying schools.

For ten years the entrepreneurial Geoffrey de Havilland had been turning out aircraft at Stag Lane — his interest in entomology reflected in the name of what was to become, in all its variants, his most famous: the Moth. The flying school had seven or eight of the open-cockpit biplanes, all painted silver and bright yellow, and it was at the controls of one of these wood and fabric machines that Batten got her first taste of aerial freedom.

As a woman, she was by no means unusual in wanting to fly. A sizeable number of female students were taking lessons at Stag Lane and elsewhere in Britain, though Batten was the first from New Zealand. Nor was her long-distance ambition unique. America's first female pilot, the glamorous Harriet Quimby, had flown solo across the English Channel just three years after Blériot and her compatriot Amelia Earhart, who in 1928 had become the first woman to fly the Atlantic (as a passenger), was about to launch into her spectacular, and ultimately tragic, solo flying career.

The London Aeroplane Club trained, or had as members, a star-studded list of female fliers, including Lady Heath, the first woman to fly to South Africa, Lady Bailey, the first woman to make a return flight to Cape Town, and the remarkable Duchess of Bedford, who learned to fly in her sixties. The Duchess made several forays to India and Africa, often knitting or admiring the view from the comfort of a deck chair in the cabin of a big Fokker flown by her personal pilot.

While Batten was taking lessons at Stag Lane, another of its graduates, inspired by Bert Hinkler's solo flight to Australia, scraped up enough money to buy a Gypsy Moth and became the first woman to trace his journey. Her name was Amy Johnson, and she returned to England to find herself hailed as the 'darling of the people'. Though Johnson's feat wasn't exceptional — eight others had already flown the distance solo and had covered the ground faster — the Yorkshire typist had demolished the myth of the dare-devil pilot, the expert, the stubble-jawed aviator with superhuman skills.

Meanwhile, Batten doggedly persevered with her own training — and it was a slow business, despite what she later claimed. In her 1938 autobiography, *My Life*, and in newspaper interviews, she hinted at rapid, effortless progress: 'I took to the air like a penguin to water. . . I learned to fly fairly quickly and found . . . that I had a natural aptitude for it.'

An anonymous fellow New Zealand student saw things differently. In a letter to a friend he wrote of Batten: 'She says that some day she is going to fly from England to New Zealand. But it doesn't look much that way yet for she is having such terrific trouble with her landings. This morning she crashed into a fence; fortunately she wasn't hurt, just a little bruised, but the pluck of the girl is astounding.' Flying solo, Batten had overshot the field and her Moth had hit a wire fence and flipped. Ashamed of the accident, she took some time to regain her spirits and never spoke of it to anyone.

At Stag Lane she had three instructors — word was that two of them had given up on their plodding pupil. The third, Major Herbert Travers, had more staying power. Travers had taught Amy Johnson to fly and Batten warmed to him, calling him 'a born instructor with the rare gift of divine patience'.

Her perseverance paid off. In the autumn of 1930, Batten gained her private pilot's licence. Straight away, and rather naively, she tried to interest potential sponsors — some mere acquaintances — in funding a solo flight to the antipodes. Not surprisingly, she drew a blank in England. Undeterred, she sailed back to New Zealand to test the waters there.

Ground down by what had by this time developed into a worldwide depression, New Zealanders showed little enthusiasm for Batten's extravagant scheme. Unexpectedly, however, Fred had come to terms with his daughter's single-minded ambition, and he paid for her to take instruction at the Richmond Navigation School. Having done this, she sailed again for England to follow a new line of attack: the better to woo sponsors, she would study for a commercial licence.

In her unreliable autobiography Batten wrote: 'I was just able, with mother's help, to scrape enough money together for the fare to England and it almost broke my heart to leave her behind.' The truth, as biographer Ian Mackersey discovered, was quite different. Her brother John, then back briefly from film work in London, had financed her passage. It was an act of generosity, like countless others from the parade of men in her life, that Batten would never acknowledge.

Even more problematic than her dealings with John was Batten's treatment of Fred Truman, a 29-year-old New Zealand pilot serving with the Royal Air Force in India. Batten met Truman on the voyage to New Zealand and he fell for her utterly. They saw much of each other in Auckland, where he was on leave, then when he had returned to Quetta, on India's Northwest Frontier, she wrote to him from London. Truman, who entertained notions of marriage, was persuaded to make Batten a series of loans, culminating in his entire airforce gratuity of £500. It was never repaid.

'Once my mind was set on anything, it was quite useless to attempt to swerve me from my purpose or dampen my enthusiasm in any way,' she later wrote.

On 9 April 1933, soon after gaining her commercial licence, Jean Batten stepped out onto the tarmac at Lympne airport in Kent and stood in the pale dawn light. She was clad in a brown fur-lined flying suit, her gear in a brown paper shopping bag. Beside her was an attractive blue biplane with silver wings, a spare wooden propeller strapped to its centre struts.

A morning newspaper carried a photograph of her in flying helmet, headlined: 'GIRL'S LONE FLIGHT — TO AUSTRALIA IN THE PRINCE'S OLD PLANE.'

Unswerving. Undampened.

A white knight in the form of Victor Dorée, son of a prosperous English linen merchant, had paid her Stag Lane subs, lent her his plane, and settled fuel bills. He had gone further, borrowing money from his mother to buy her a Gypsy Moth of her own. Ostensibly, it was a business deal, with Batten

agreeing to hand over half of any proceeds from the flight, but in effect the sober Dorée was a willing benefactor.

Her machine came with an impressive pedigree. Its previous owner was the Prince of Wales, later King Edward VIII, and Dorée had bought it from the King's Flight.

In preparing for her long-distance attempt, Batten revealed the organisational skills that were to distinguish all her record-breaking flights. To extend the aircraft's meagre 400-kilometre range, she had two extra fuel tanks fitted, one in the front cockpit, which was then sealed over, and a second behind the pilot's seat.

She then arranged visas, fuel supplies and landing authorisations in the fourteen countries she would fly through, as well as noting the flash codes of all the lighthouses along the 16,800-kilometre route she planned to follow — a line from Europe through the Middle East, India, Burma, Singapore and the Dutch East Indies (now Indonesia). Some of the maps had been lent by her old hero Kingsford-Smith, who had flown the route three years earlier, breaking Hinkler's record in the process. Along with the maps, Kingsford-Smith had passed on two pieces of advice: don't attempt to break men's records, and don't fly at night.

Batten was pointedly to ignore both of them.

At Lympne, having hastily collected a few handfuls of cigarettes from those around her — 'useful if I am captured by Arabs' — the slender 1.62-metre-tall aviator climbed up into G-AALG. It was 6.25 am. Someone flicked the propeller and, with an affectionate farewell from her mother, Batten taxied out and lifted off into the clear morning sky.

Things began well. Having made good time to Marseilles, Batten decided to press on to Rome without stopping, tearing at a chicken leg and trying unsuccessfully to pour from a Thermos as, beyond sight of land for the first time, she crossed the Mediterranean. The frequent need to top up the main wing tank by hand-pumping fuel from the auxiliaries, along with steering a compass course, updating the log and checking her map position, lessened the monotony of the ponderous flight at 130 kilometres per hour. Working the pump also left her with a blistered right hand.

Having flown as far as Naples on the first day to refuel, she took off in darkness early the next morning, reading her instruments with the aid of a

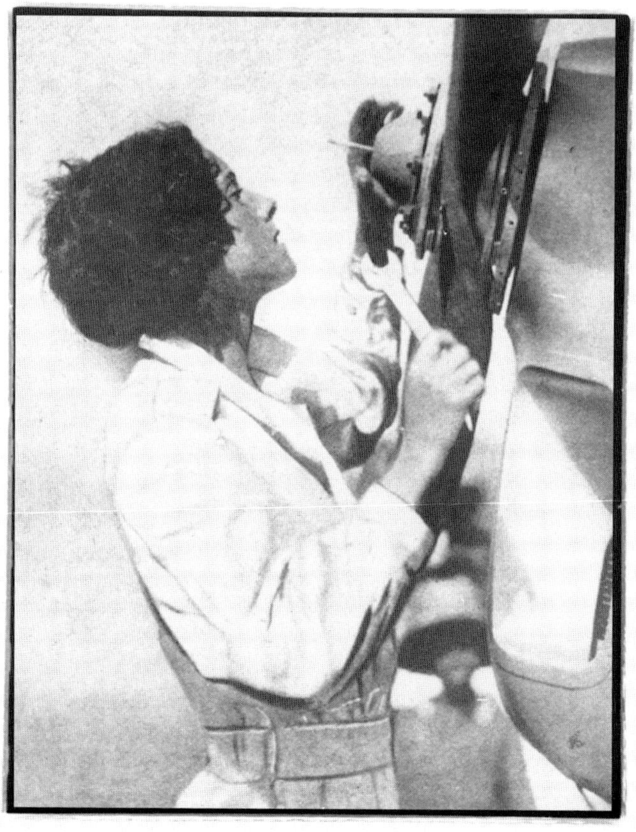

torch. In the lee of the Taurus mountains she struck violent turbulence, and then dense cloud. Unlike Amy Johnson, Batten carried no parachute, but seemed never to be fazed by danger (newspapers would speak of her 'cool contempt for distance', her 'cheerful defiance'). She pressed on, landing at a French military airfield in Aleppo, Syria.

After a convivial lunch in the officers' mess, she flew off again towards Baghdad — and straight into one of the most terrifying ordeals of her life. Some 160 kilometres out from Aleppo a storm struck with unimaginable fury. 'The whole desert seemed to rise like a solid wall before me,' she wrote in *Solo Flight*, her 1934 account of the journey. 'Flying entirely by instruments, with the sand pricking my face and cutting my lips, there was nothing for it but to fly on a compass course and land as soon as possible . . .'

After a gruelling hour, she broke through the storm, only to hit another. 'Suddenly the machine was being tossed into what felt like an upward roll. Then, with a shudder that made all the wires ripple, it pitched into a spin.' Regaining control only metres above the ground, and badly shaken by the experience, Batten decided to land in the desert and sit the storm out. She spent nearly an hour on the ground, wrestling with the Moth's wings to stop the wind flipping it. Then, when the wind died and the skies cleared, she calmly climbed aboard and flew on — her only regret, the loss of valuable time.

Well short of Baghdad she was overtaken by darkness and, chancing on a camel track lit by the moon, decided to risk a landing on the uneven ground. She glided down, the plane's wheels bouncing then rolling to an uneventful stop.

'For a few minutes I remained sitting in the cockpit with my eyes closed, thanking the Almighty for my safety. Then I slowly crawled out of the machine, tired and bruised, my face chafed and lips bleeding from the sand . . .'

She twisted screw pickets into the ground to secure the aircraft, then went looking for a stone to break open a tin of food. In the darkness, she stumbled into a dead camel. Heard some creature moving nearby. Gritted her teeth against the piercing cry of a jackal. With 'cheerful defiance' she bedded down as best she could beside the Moth.

The next morning, after a brief encounter with a band of hostile-looking Arab tribesmen (during which, with trembling hands, she distributed the cigarettes), she fought the engine into life and got airborne once more.

At the RAF officers' mess in Baghdad she learned that a sandstorm there had closed the city's aerodrome the previous night. Had she battled on to reach it, she would not have seen it amid the dust and most likely would have crashed.

Later, a stage or two nearer her Australian goal, she changed into what was to become her trademark rig — a white flying suit — and, in fierce heat over the Strait of Hormuz, strapped on a pith helmet.

The tropical interlude was not to last. Half an hour short of Karachi the Moth flew into another sandstorm, which sent it careering along like a scrap of paper in a gale. Again Batten sought the relative safety of earth, but this time her luck ran out. Touching down on a strip of cultivated land, the aircraft eased into a patch of Baluchistan mud, damaging the propeller.

She was quickly surrounded by villagers. 'I soon realised they were most kindly and obviously regarded me as a sort of goddess' (this is said straight-faced). She somehow persuaded them to lift the plane free and, by a commanding display of resourcefulness and perseverance, set about finding a replacement prop in Karachi — inexplicably, the spare was no longer to hand.

Getting the new propeller was a process of Pythonesque indirectness. Batten mounted a horse which promptly bit her, transferred to another which ran like the wind, and ended up at a village, where she was given curried prawns and goat's milk and set on a camel with a driver. She swayed off into a crimson sunset to fetch up nine hours later at a place called Bela. It was 3.30 am.

On arrival she discovered that it was impossible to arrange for anything to be flown out from Karachi to the landing site, but help was at hand in Bela in the shape of an old Chevy truck. Unfortunately, the truck was short of petrol for the journey to Karachi, so Batten decided to drive back to her Moth and drain fuel from its tanks. The truck ran dry before reaching the aircraft and the Baluchis accompanying her rose to the solemnity of the occasion, brewing tea and whipping out a small wicker table and chair for their guest.

Camels carrying petrol cans soon arrived and 90 minutes later, fortified with curried fish, Batten was disconnecting the Moth's carburettor and filling the cans. Some four hours on, she was once more at a standstill, watching from the Chevy as helpers toiled to dig a ramp down to the bed of a river which blocked the way, then construct a causeway. The exercise was gone through at five rivers in all before Batten reached Karachi.

Rested, and after failed attempts to spot her Moth from the air with the

aid of the local flying club, she drove back from Karachi to within a few kilometres of her aircraft. She finally reached it on camel-back, some lads running ahead with torches, others running alongside, shouldering the new propeller.

The next morning, having given the Baluchis money for their help, she had her aircraft pulled into a corner of the field. Though the machine was light on fuel and there was a wind blowing, the take-off was touch and go. Unable to lift off in the small space, Batten vaulted the Moth over a bank at the far side and dropped into the next field, from where it was able to claw its way into the air. Elated, she turned towards Karachi to refuel before flying across India.

Half an hour later, her world caved in. 'There suddenly came from the engine a noise that seemed to freeze my blood. A sharp report like a clap of thunder, followed by the sound of tearing, rending, splintering metal.'

A faulty con-rod had snapped and been driven through the crankcase.

Batten cut the engine and quickly looked for a place to land. She was only 150 metres above the ground — too low to reach the nearby aerodrome. Instead, she picked out a narrow road which ran between dunes and dropped towards it.

Too late she noticed the stone markers which ran along either side of the road. One of the Moth's lower wings struck and the aircraft flipped, coming to rest upside down in sand beside the road.

'But for the fact that I was wearing a harness and had the presence of mind to cling to a strut on the floor of the cockpit as we turned over, my neck would have been broken as surely and suddenly as the connecting rod. When I managed to undo the straps, lower myself onto my shoulders and crawl out from beneath the plane, I found it very difficult to hold back the tears.'

Batten was lucky to be alive, but the Moth had been reduced to a pile of twisted metal and splintered wood. The journey was at an end.

A demoralising year of near-poverty in England followed. Then fate offered up a second chance. Armed with a letter of introduction from Geoffrey de Havilland, Batten approached Lord Wakefield, the founder and governing director of Castrol Oil, for assistance. He had generously helped her get back from Karachi and, after chewing the matter over for an agonisingly long time, he agreed to sponsor another flight attempt.

So on 21 April 1934 she repeated her first flight, taking off from Lympne in a rebuilt fifth-hand Gypsy Moth. Painted an attractive silver with green registration lettering, G-AARB would get her to Australia.

But not this trip.

Things quickly turned bad. Disregarding advice from officials at Marseilles airport to wait, the impetuous Batten pressed on towards Rome in deteriorating weather. Caught in fog, she could not turn back, so bore on into a strengthening headwind. Unaccountably, passing up the chance of finding somewhere to put down in Corsica as evening approached, and then again at a naval base on the Italian coast, she persevered with what she must have known was a suicidal attempt to reach Rome. Her competitiveness, the single-minded determination to break Johnson's record, had clouded her judgement.

Over the outskirts of Rome the inevitable happened. The engine cut out and in darkness Batten ghosted down eerily over buildings and streets. Suddenly, above her, she saw the flash of a red light. Then another. The beam of her torch picked out a wireless mast directly ahead.

Batten flung the aircraft to the right, then to the left as another mast loomed up. With what little momentum was left, she managed to pull up over a line of trees and drop the stalled Moth to the ground. The aircraft pitched onto its nose, throwing her against the windscreen.

With one eye swollen to a mere slit and a badly cut lip, she surveyed the crash site. Around her reared the 200-metre-high masts and high-tension cables of the San Paolo wireless station. Less than 300 metres away stood the Basilica of St Paul's.

G-AARB was in a bad way, its undercarriage and lower wings crumpled, the propeller smashed.

A lesser mortal would have decided there and then on a more risk-averse occupation. The astounding thing is that within sixteen days Batten — already dubbed the 'Try Again Girl' by the press — was setting off from Lympne in the repaired Moth on her third attempt to reach Australia.

In notebooks she had recorded the distance between fuel stops, approximate times of departure, times of sunrise and sunset (which she checked during a special trip to Greenwich Observatory), the daily maintenance schedule, the conditions of airfields en route and the distances to the nearest towns. Names and addresses of oil and fuel agents. Local exchange rates. As an added precaution, she typed everything out again and glued the duplicate details onto the back of her maps.

In the cramped cockpit she stowed her cork sun helmet, canvas covers for the Moth, a little food and water, first-aid kit, ropes and screw pickets, the torch. Some things, too, that would have brought a smile of approval from Ellen: a fishing line and hooks, a flint and a magnifying glass.

In a small canvas bag she packed underwear, silk frock, tropical flying suit and toiletries, and in her breast pocket that essential triumvirate for female aviators: eau de cologne, a powder compact and lipstick.

A stockbroker by the name of Edward Walter had offered her a heap of gear, including a mosquito net, collapsible canvas bucket, jack-knife, axe and revolver. She laughed at the revolver, took the axe —handy for hacking off a wing to float on after a sea ditching — and declined the rest.

She also took his ring. Edward Walter, Ted, was the only man to whom Batten was ever formally engaged, although it was a short-lived affair which did neither of them any favours.

Walter lent Batten the lower wings from his own Moth to replace G-AARB's damaged ones, and the restored machine performed well on this third attempt at fame, not missing a beat on the 17,400-kilometre journey.

At Rutbah Wells, an idiosyncratic desert staging-post in the Middle East run by Imperial Airways, she was treated to a four-course meal in the company of some Orient-bound KLM passengers. Elsewhere she had to pull rank. At Basra, for example, a London-bound airliner had taken up all the accommodation and Batten had no qualms in edging out a passenger 'who very kindly gave up his room to me and sat up all night, so I was able to enjoy my usual good night's rest'.

Then there was the weather. A blowtorch of a sun melted the soles of her shoes and the rubber of her goggles on the stage between Karachi and Calcutta. South of Burma she hit a monsoon 'wall of death', a vast black mass sparking with forked lightning which instantly turned day into night. Reading the instruments by torchlight, she was drenched in seconds and the cockpit awash with water.

In Batavia (now Jakarta), an energetic fuel agent dispersed thick ground fog at the airfield by driving his car up and down the runway, creating a corridor of clear air for Batten to fly through. She fought off insects while resting at Rambang and further on was showered with hot cinders from a volcano on Flores Island.

Over the Timor Sea — at 890 kilometres, the longest sea crossing she had yet attempted — the Try Again Girl dropped a bag of aluminium shavings to judge the aircraft's drift, belatedly correcting for compass deviation caused by the metal of her long-range tanks. She altered her course by seven degrees and tried not to think of sharks.

Meanwhile, back in London, Ellen gave the press stories of her daughter's self-reliance and repeated the fiction of having sold property of her own to help finance the trip. The silver-haired Ellen revealingly told one reporter: 'She is doing just what I would have liked to do myself. We have much in common. We are really more like sisters.'

At 12.45 pm — much later than she expected — Batten sighted a dark smudge on the horizon, scratching an exultant 'hurrah land hurrah' on her knee-pad log. A little later, at 1.30 pm on 23 May 1934, she touched down at Darwin aerodrome, her arrival and rousing reception captured by a Fox Movietone News cameraman.

Batten had taken fourteen days, 22 hours and 30 minutes for the trip, shaving more than four days off Amy Johnson's time. Weary but exhilarated, she cabled Ellen: 'DARLING WE'VE DONE IT. THE AEROPLANE, YOU, ME.'

Britain's morning papers were quick to trumpet her achievement. Under the banner 'Miss Jean! Splendid!' the *Daily Express* praised her 'skilful piloting and astonishing persistence'. The *News Chronicle* spoke of 'sheer grit and determination'. 'She has accomplished a feat which deserves to be acclaimed throughout the Empire,' blared the *Morning Post*.

Cables flooded in from prime ministers and governors-general. From the British Secretary of State for Air. From Lord Wakefield. Batten was deluged by congratulations from unknown well-wishers and from her peers Amy Johnson and Amelia Earhart.

The 24-year-old Jean Batten had arrived.

She had never worked for wages in her life. Now that the world had set her on a pedestal she would never need to contemplate doing so in the future. The press hounds were at her feet. The circle of the rich and influential parted to accommodate her. Doors of opportunity would open . . .

Amid the fuss, it was perhaps unsporting of the aviation magazine *Flight* to point out that her record flight time was due largely to improvements in ground facilities along the route. Or of the staid *Times* to suggest that such endurance stunts, which in its opinion were little more than tests of pilot stamina, would soon 'fall into the category of Channel swimming and motorcar reliability trials'.

They were right, of course. Batten's claim to be trail-blazing commercial

air routes had little credibility — the route-proving flights of professional airline and air force pilots did far more of worth in that direction, and already there were regular air services between Europe and the Far East. Nor was she anywhere near making the fastest England–Australia passage. Two years earlier, a sleep-deprived Charles Scott had taken less than nine days to cover the same route in a similar aircraft.

Despite Batten's undoubted courage and flying skills, her celebrity status was almost entirely due to her being a female aviator — and a glamorous, knowing one at that.

Newspaper correspondent Mary St Claire put her achievement into perspective: 'Once, and not so long ago, the only time women brought the name of their country into prominence was when they won a beauty competition or figured in a sensational divorce case,' she wrote. 'Now things are different.'

Batten was one of a select company of women to make the gruelling solo flight. Apart from Johnson, only one other had done so — the German Elly Beinhorn, and she hadn't really entered into the spirit of things, taking a dawdling and distracted 110 days to reach Darwin.

Escorted by a Wakefield company aircraft on the dangerous 3200-kilometre flight across the barren Australian heartland, Batten reached Sydney to an even more rapturous welcome. Declared a guest of the state, she spent four weeks at government expense, receiving adulation of an intensity that strains belief.

She attended balls, receptions, banquets and press engagements with the relaxed confidence of someone born to it. But insiders were already beginning to glimpse the aloofness and arrogance, the demanding egotism, that fame would increasingly lay bare. In years to come, Jean Batten would elicit little love, just a reputation as a cold, transient star.

Having freighted G-AARB across the Tasman courtesy of the Union Steam Ship Company — frustratingly, the Moth didn't have the range to fly it — Batten travelled through New Zealand to equal acclaim. Joy rides, a 20-town lecture tour and a controversial £500 state grant all swelled her income enormously so that, by the time she returned to Australia, she had more than recouped her expenses.

She was, too, becoming adept at playing the sponsorship game, calling Lord Wakefield 'the patron saint of flying', and endorsing a string of products. Batten used KLG spark plugs, declared there was 'none better' than Castrol XXL motor oil, found Ovaltine 'wonderfully sustaining', drank Roma tea

('a cup of good tea is always the first thing I want after a flight') and praised Bidomak nerve tonic for strengthening her powers of endurance.

Perhaps the Bidomak also helped steel her against entrapment. Despite having developed a strong attachment — a love, perhaps — for an easy-going Australian called Beverley Shepherd, on 8 April 1935 Batten climbed aboard her long-suffering Moth and set off for England. Having decided to break her own long-distance speed record, she was determined not to let anything get in the way.

She had already cut the tie with Edward Walter, and made no secret of it. Indeed, her later account in *My Life* is lit by an undisguised pride: 'Now that I had tasted the fruits of success and felt the urge to rise to even greater heights, any responsibility, however light, that would in any way hinder or deter my progress was not to be considered. In short, I suppose ambition claimed me . . .'

In contrast to the adulation that had greeted Johnson's return to London, Batten arrived — after a non-too-fast journey from Darwin — to a modest reception at Croydon aerodrome. The press lauded her still and she moved in high society as never before — one society magazine was later to photograph her 'ready for a race meeting, in an early winter hyacinth-blue wool frock, and loose jacket, the collar and turban dappled with ocelot'. But the flier sensed the need for spectacular new achievements if she was to keep her incandescent star aloft — and that meant something more adventurous than the Derby and more powerful than a 100-horsepower biplane.

Five months later, she had her hands on G-AARB's replacement.

Visitors to Auckland International Airport at Mangere can get close to Batten's new instrument of choice. There, under one of the terminal's flat ceilings, suspended above departure signs and a ring of duty-free shops, hangs the machine itself — a sleek, low-wing Percival Gull monoplane.

With a 200-horsepower six-cylinder engine, the three-seat Gull 6 was almost twice as fast as the Moth and could cover 3200 kilometres before refuelling. Designed by Australian pilot Edgar Percival, it came with a host of refinements, including a starter motor (no more swinging a heavy prop by hand), electric fuel pumps (no more blisters), brakes, flaps and a metal propeller.

Yet, for all its sophistication, the Gull looks fragile hanging from wires in its glass-lined enclosure — a mere toy compared with the massive commercial jets loading and unloading beyond the windows.

Batten took delivery of her new machine, G-ADPR, on 15 September 1935 — her 26th birthday. Less than two months later, on Armistice Day 1935, she changed into a new white flying suit and white helmet — white for purity, white for stardom — wrapped a silk New Zealand flag round her neck as a muffler, and climbed aboard the Gull for another assault on the record book. The route this time was England to Brazil via West Africa and the South Atlantic.

The day Batten left, news broke of the disappearance of Kingsford-Smith and his co-pilot Tommy Pethybridge off the coast of Burma. Hard up, her old flying friend had been desperate to earn money by attempting a new England–Australia record. His body would never be found.

Batten was unsettled but not deterred. No matter how high the casualties mounted — and in her game they came thick and fast — Batten seemed unflinching in her courage and tenacity. Even her own serious crashes — including an embarrassing and hastily covered-up smash in the Gull in a Sussex field — didn't dent her resolve.

Having arrived at a military airfield in French Senegal and taken on board 147 gallons of fuel and ten gallons of oil, she fretted about G-ADPR being too heavy to take off from the small field. She ditched a signal pistol, revolver, rockets, cartridges, torch, engine parts, water drums — then took a step back.

'I surveyed the assorted collection and selected two evening dresses . . . and to the surprise of all present put them back into the locker. After all, if I crossed the Atlantic successfully they would be more useful than the tool-kit . . . And if I didn't — well . . .'

Despite a poor forecast, Batten launched the Gull at South America early the following morning, lifting off by the headlights of the military commandant's car. Unable to detour around a storm mass a few hundred kilometres north of the equator, she flew into it, keeping unflinchingly to a magnetic heading of 242 degrees 15 minutes. A deviation of just one degree, she had earlier calculated, would result in an error of almost 55 kilometres at her destination.

Here lies Batten's greatest gift as an aviator: an uncanny instinct for navigation. Her technical flying skills had steadily improved since her student days, but it was her ability to find her way across vast expanses of sky, sea and featureless desert using primitive instruments — little better in the Gull than in the Moth — that put Batten in a class of her own.

An eternity after leaving the coast of Africa, she sighted a bleak coast of dunes and trees and, searching for a landmark to fix her position, noticed a clump of palms to the north. Reaching into her pocket she pulled out a small picture someone in London had given her of her destination, Brazil's Cape San Roque. The photograph was identical to the view through the Gull's perspex. As further confirmation, there too was the lighthouse.

After flying for more than thirteen hours across 3200 kilometres of empty ocean, and having encountered a prolonged magnetic disturbance near the equator which swung her compass wildly in all directions, she had made landfall less that a kilometre from her intended destination.

The 'famosa aviadora', this 'carnation of the sky', as the jubilant Latins styled her, had also set a batch of new records: the world's fastest flight from England to Brazil, fastest South Atlantic crossing, first woman to fly from England to South America.

The Brazilian President draped a gold cross over her, the British Chamber of Commerce pressed money into her palm, she was made an honorary officer of the Brazilian air force and navy. Hot-blooded crowds worked themselves into lathers of adulation. And through it all, Jean Batten presented an air of unassuming modesty.

The next year, 1936, after taking Ellen on an aerial tour of Spain and Tangier, Batten again flew out to Australia. This time, she could glance at her 22 metres of joined strip maps in the comfort of a heated cabin and cruise above the worst of the weather that she had encountered two years earlier in the Moth.

Batten drove herself remorselessly, taking just five days and 21 hours to reach Darwin. She landed in hair-raising fashion when first the Gull's throttle jammed open, forcing her to overshoot the aerodrome, and then, on touch-down, a wheel brake locked, spinning her aircraft spectacularly before it came to rest.

Utterly exhausted, she could nevertheless feel pleased with herself. She had set an absolute record for the trip, one that was to stand for 44 years. After a two-day delay in Sydney caused by bad weather, she squared off to face her supreme challenge: the notorious 2200-kilometre-wide Tasman Sea.

A great many people tried to dissuade her. The Australian civil aviation department, fellow aviators, countless well-wishers. The Mayor of Auckland. Kingsford-Smith's business manager, Beau Sheil. Chauvinism undoubtedly played a part, but there was also a solid argument against flying a single-engined aircraft with no radio over such a hazardous stretch of water.

'It is not for ground fowl to dictate to the eagles,' said one newspaper meekly, 'but New Zealand remembers Kingsford-Smith and Ulm, who conquered the air and were claimed by the sea.'

Undaunted, Batten replied by requesting that no search be made if she went down.

Declining a staggering £5000 offer by media magnate Frank Packer for her to abandon the attempt and embark on a lecture tour, Batten loaded the Gull down with half a tonne of fuel and braced herself for what lay ahead.

What did lie ahead — apart from a brief wavering of nerve over the Tasman — was unprecedented acclaim. The flight went without a hitch, and Batten touched down to a rapturous reception at Mangere aerodrome shortly after 5 pm on 16 October 1936, having made the crossing in a record nine hours and 30 minutes (she had reached New Plymouth an hour earlier, then flown north to Auckland). Caught up in the sense of occasion, thousands of Aucklanders drove out to glimpse the woman whom the *New Zealand Herald* was to call 'Her Serene Highness'.

There was money again — lots of it. A graceless snub for her father on landing. A repeat of the now-familiar rituals of public hero worship. But also an increasing edginess in her manner. A weariness with the roar of aero-engines, with vibrations and the intricate demands of navigation. With insatiable media attention. In her memoirs, she wrote of the 'rarified atmosphere' of fame, of its 'lonely solitude'.

Its empty, echoing chamber, she might have said. Its poisonous locomotive breath.

Strained by the demands of flying, and of what was unleashed after touch-down, Jean Batten broke down. The wealth she was so avidly accumulating yielded little in return. Worse, her popularity was quickly fading. Lectures had not been well attended. Newspaper coverage fell away. She was packed off to the South Island to recover.

The resilient slip of a thing from the Dominion who liked nothing better than steak for breakfast, the brown-eyed brunette who seemed impervious to hardship and lack of sleep, had tested the limits. In time, and after a fashion, she mended.

The next year, on the eve of her last great flight, the attempt to break the Australia–England record, journalist Colin Simpson called at Batten's flat, unannounced, to put some questions to her. Barred by an exclusive contract from granting him an interview, she was reticent. Simpson, nevertheless, got to the heart of her dilemma.

'Why is Jean Batten flying for another record?' he mused. 'What urge, what purpose, what profit or what aim is there in her going on and on?'

'When you have drunk the champagne of life, it is not human nature to decide that henceforth you'll quit champagne and stick to barley water, because barley water is better for your health,' he wrote. 'But . . . the world grows jaded. What has been done is over, no longer awesome, no longer something for clamorous congratulation. So you have to go one better . . .'

The trouble, as Simpson well knew, was that for Batten and her kind the curtain was already dropping. 'Aviation is now a business like shipping and railways. There will always be speed-flying and air races just as there

are motor speed records and motor track races — thrilling, courageous spectacles. But the day of the adventure flier draws to a close.'

Outbound from England, Batten had noticed the ripple of change Simpson was talking about. Endless customs formalities at Karachi. Allahabad's new control building. An all-weather bitumen runway at Akyab. The Gull's cabin sprayed by health officials. And everywhere detailed weather reports for the asking.

Six days after speaking to Simpson, Jean Batten was back in England, a meteor come to earth, her spectacular career at an end. She had broken the return record too, but it was to be her last long-distance flight.

Once more she moved in society circles, and for a time thrived. But with the exploits over, there was little to sustain her — certainly no enduring friendships. She and Ellen, seemingly happy in each other's company, quietly withdrew. They slipped under the radar and went abroad, first to Jamaica, where Batten built a house — 'Blue Horizon' — then for seven years of sightseeing in Europe.

At Jean Batten Primary School in Mangere, a short distance from where the aviator landed her Gull to such acclaim in 1936, school secretary Raewyn Smit unlocked the sound room and led me inside past storage shelves and cabinets. 'This is quite precious,' she said, handing me an album of photographs and correspondence.

'Give my love to all the children,' Batten writes in one letter. Another asks Mrs Satherley whether the tree she planted at the school has survived. There are the familiar images of the legend — as a conquering white-helmed Joan of Arc, on the celebrity circuit.

The school, whose commemorative name was suggested by founding principal John Sinclair, opened in 1970. Its motto, 'Faith in God and confidence in oneself', is taken from a remark Batten made after one of her headline-making flights.

When she learned of the gesture Batten was touched, calling it one of the greatest honours she had ever received. 'She maintained a steady contact with us and when she visited she read stories to the children,' Smit recalled. 'She was very graceful, of course, and refined. Beautifully spoken.'

Nevertheless, the school was surprised, years later, to receive a substantial legacy from Batten — one she stipulated should be used to encourage reading, oral language and music — three subjects close to her heart. The gift now funds annual competitions in her honour.

'She is portrayed as selfish and egotistical, but she had this other side,' said Smit. She repeats this anecdote: for many years an elderly woman and former flier in Te Awamutu would courier to the school the first of the season's blooms from her garden. Lily of the valley — Jean Batten's favourite. A tribute from one aviator to another.

It is a rare expression of warmth.

In 1977, while in Auckland to open the Museum of Transport and Technology's pioneers pavilion, Batten attended the funeral of Sinclair, the school's principal, who had died suddenly. Then, after brief return visits, the latest in 1980 as a guest of Qantas, she dissolved from view. Indeed, since Ellen's death — in Jean's arms — at the age of 89 in 1966, Batten had been living an ever more guarded, reclusive life. Her short-lived re-emergence, with facelift, bottle-blonde hair and youthful, short-cut dresses, a temporary aberration, a wrong-footed attempt to recapture the limelight.

The school wrote to her proxy address in England once a term telling her of local happenings, but without reply. It was not until a decade later, and after much searching, that biographer Ian Mackersey uncovered the wrenching truth. He tracked her down to an unmarked pauper's grave on the Spanish island of Majorca. There was enormous irony in finding the woman who craved privacy lying with 149 others in a concrete-walled pit.

It transpired that Batten had died an anonymous death in a small fifth-floor hotel room in Palma in November 1982. The cause: a dog bite, leading to a lung infection and pulmonary abscess. It was a needless death, easily treatable if Batten had seen a doctor. Stubbornly, she didn't.

New Zealand had belatedly reclaimed one of its finest long-distance fliers. But, in truth, her life had ended long ago when she stepped from G-ADPR at Croydon.

For 45 years this aviator had been running on empty.

August 2002

Illustrations

Breakout – The Saga of the German 'Sea Devil': Felix von Luckner

For Lieutenant-Colonel Charles Harcourt Turner, 5th Wellington Regiment, the evening of Thursday, 13 December 1917 had begun as pleasantly as any other. In the face of a freshening breeze he had stepped aboard his launch, the *Pearl*, and set off from Queen's Wharf in downtown Auckland for the internment camp on Motuihe Island, of which he was — nominally — in charge. With him on the sixteen-kilometre journey were his orderly, Frank Wainwright, and two German prisoners-of-war, Albert Paulsen, who served as a deckhand, and a man named Freund, as engineer.

It had been Wainwright's job to chaperon Paulsen and Freund while his commandant attended to some pressing business in the city, though it was anyone's guess how passers-by would have reacted had they known the identity of the trio in their midst. 'Just as well people didn't know,' Wainwright's mate Bill Wiggins, another Motuihe guard, was later to say. 'If you told them that prisoners-of-war were up in Queen Street doing their shopping, that would be the end of it, wouldn't it?'

For Charles Turner, however, Paulsen and Freund were useful. In a way, he had them and the other German prisoners on Motuihe to thank for the *Pearl*, which had been placed at his disposal. They were also to thank for his rapid promotion to lieutenant-colonel (and, though no one could have foreseen it then, in something under six weeks, for his own court martial). All these 'thanks' fell to one man in particular: a powerfully built seadog, a pipe-smoking captain in the Kaiser's Imperial German Navy with an unquenchable thirst for adventure and a reputation for daring and resourcefulness. A man whose name — and nickname — was to become a household word in New Zealand: Count Felix von Luckner, the 'Sea Devil of the Southern Seas'.

Just months earlier, having left a trail of ships captured or sunk the length of the Atlantic Ocean, von Luckner had rounded Cape Horn in his disguised windjammer, the *Seeadler*, and burst into the Pacific. There, after much effort, he had been arrested, along with several of his crew, and brought south to New Zealand. Shortly after his arrival, the Count had been transferred to Motuihe Island, along with his second-in-command, Lieutenant Carl Kirscheiss, while another four of the *Seeadler*'s crew were transported to Somes Island in Wellington harbour.

Until his arrival, Motuihe internment camp had held only German nationals living in New Zealand at the outbreak of the war, and others captured when the New Zealand Army occupied German-held Samoa and other islands in the Pacific. Among the detainees were the former governor of German Samoa and 20 or so merchant navy cadets of the North German Lloyd line, who had earlier made an intrepid escape from Pago Pago in a stolen boat, only to be captured in Apia.

Bill Wiggins remembered Motuihe as a 'happy little camp'. The Germans had their own cookhouse and would offer coffee and freshly baked cake to the sentry each morning. The prisoners were allowed visitors from the mainland, and were readily granted permission to stroll around the island. On one of its tranquil beaches they fashioned a retreat out of manuka, and when the weather grew hot they would often go there and recline in chairs contemplating the dazzling waters of the Hauraki Gulf.

The prisoners spent time tending the camp vegetable gardens and looking after poultry, and to supplement their modest rations they caught snapper and gathered oysters, mushrooms and apricots. One of the privileges they enjoyed was that their quarters, a few hundred metres from where the soldiers were stationed, were off-limits to almost all military personnel except Turner himself. 'It was a very quiet, staid camp,' recalled Wiggins. 'The war never seemed to enter that kind of place.'

At least, not until Felix von Luckner's shadow touched it.

With the appearance of the Count — a jewel in the crown for any camp commandant — Turner got a promotion, a telephone line to the mainland, and a fast motorboat — the *Pearl* — for patrol work and as a back-up in case the vital telephone failed. The guard was increased from 60 men to 80, a report was to be telephoned through to the mainland without fail every hour, and for a time everyone in uniform wore a determined look.

Vigilance was the watchword. Some weeks before von Luckner's arrival, informants had volunteered disturbing information about plans to liberate prisoners using a chartered scow, and the Bohemian community at Puhoi on the mainland, 40 kilometres to the north, had come under suspicion. Mysterious lights had been seen flashing from the vicinity of the internment camp on Motuihe's north-western clifftops — where certain prisoners had, for the sake of their health, been permitted to live — but despite thorough searches on that forested headland, nothing had been uncovered.

Offshore patrols around the island were increased, and a landing made on nearby Rangitoto Island, where answering points of light had been detected. Despite every effort, however, the military had drawn a blank and, once the nocturnal signalling ceased, the night patrols had been wound down.

Lieutenant-Colonel Turner and his shopping Germans reached the Motuihe wharf without incident on that December evening, at 6 pm. Turner paused to remind Paulsen and Freund to bring the spark-plugs to him once they had moored the launch, then stepped ashore with his orderly. Part-way up the rise to the camp the lieutenant-colonel turned once to see the vessel being made fast to its mooring. Some way further on he unexpectedly encountered von Luckner, who was advancing in an unusually stiff-legged way. A bout of rheumatism, the Count explained as he limped past.

There had been a fair amount of coming and going around the island in the previous days. Von Luckner had obtained Turner's permission to stage a Christmas play, and the prisoners' barracks had been the scene of energetic and lavish preparations for the show. Turner was pleased the prisoners were taking an interest in providing their own entertainment. It spoke of motivation and good morale. It reflected well on him.

Suddenly, Turner's orderly rushed into his house and agitatedly reported that a fire had broken out in one of the barracks. Turner was instantly galvanised into action, furiously blowing his whistle to raise the alarm. A fire on such a small island was a serious matter. Running to the blaze, Turner noticed von Luckner in the thick of it, fighting the flames with a passion and directing his men to do likewise. Then, in the smoke and confusion, Turner lost sight of him.

As told by von Luckner's biographer, Lowell Thomas, the Count and ten of his men slipped away under cover of darkness, stole the motorboat and headed for the open sea. It was an escape bid worthy of the audacious Sea Devil, and has assumed the status of legend. And it is, in all likelihood, completely untrue.

Thomas, it seems, was not the sort of writer to let facts get in the way of a ripping yarn. The circumstances of the Motuihe break-out and other events in the Count's crowded and heroic life were magnified and distorted shamelessly by Thomas in the hagiography he published eleven years later, entitled *Count Luckner: The Sea Devil*. But then, what else would you expect, or demand, from the man who elevated another figure to legendary dimensions when he wrote *With Lawrence in Arabia*?

The reports of Turner and other Motuihe eyewitnesses paint a less dramatic, but no less remarkable, picture of the events of 13 December. According to these sources, after dinner, at around 7.20 pm, the telephone rang at Turner's house. The *Pearl*'s dinghy was adrift in the channel beyond the barracks and slowly sinking, and the launch, with Paulsen and Freund on board, was away after it. Turner went down to the wharf, expecting at any moment to see the launch return. When after half an hour there was still no sign of it, he ordered a check of all prisoners.

In addition to the two men on the launch, another known to be out with the transport cart at the wharf and a fourth away pumping fresh water, seven other prisoners — including von Luckner — were unaccounted for. The Count himself, it turned out, had dined early and was absent at the evening meal.

It soon became clear that all eleven had got off the island. Von Luckner and his second-in-command had been on Motuihe only a matter of weeks.

Turner surmised that the seven — among them a plantation owner from

Samoa — had crept through bush to the south-east of the island, from where they had been picked up by the *Pearl*. Others felt it likely the prisoners had made their way down the cliff from the compound. It was later revealed that von Luckner had hidden in a boatshed near the wharf before clambering aboard.

Turner at once tried to telephone news of the escape to Auckland, but found the line dead. His nightmare was worsening. As it was by now dark, he had a large bonfire lit and flamed with kerosene to attract attention. About 10 pm, several rockets went up in Auckland, possibly in answer to the fire, but two boats seen coming down the harbour shortly afterwards passed by without stopping.

Just before midnight, the sabotaged telephone line was repaired and at last Lieutenant-Colonel Turner could unburden himself. He rang Major Price, acting commander of the Auckland district, and the efficient major immediately ordered a pursuit by sea.

Meanwhile, aboard the overloaded and labouring *Pearl*, von Luckner and his cramped crew were butting into a gale somewhere off Cape Colville. The Sea Devil, with a sure sense of theatre, had clad himself in the uniform of a New Zealand army officer, taken from Turner's quarters, along with the commandant's own dress sword. It was this sword, concealed down his trouser leg, which had given the Count such a pronounced limp earlier in the evening.

Turner was, for now at least, spared the knowledge of just how thoroughly he and the island's guards had been duped by their captives. All too soon, however, the facts of the case would surface to embarrass the military. Life in Motuihe internment camp, it turned out, was a comedy of deception.

Even before the arrival of von Luckner and Kirscheiss, the enterprising cadets had stolen and hidden tools from the prison workshop and had retrieved fuses and gun-cotton from a derelict floating mine to make bombs — one fearless cadet sleeping night after night on a mattress stuffed with the explosives. The party had even acquired charts showing the location of minefields in the Hauraki Gulf by bribing guards. These charts were later supplemented by maps of the Pacific taken from the camp library.

With the arrival of the two naval officers, the vague impulse to escape coalesced into a definite plan. With what one report described as 'Hun foxiness', von Luckner and Kirscheiss orchestrated their bid for freedom. A sextant was laboriously crafted from an old launch steering-wheel cut in half, and bombs were fabricated from a cache of explosives left over from roadworks on the island.

Von Luckner even managed to have one of his *Seeadler* crew transferred to Motuihe from Somes Island on the pretence of needing a batman. The real reason was that, apart from being a highly trained gunner and signaller, the leading seaman looked English and spoke the language flawlessly.

To disguise his preparations, the Count had contrived to stage a Christmas play — Thomas got that right, at least. Once permission had been given, von Luckner's men got busy making the necessary 'props', including several German naval ensigns and a realistic-looking Lewis machinegun fashioned

from wood and jam tins. When one of the guards drew his superior's attention to what looked like the making of sails, he was told all was in order. They were curtains for the Count's dramatic production. Which, in a way, they were.

At about this time the commandant's sword was stolen from underneath its waterproof cover in the orderly room and replaced by a length of pipe with a meat-tin handle. Chickens from the camp run were surreptitiously killed and canned to supplement the hoard of provisions. Even stale beer has a use: as flux for soldering.

Whatever was not procurable on the island was got through a surprisingly simple ruse. Whenever the prisoners needed something legitimate from Auckland, they filled out a requisition form, leaving a space at the bottom. Once the commandant had signed it, they added copper wire, fine canvas, solder or whatever else was wanted. The commandant's launch, the fulcrum of the escape plan, had for weeks plied the waters of Auckland harbour with all manner of munitions and spare engine parts concealed in its bulkheads.

In their bid for freedom, the prisoners were heartened to see an off-handedness creep into the behaviour of their jailers. The guards had abandoned their rifles and instead affected small canes. 'If a prisoner objected to following orders,' von Luckner was later to claim, 'the guard would threaten to blow his whistle.'

After ten expectant days the opportunity for escape came, and von Luckner seized it. Now, as he and his men nursed their leaking launch through the storm, at their backs confusion reigned. Every available vessel, including many civilian craft animated with the spirit seen later at Dunkirk, had put to sea to scour the Hauraki Gulf. In the heavy seas a steamer ran ashore. Other boats collided. At least one was fired at from another launch. On land, searchlights put on a show of piercing the night. But when rumours spread that the *Pearl* had capsized and sunk with all hands, the fatigued search crews thankfully turned their prows for home.

It was in just such a storm one year earlier, almost to the day, that von Luckner had punched through the British North Sea blockade to hunt and destroy Allied merchant ships bringing food and raw materials to Europe from Australasian ports, which were beyond the range of German submarines.

The Count, who had brought attention to himself as a quick-minded officer on a German battleship in the battle of Jutland, where he had been wounded, was singled out for this unusual and demanding task. As Germany had no overseas coaling stations, he was given command of the 83-metre-long *Seeadler*, a captured American three-masted sailing ship formerly named the *Pass of Balmaha*.

In Germany the steel-hulled *Seeadler*, the last square-rigged ship ever to be commissioned as a warship, had been fitted out for commerce raiding with two 105-mm guns, one hidden on deck under a false canvas pigpen. Two concealed diesel engines had been installed, along with a hidden radio transmitter and secret accommodation for hundreds of prisoners. The ship's main saloon was equipped with a diabolical trap for any enemy boarding party: an ingenious hydraulic floor designed by the Count himself to plunge suspicious visitors into the arms of gun-wielding sailors four metres below.

The *Seeadler*, which carried a deck cargo of timber, flew the Norwegian flag and was manned by a hand-picked and well-armed crew — 64 in all — masquerading as Norwegian sailors. Portraits of Norwegian and British royalty hung in the cabins, and the crew learned to forget their disciplined naval habits. Von Luckner grew a beard and gave orders in the foreign tongue.

Born into an illustrious titled and military family, he was just the man for the job. His great-grandfather, a mercenary, was made a Marshal of

France for services rendered. Von Luckner even claimed the French national anthem, the *Marseillaise*, had been dedicated to his ancestor. Fame is not always durable, however, and he died under the guillotine during the French Revolution.

The Count's father was a military man, and had been fighting for King and country since 1848. With the outbreak of war in 1914, he had volunteered to take up arms again — at the age of 90.

As a child, von Luckner had once been sat on the knee of Queen Victoria while the monarch fed him sweets and tried to discover what toys he liked best. He and several others had been part of an unusual experiment to discover which of the products of the world-renowned German toy manufacturers should be sent across the Channel for the delight of British children.

When he was a little older, he spent truant hours hidden in the courtyard of the Dresden Natural History Museum shooting at the stuffed wild animals which, in fine weather, were brought outside for an airing. He was discovered only when one of the pellets from his airgun smashed the glass eye of an imposing lion.

In 1894, at the age of thirteen, von Luckner ran away from home, or rather from school, 'having already been to more schools than classes', and

under a false name shipped before the mast on a Russian sailing vessel, the *Niobe*. He later explained that he got the scars on his hands and forearms after falling from the *Niobe* in a raging sea. Seizing an albatross which had swooped to attack him, he had used the bird to stay afloat until being picked up, but in the process his arms had been lacerated by its beak.

For the next seven years, von Luckner lived a *Boys' Own* adventure as seaman, prize-fighter, kangaroo hunter, beachcomber, conjurer's assistant, circus strongman, lighthouse keeper and world traveller. He became a gardener's boy with the Vanderbilt family in the United States and even, for a time, laboured for the Salvation Army, selling the *War Cry* in the harbourside pubs of Fremantle.

In America, he made a pilgrimage to meet his boyhood hero Buffalo Bill, walking 2100 kilometres of railroad track only to discover that Cody was touring Germany at the time. He was later told that, while there, this model self-made man had been a guest in the house of one of his uncles.

At the age of 20, he joined the German Navy and embarked on the career that would lead him to a prison island on the other side of the world, a captive of the New Zealand Government.

On its outward voyage, the *Seeadler* seemed a charmed ship. The vigilant British were duped time and again by the meticulously orchestrated Scandinavian charade. On one occasion, when an armed party from a blockading cruiser boarded the windjammer, a 'fair-complexioned' youth from the *Seeadler*'s crew, disguised as von Luckner's wife and feigning toothache, diverted the inquisitive enemy from a close scrutiny of the saloon and its hydraulic floor. Von Luckner, chewing tobacco and spitting in the manner of a Norwegian captain, accompanied the search crew to the strains of 'It's a long way to Tipperary' drifting up from a gramophone in the mess room. After what seemed an eternity, the boarding party returned to the cruiser and the *Seeadler* was sent on its way.

In the months of raiding on the high seas that followed, von Luckner sank 'with guile and artifice' a total of 86,000 tonnes of shipping, mostly off the coast of South America, and captured more than 260 enemy crew. A romantic at heart, he flew the Jolly Roger alongside the German ensign when attacking another ship, and took care to treat his captives well. It was to be his often-repeated boast that, despite his sending seventeen ships to the bottom, no lives, not even that of a ship's cat, were lost at his hands.

However, the Pacific Ocean was not kind to the *Seeadler*. The good fortune which had accompanied it across the Atlantic abandoned the vessel shortly after it rounded Cape Horn. In June and July von Luckner captured or sank three schooners near the equator, but his crew were weary after seven months and 50,000 kilometres at sea, and the ship was in need of repair. The Count decided to make for the uninhabited island of Mopelia in the Society Islands, 450 kilometres from Tahiti. In Mopelia, a raised island on a palm-studded reef surrounding a ten-kilometre-long lagoon, the 'Norwegians' found a type of Valhalla.

'The coral shore was snow white, and, with the sun's rays reflecting from it, it looked like a sparkling jewel set in an alabaster ring,' von Luckner was to recall. The crew dined on pork, fish, turtle and crab flesh, birds' eggs, coconuts, champagne and brandy, and lay about in the tropical sun.

Even paradise can carry a sting, however, and soon after their arrival catastrophe struck. Again, von Luckner's biographer Lowell Thomas was not found wanting when it came to an explanation. According to Thomas, the *Seeadler* was destroyed by a tsunami. A massive wall of water twelve or more metres high flung the ship onto the reef, snapping its masts and spars like so many matchsticks and turning the rigging into a mass of tangled cordage. The vessel which had been the terror of the shipping lanes was wrecked, its hull punctured by jagged coral. The small mercy was that no one had been injured.

Another version of the story is that the *Seeadler* had been careened to clean barnacles from its hull, but a heavy sea drove it onto the reef. A third, even less flattering, account, states that an American schooner captain among the ship's prisoners warned von Luckner that he had anchored too near the reef, but was ignored. A gale came up and the vessel was destroyed.

Whatever the string of events, the outcome was the same. Von Luckner, his crew and all 48 American prisoners were marooned in paradise. They salvaged what they could, including 380 tonnes of diesel, rigged a wireless aerial in the pines and built huts from timber, sailcloth and palm leaves. They even wired up an electric light from a generator for the public meeting place. The Americans, who proved adept as castaways, built a separate town for themselves, naming its streets Broadway, The Bowery, Pennsylvania Avenue. The Imperial German flag flew from the highest palm over this, the last German colony in history.

But if his subjects were happy, the 'Sea Devil King' was not. He quickly grew impatient with the constraints of Mopelia, and his crew proved less at ease in holiday heaven than their prisoners. The time had come for action.

Von Luckner had the *Seeadler*'s whaleboat scraped, corked and painted, and crammed into its six-metre length food, water, tobacco, civilian clothes, machine guns, pistols, hand-grenades and an accordion. He then picked five crew, including his navigating officer, Lieutenant Kirscheiss, christened the boat *Kronprinzessin Cecilie* and, on 26 August 1917, set off into the wide, empty Pacific in search of a new ship. The plan was straightforward: to capture a vessel, preferably in port, then return to rescue those who had remained at Mopelia, before resuming a life of buccaneering on behalf of the Kaiser.

The *Cecilie* leaked badly and had only 300 mm of freeboard amidships. Nevertheless, within a few days they had reached Atiu in the Cook Islands, where they passed themselves off as Dutch Americans sailing from Honolulu to the Cooks and back for a wager of US$25,000. Von Luckner transformed himself into Van Houten, 'of cocoa fame', while Kirscheiss became an American tourist. The resident agent, whom they found indolently stretched out in a chair on his porch, was taken in by the story and allowed them to secure fresh supplies.

Soaked by tropical downpours and heavy breaking seas, they then made for Aitutaki, which again they reached after several days at sea. They found the resident agent at Aitutaki pleasant, but suspicious. Von Luckner's answers seemed to allay his fears, but the Cook Islanders were not taken in and pressed the resident to take action. He gave the boat's log a cursory inspection while a hostile crowd numbering several hundred gathered outside his house. Von Luckner, forced at last to drop the deception, took the nervous resident on board and revealed the store of arms. The resident urged the Germans to leave to avoid bloodshed, while making out to the Islanders that all was well.

Extracting themselves from an unsatisfactory situation, the Dutch-American-Norwegian-Germans decided against taking the island by force, which would have been easily done, and capturing the next ship to arrive — only a few days away, as it happened. Instead, they again put to sea, this time steering a course for Fiji, more than 3000 kilometres away. It was to prove a fatal mistake. Forgetting that it was the stormy season, they let themselves in for seemingly unending days of rain and bitterly cold nights. They jettisoned their mattresses, which had become unbearably sodden, and slept on the wet planks of the hull. Whenever the sun appeared, it stiffened their clothing into boards of salt which cruelly chafed their skin. Then the clothes would be soaked afresh and the salt would seep into the raw wounds, setting their flesh on fire.

On 23 September, a half-caste youth in a cutter landed at Levuka in Fiji in the teeth of a tropical storm with news that a strange launch had arrived at Wakaya Island, some eighteen kilometres away. Sub-inspector Harry Hills, a 33-year-old former New Zealand customs officer serving with the Fijian constabulary, questioned him and discovered that the launch had a fender around it like that of a ship's boat. Moreover, its crew spoke English in a peculiar way — like Mr Straub, the former German Consul at Levuka.

Suspecting it was linked in some way with the launch which had been seen in the Cook Islands the previous month, Hills left for Wakaya that day, but was driven back by the storm. He then telephoned his superiors in Suva for permission to arm his Fijian Indian police and try for Wakaya the following day. The request for weapons was turned down, but Hills was told that he could pack his service revolver — at his own risk. Having learned that the cattle steamer *Amra* had arrived at Suva, Hills persuaded the governor there to charter it. The next day it arrived at Levuka, and Hills set out with his small force.

Von Luckner and his party, meanwhile, had been eyeing suitable shipping in Wakaya. Posing as day-trippers from a vessel in Suva, they were instantly attracted to a new twin-engined schooner, *Gleaner A*, which had taken refuge there from the storm. Learning that the schooner's owner would be returning from Suva shortly, von Luckner decided to ask for a tow, then board and capture the vessel once they were clear of land. With that in mind, he instructed his crew to keep their uniforms and arms always near at hand.

It was then that the *Amra* hove into sight and anchored in the bay. Von Luckner had already upped anchor and was heading for the reef opening and the open sea. A boat was swiftly lowered from the *Amra*, and Hills's men pulled hard across the lagoon to cut the whaler off. Hills stood up in the bow and waved his hat three times — an Island signal to stop. Von Luckner slowed, but kept on. As Hills got within hearing, he shouted: 'Stop! That steamer has you covered with her guns.' A surprised von Luckner obeyed, and Hills's boat drew alongside. With a hand on what was in fact an empty service revolver, the sub-inspector ordered the Germans to surrender.

'I looked and saw his armed natives, but could do nothing, as our small arms were packed in our kit bags, and the machine-gun, bombs, etc. were hidden under canvas, rugs and other gear,' the Count said later. 'Had I suspected [the *Amra*'s] purpose she would have been at the bottom of the

Koro Sea in a few minutes.'

Lieutenant Kerscheiss stepped aboard Hills's boat, identified himself and handed over his automatic pistol. Hills removed the magazine. Two bayonet-wielding Fijians then jumped aboard the whaler, and Hills called on the man at the stern to surrender. The man handed Hills his pistol and said: 'My name is Count von Luckner, commander of the *Seeadler*. I surrender.' The rest of the crew then did the same. The whaler was found to be carrying a machine gun and 5000 rounds of ammunition, six Mauser pistols, six rifles and a cache of hand-grenades.

Once on board the *Amra*, von Luckner was keen to learn about the vessel's armaments. When he discovered there were none, he grew indignant — more so, when he discovered the ship was down to a few bags of coal and would have been in no condition to give chase.

It was 24 September, two days short of a month since, in high spirits, they had left Mopelia. After an open-boat voyage in the manner of Captain Bligh's after the mutiny on the *Bounty*, the Sea Devil had been caught. And not merely caught, but fittingly caught. Got by bluff. Duped.

Some claimed that the Count had mistaken the prominent cattle pens on the *Amra*'s deck for camouflaged guns. Others that he took ventilation slots in the cattle ship's sides for gun ports. Von Luckner later made an unconvincing attempt to deny it. His marine glasses, he said, had shown him exactly what the *Amra* was.

In Thomas's version of the capture, it came down to naval code. With their uniforms still stowed below, the raiders would have been forced to fight off arrest as civilians: 'and as civilians we would have to raise our weapons against soldiers. That not only went against the grain, but it went against the unwritten laws of the game.'

In other words, theirs would have been the fate of civilian snipers, spies or common bandits: a hanging, or worse.

After a brief stay in Fiji, the six crew were shipped to New Zealand, where they were confronted by hostile crowds who had got wind of their arrival. At about the time von Luckner had been captured, the Cunard steamer *Port Kembla* had been sunk eighteen kilometres off Cape Farewell, and war had entered New Zealand waters. The passenger steamer *Wairuna*, too, had been lost at sea, missing since May, and von Luckner, commerce raider, slayer of the innocent, was surely to blame.

In reality, the two ships had been the victims of another German raider, the *Wolf*, which was also active in the Pacific. Passengers and crew had been taken on board the German vessel as captives. This truth was slow to arrive, however, and the Count was hidden away for a time in the Devonport torpedo yard barracks at North Head. From there he was taken by train to Wellington for interrogation before being transferred, with his second-in-command, to Motuihe.

It was less than two months later that he and ten other prisoners rounded Cape Colville in the stolen *Pearl*. They made for the Mercury Islands, where, finding a sheltered bay, they set a lookout and lay low to attend to the launch's faltering engine and to see whether they could surprise and capture a seagoing vessel. They were now 112 kilometres from their island prison. Von Luckner's plan was, after hijacking a suitable vessel, to put its crew ashore on the distant Kermadecs and head for South America. However, time was not on their side, as by now some 29 vessels were patrolling the waters of the Gulf in search of them.

On Sunday, 16 December the lookout saw two ships standing off the coast, and von Luckner called all hands to the *Pearl*. The ships proved to be scows — sturdy, flat-bottomed coastal traders of a type unfamiliar to the Germans. They were some eight kilometres apart and both heading north under full sail. It was decided to attack the rear vessel, the *Moa*, as the other, the *Rangi*, appeared faster.

Once outside the three-mile (five-kilometre) limit, von Luckner swore the cadets into the Imperial German Navy and, still flying the New Zealand flag, ordered the scow to stand to. The *Pearl* was made fast and von Luckner, bearing a German battle ensign made from painted flour sacks, sprang aboard. Brandishing hand-grenades and rifle, he demanded the ship's surrender.

Knowing nothing of the Motuihe escape, William Bourke, captain of the *Moa*, was mightily displeased at this blatant act of piracy. Von Luckner informed him and his five crew — including eleven-year-old Joseph Grogan, on the voyage for his health — that they were civilian prisoners of the Kaiser. The Count advised them to obey orders and offer no resistance. They would, he added, be paid for the time spent in the Kaiser's service.

Unhappily for von Luckner, the *Rangi*'s captain had seen the capture and, as the *Pearl* had been damaged getting alongside the *Moa*, his scow proved too fast to be overtaken. It was to be a costly failure. Von Luckner abandoned the chase, jettisoned as much of the *Moa*'s cargo as possible — more than half its 80,000 feet of sawn rimu timber — and crowded on sail for the Kermadecs. En route, the *Pearl* capsized and sank in heavy weather.

Meanwhile, the *Rangi* had intercepted the cable ship *Iris* off Cape Colville, and the news was passed to Auckland. The *Iris* then itself returned to Auckland to take on board two six-pounder guns and their gunners. (How the high command must have craved air power. It was to be a pursuit in slow motion.)

On 21 December, after five days at sea, the crew aboard the *Moa* made landfall in the Kermadecs, 960 kilometres north-east of New Zealand, and hove to off Curtis Island, which, in a defiant gesture, von Luckner claimed for Germany. His men were taking aboard provisions after pilfering stores kept on the island for shipwrecked mariners — bacon, butter, lard, canned beef, blankets — when Kerscheiss saw smoke on the horizon: the *Iris*.

Not wishing to be embarrassed as he had been in Fiji, von Luckner set sail at once, ignoring the steamer's signals and determined to outrun it. A shell fired across the *Moa*'s stern soon convinced him otherwise. It was the first shot of the war in New Zealand waters. The Count ordered the scow

brought to, and he and his crew were taken aboard the *Iris* at gunpoint and searched. The bid for freedom had failed.

As if justifying his actions, von Luckner told his captors: 'You left your door open; you cannot blame me for walking out.'

The *Moa*'s original crew were found to be unharmed, and admitted to having been well treated. The Germans had even given the ship's boy sweets and chocolates taken from the internment camp. The crew had just one complaint to make about the episode: the Count had inexcusably replaced their picture of Lord Kitchener with one of Field Marshal von Hindenburg.

By comparison, the Germans felt hard done by. Sentenced to fourteen days in Mt Eden prison — like old drunks, in the Count's opinion — they began their confinement on Boxing Day. It was the day of an important race meeting, he later recalled. 'We were hustled into the cold, cold cells in order to allow the saucy-looking major to be in time to see the first race. "Hurry up, Count", said he, "and hop in or I will miss it," and, despite my protests, I had to "hop in".'

Von Luckner and Kerscheiss were transferred to Ripapa Island in Lyttelton harbour, where for six months they were kept in close confinement. 'I verily believe that had we stayed there much longer we would have died of ennui,' said the Count, who entertained thoughts of escape in an empty tar barrel.

To their delight, the two prisoners were then returned to Motuihe, where they found camp life relatively unchanged. There was a new commandant, of course — one who was alert to any signs of 'Hun foxiness'. To be sure, some of the Count's countrymen, who had in vain spent such time learning their lines for his Christmas play, seemed to hold a grudge. Most prisoners, however, greeted the escapees enthusiastically.

When the war ended on 11 November 1918, the unstoppable Count was on the verge of another escape attempt. Before being repatriated, he showed guards a camouflaged dugout in the side of a dry river bed on the far south-east of the island, which had been painstakingly stocked with food, clothing and weapons. He and others, including the former governor of German Samoa, had anticipated lying low there for up to six weeks before setting out to capture yet another ship.

It was only on his return to Germany that von Luckner learned the fate of the 58 *Seeadler* crew he had left on Mopelia. They had succeeded in capturing a two-masted French schooner, the *Lutece*, which had sighted their wreck. Renaming it *Fortuna*, they made for Easter Island, where they were forced to sink their leaky vessel. Two months later, on 25 November 1917, they were taken aboard a Chilean steamer and spent the rest of the war in Chile as guests of the country's German community.

In 1938 von Luckner, now an international celebrity, returned to New Zealand with his Swedish wife aboard their yacht, *Seeteufel* ('Sea Devil'). They were warmly received by a public enamoured of the Count's colourful exploits. He was strong as an ox, and his favourite crowd-pleaser was to rip telephone directories apart. Accused by some of spreading Nazi propaganda, he replied: 'I respect Herr Hitler, as I do the German Government, but I take no part in it. If I am an ambassador, let me be one of peace.'

Nevertheless, the beginning of war in 1939 cast a shadow of suspicion over his Pacific travels in *Seeteufel* — the two-year voyage was widely seen as one of espionage — and clouded the reputation of a man once described by the Pope as 'a great humanitarian'. He spent World War II in retirement in Germany and died in 1966 in Malmo, Sweden at the age of 85.

An incident that could well serve as his epitaph occurred in England in 1935. There on a goodwill visit, he had been invited aboard a British battleship as an honoured guest by a group of naval officers, some of whom had once hunted him across half the oceans of the world. At one of the festively decorated tables on the quarterdeck, an admiral rose and, after a

speech of welcome, turned to Captain Holland, the man who years earlier had unsuspectingly let von Luckner slip through the North Sea blockade.

'Well, Holland,' said the admiral. 'Today you are again with him. Are you sorry you let him go?'

Holland is said to have stood and replied: 'From all accounts, sir, and that includes even our own official history, it is quite clear that the operations of *Seeadler* represented the only really romantic episode of the war at sea . . . If I hadn't let Count Luckner and his ship go, naval history would have been the poorer.'

Loud applause. A clatter of chairs. Shouts of 'Three cheers for the last of the pirates!' And fade.

September 1997

Motuihe Island

With its sheltered white-sand beaches and impressive mudstone cliffs, its reefs and rolling farmland, Motuihe Island made an idyllic holding-pen for Count Felix von Luckner and his fellow prisoners. For some New Zealanders, the island two-and-a-half kilometres long and nestled amid a huddle of islands in the inner Hauraki Gulf, will be for ever connected with the memory of von Luckner and his flamboyant escape. But there is more to Motuihe than that. At one time or another, it has been fitted out for almost every job an island near a major city can take on.

A summer Mecca for tourists and day-trippers since the 1930s, Motuihe still carries evidence of the substantial Maori occupation that began in the thirteenth century. Some 37 marked archaeological sites can be visited, including the remains of fortified pa which date back to the Ngati Paoa and the earlier Ngati Huarere. The island was originally known as Te Motu o Ihenga, after the nephew of the Arawa canoe's navigator. With the coming of the Europeans, however, human activity began to leave more obvious traces.

Most of them are to be found on the attractively formed western headland. A short way up the winding road from the beach is a grove of gnarled and prolific olives, said to have grown from seeds brought out from Scotland in the middle of last century by John Logan Campbell. Campbell, remembered as the 'Father of Auckland' for his many gifts to the city, bought Motuihe with his business partner William Brown in 1843 and farmed it until 1858.

They and a later owner energetically planted ngaio trees, cereals, vegetables and gorse and shipped over horses, cattle, sheep, pigs, goats, partridges, turkeys, pheasants, quail, geese 'without number' and herds of deer. By 1868 Motuihe had become something of a game park masquerading as a farm.

The mood on the island, however, soon became less sportive. In 1872, Motuihe was bought by the government, and the following year, when a sailing ship arrived in Auckland with smallpox on board, the entire island was pressed into service as a human quarantine station. Buildings were hastily thrown up on the northern headland, some of them fashioned from materials salvaged from the demolished Albert Barracks, which had been built in central Auckland during the war against Maori in the Waikato.

Around two large, two-storeyed accommodation buildings known as 'The Barracks' stood a sprawling array of other buildings, including hospital wards, stables, a caretaker's house and a brick structure with a high chimney used for fumigating clothing and baggage. A sizeable part of the island also became an animal quarantine station, and until 1941 this area was permanently closed to the public.

Human quarantines were rare, however, and ferries regularly brought over picnic parties — some complete with their own bands. People with influence were even able to rent The Barracks over the summer. At one point the quarantine station became home to psychiatric patients for six months when the Avondale Mental Hospital was damaged by fire.

In 1929, an uplifting organisation called the Community Sunshine Association was permitted to use the quarantine station for children's health camps, and in 1931 it cared there for many children who had been evacuated after the Napier earthquake.

In 1941, with the outbreak of war in the Pacific, a new phase of island life began when the navy moved in, converting the station to a training establishment and, in accordance with naval custom, transforming it into a ship: HMNZS *Tamaki*. The navy set about moving in guns, erecting yet more buildings, improving roading and drainage, building parade grounds and tennis courts and generally introducing an air of military bustle. During the war, some 6000 recruits — almost two-thirds of all New Zealanders who saw active naval service — had learned to stow their belongings, make fast their ropes and deliver a powerful opening volley on HMNZS *Tamaki*.

In 1963, the navy upped anchor, leaving a vast establishment of more than 70 buildings and a question mark over the fate of the island. While the Auckland City Council was chewing over the vexed question, an inspection by its diligent Parks and Library Committee discovered that the navy had, in an act reminiscent of Joseph Stalin's slash-and-burn policy of retreat, stripped the buildings of all their plumbing and fittings. Though the Russian leader's actions had helped win the war, the navy's emulation of them merely provoked outrage at what was seen as 'criminal wanton destruction by a Government department under bureaucratic control'.

Two years later, broadcaster Shirley Maddock described what was left of the base: 'Fat boilers sit in the whitewashed galley, caught fast in rust and cobweb, a flypaper spattered with little cadavers hangs from the light cord and a mouse scutters in the cupboard. Nothing is left in the barrack rooms but rows of hammock hooks and a sheepish lavatory pan lurching by a door.' Though most buildings were demolished, some survived, including the water tower which escaped destruction largely because of the awkwardness of pulling it down.

In the years following the navy's withdrawal, day-trippers again discovered the delights of Motuihe, with 6500 visitors arriving by green-hulled ferry and private pleasure-craft over a single weekend in the summer of 1964. At the height of the picnic season, Sunday schools, fire brigades and watersiders took to Motuihe's beaches for their ritual outings — on one occasion a company of sausage-sizzling police found themselves just up the beach from a party of card-carrying communists.

The camp high on the promontory, which once held von Luckner's crew in its soft embrace, has now been abandoned to pukekos, ducks and fantails. Scattered round about are the remains of base life: rubble, timber, patches of asphalt, the water tower near to collapse, the concrete pad of a gun emplacement. And nearby, on the northern tip, a touchingly informal cemetery contains a dozen or so graves — many dating from the influenza epidemic of 1918, when the RMS *Makura* was quarantined there. Among the graves is that of Ethel Browning, the 28-year-old wife of the *Makura*'s captain who died while voluntarily nursing patients from the ship.

Through the foliage at the cliff's edge the conical tip of Rangitoto Island is clearly visible, and a little to the right, just beyond a narrow stretch of water, lies Motutapu, its cliffs and sheltering trees — a daily sight to von Luckner — temptingly close.

Illustrations

The Birdman of Upper Waitohi: Richard Pearse and the Quest for Flight

In the depths of the winter of 1951, a frail, elderly man with long white hair and an unkempt moustache was helped from his home in Woolston, Christchurch, and taken to Sunnyside Hospital, a psychiatric institution in the city's south-west. Weak and distraught, he muttered about attempts being made on his life. People were out to steal his inventions, he said.

His background was a mystery. About all that could be deduced was that he was a retired farmer, of Irish extraction, unmarried and with no known relatives in New Zealand.

On the afternoon of 30 June, the day of his admission to Sunnyside, the muddled, disoriented old man, who gave his name as Richard William Pearse, was subjected to a clinical examination. 'He knows his age and year of birth but does not know what year or month it is at the present time,' recorded the examining doctor. 'His spontaneous conversation is jumbled and largely incomprehensible. He jumps from speculations about planetary collisions and vague ramblings about astronomy to fragmentary accounts of his everyday affairs.'

The diagnosis was arteriosclerotic psychosis, a common ailment among the elderly. Pearse was not insane, just confused, hard of hearing and no longer able to care for himself.

The 73-year-old soon grew accustomed to Sunnyside life, liking the food — or at least eating without complaint — and taking part in basket-making and other occupational therapy classes. Yet the paranoia persisted, and at times drove him to distraction. His inventions were at risk. Schemers plotted even now to snatch them away. The Wright brothers had illegally used his ideas, as had American helicopter designers. He fretted over his Australian patent rights and told the medical superintendent that he wanted them extended.

Talk of patents was news to the superintendent, as was the discovery by the Public Trust Office that the apparently impecunious Pearse owned three houses in Christchurch, all of which he had built himself, and that he was collecting rent from each of them.

A property inspector was sent to investigate complaints by tenants at the Woolston house where Pearse had for years slept, cooked and lived in a small front bedroom. On the other side of the door to that room something, perhaps leftover food, was decidedly off. The inspector entered but found nothing untoward, and little of worth: a gas cooker, a cycle lamp, a cased cello. Out in the locked garage, however, he came upon something unexpected. There, among the tools and farm implements, and an odd home-built power-cycle, were a set of wings and the assorted fabric-covered parts of what the Public Trust man construed to be an 'improvised autogyro'.

Richard Pearse, self-taught inventor, trail-blazing aviator and eccentric visionary, was about to be rediscovered.

In the half-light of an early autumn morning I arrived at the home of South Canterbury farmer Evan Gardiner, which rests on a spur overlooking the valley of the braided Opihi River. Eighteen kilometres east is the old ceramics town of Temuka, and 25 kilometres or so south-east lies Timaru, picturesquely elevated about Caroline Bay. The Opihi valley itself is hatched with straight businesslike roads that connect a scattering of homesteads with Waitohi and with the small service town of Pleasant Point on the far bank, near a fork in the river.

I had come here to learn more about the retiring and enigmatic Richard Pearse, who left few clues to his life and even fewer about his lifelong pursuit of the Holy Grail of flight. No diary, no journal, no personal letters or scribbled memos survive. Not even a photograph of him beyond 1917. Gardiner, Pearse's great-nephew, had offered to fly me over the countryside Pearse grew up in, and of which, if the claims are true, he snatched tantalising glimpses in a few brief airborne moments early this century.

For a big man — he stands a solid 190 cm tall — Gardiner's choice of aircraft is surprisingly compact: a dacron-skinned microlight, housed out in a shed alongside the farm tractor. I had seen a reconstruction of Pearse's first flying machine in Auckland's Museum of Transport, Technology and Social History, and could not help thinking the microlight was a perfectly fitting vehicle for the journey back into history. Pearse's contraption, the creation of a young man just into his twenties, bears an uncanny resemblance to the early microlights that first began labouring across the country's beaches and fields in the 1970s.

Gardiner swung open the paddock gate and we got down to business, taxiing into position, then, with a surge of power, belting along the grass strip for a few seconds before leaning back into the pale autumn sky. Farmhouse and shed, field and fences all dropped effortlessly away, leaving us an infinity of South Canterbury sky to roam about in.

It was so easy that I felt like a cheat. Pearse had worked tirelessly to get his machine built, making countless trips to Temuka along the once-dusty straights we now drifted over, his pushbike laden on the return ride with bamboo and other materials. Putting together a makeshift engine from odds and ends he found about the farm. Forgoing settled family life, and for years enduring the ridicule of uncomprehending neighbours, the more charitable of whom dismissed him as merely eccentric.

'Mad' Pearse did not fit in. An indifferent farmer, he let his property go while toiling at his workbench or doing complicated calculations at the kitchen table. Much of the farmwork, such as crop harvesting, he contracted out, and when he did venture into the paddock on farm business he invariably carried with him some book of a technical nature to pore over.

From 50 metres up, Waitohi is a place of modest dimensions. It does not take long to get from the rolling hills down to the flats with their patterned fields of animal feed. Part-way along Main Waitohi Road is the site of Pearse's farm, a satisfyingly regular 40-hectare rectangle of land backing up to the ridge of higher ground beyond. Here, Pearse was said to have made his historic first flight, wheeling his homemade machine out past the schoolhouse, and taking off noisily along the road. He was airborne for 100 metres or so, if witnesses are to be believed, before crashing unceremoniously into a tall gorse hedge.

We skimmed the road, lined at this time of year (it was the season of Pearse's early attempts at flight) with cylinders of cut hay, and flew over the monument put up belatedly in the aviator's honour — a scale replica of his machine on a steel post, set off by a half-circle of white stone. From the driving seat of a passing car it has a momentary presence, but seen from the air it appears as flimsy and insubstantial as a wind-blown seed. All around was brown earth turned by the plough.

Eight kilometres south-east, on the terrace overlooking the Opihi River — no one knows exactly where — Pearse is said to have made another, more spectacular, attempt at flight. He somehow managed to get his small machine, with its iron frame and cloth-covered bamboo wings, from the farm all the way down to this stretch of land, nine metres or so above the river bed. There, after an abortive first try, and watched by half a dozen eager lads, he succeeded in launching himself off the terrace. A kilometre upstream the machine came to grief on the rocky river bed and Pearse was seen to scramble up the bank among the blackberries.

We flew on upriver, then cut across in the direction of the monument. Here, the broad river flat has been brought into pasture for grazing deer. On the lip of the 30-metre-high terrace which marks its edge, in tree-studded grounds with a tennis court and a long birch-lined driveway, is Trewarlet, the old Pearse homestead.

Gardiner circled once or twice to let me admire the solid building, now much enlarged, where Richard spent his dreamy youth. Magpies lifted lazily

into the air as our shadow flickered across a field of kale. Sunlight glanced off the white stone walls. Pearse's parents, Digory and Sarah, bought land here in 1865 and built Trewarlet — named for a family estate in Cornwall — from local limestone around 1888.

It must have been an entertaining childhood. There were peacocks and pheasants at Trewarlet, as well as a parrot that would greet the day by screeching: 'Time to get up and get the breakfast!' There were also guineafowls, goats, ferrets, various dogs and a monkey which lived in a box on top of a pole. The creature had been bought from an organ-grinder in Temuka, and on the way to the homestead had grabbed at the reins of the gig and steered it into a ditch.

And there was an intriguing landscape for young legs to explore: the river terrace with its speargrass and thickets of flax and toetoe, limestone outcrops, the countless streams descending from the hills, in summer the shingled bed of the Opihi.

The Pearse family was uncommonly musical, even for an age when entertaining oneself was the norm. Richard's brothers and sisters — he had four of each — all played instruments; some the violin, one, Margaret, the harp. Richard himself mastered the cello. It accompanied him throughout his life, and he often sought relief in its mellow tones from the unending work of invention.

The family not only fielded a sizeable orchestra but, if pressed, could put together a powerful tennis team. Digory played enthusiastically into his 70s, and the grass court at today's Trewarlet is a legacy of the game's grip on the family. At harvest time, when normal folk laboured in their fields until dusk, the Pearses would sometimes call a halt at four in the afternoon for a few sets. Their neglected hedges grew to be the highest in the district and when they were 'trimmed' it was with matches rather than shears. 'Gentleman farmers', neighbours called them.

Richard, who was less farmerly than most, achieved some notable successes at tennis, and perhaps could have done more if the siren of flight had not claimed him utterly. Once, when he failed to show for a tournament, he was found hammering determinedly in a shed. His brother Warne was more devoted to the sport, and achieved a national reputation, winning the South Canterbury singles title a dozen times, as well as other provincial contests. Once he cycled all the way to Nelson for a tournament, then, when it was over, cycled back home again — a round trip of 1100 kilometres.

Warne's grandson, Jeffrey Pearse, owns Trewarlet now, and keeps the flame of tennis alive by playing once a week in Temuka. I had arranged to meet Jeffrey at the homestead and, having cased it from above, drove to the house across the flats. The 200-hectare property is run as a deer farm and, as we talked, Suzie, a three-month-old doe, wandered through the house delicately nuzzling papers on a sideboard and taking a passing interest in a television programme watched by Jeffrey's children — fifth-generation Pearses.

Despite the alterations, the original dimensions of the homestead can still be traced, its modest rooms enclosed by weighty 380-mm limestone walls. In Richard's childhood, Trewarlet was a plain home, austere even, with low-silled windows and a scatter of shrubs out front to keep the ragged grass at bay.

It was here, among family, that Richard's inventiveness first began to blossom. He made a needle-threader for his mother, a zoetrope for his sisters, and one day arrived at school with something he had cobbled together from a cotton reel, a nailed board, a piece of string, and the top of a herring tin cut and twisted into a propeller. He wound the string around the reel, tugged it and the thing shot off the nail and was airborne. Richard had built a copy of the earliest airscrew known, a mechanical toy first pictured in the pages of a fourteenth-century Flemish manuscript.

Far from being a star performer at school, the boy had just one strong suit: engineering. Unhappily, when school ended his father refused to let him hone his talent by studying at Canterbury University College in Christchurch. Digory had invested in his oldest son Tom's medical degree. Richard and his other brothers would have to work the land.

In 1898, at the age of 21, Richard took up the 40 hectares on Main Waitohi Road that he was to farm fitfully for thirteen years. He lived on at Trewarlet, though, converting his new property's thatched cottage into a workshop and making himself a lathe, then a forge and bellows, from cast-offs found at the tip. There, in the workshop behind the screen of an overgrown gorse hedge, he worked into the night on his inventions and began his slow slide into seclusion.

The first fruit of that solitary toil was patent 14507, gazetted in late 1902, for a new type of bicycle. The *Temuka Leader* of 21 May 1903 was sufficiently impressed to find room in its pages for a mention when Richard rode to town on sale day that month. The *Leader* was particularly taken with the cycle's novel driving gear. 'In place of the sprocket wheel the machine is fitted with cranks about half as long again as those of the ordinary bicycle, and these go up and down in arcs instead of revolving in cycles,' the paper told its readers. 'It is claimed for the invention that it makes riding easier as there is no waste of energy, the rider being able to keep a steady strain on the machine the whole time.'

The paper went on to discuss the bicycle's unusual gearing system — adjusted by means of a pin — but not its unusual back-wheel rim brake or its automatically inflating tyres. Through the clotted prose of a patent attorney, Pearse explained how the tyre pumps worked: 'The eccentric disc [mounted on each wheel axle] is furnished with a projection or knob that engages with a stop that is actuated by the rider. By these means the eccentric is caused to remain stationary, and the pump is thereby actuated through suitable connections as it evolves with the wheel around the eccentric disc. When desired by the operator the eccentric may be released and it will then revolve with the wheel and the pump cease working.'

In an age of rough roads, when cars were rare and bicycle tyres of poor quality, Pearse's patent offered genuine advances. That impractical Victorian icon, the penny farthing, had been superseded by the safety bicycle only sixteen years earlier, and pneumatic tyres had appeared two years after that. Yet the new machine was not put into production and Pearse's bamboo prototype disappeared. Perhaps its potential was overtaken by the inventor's consuming fascination with flight.

It is hard now to grasp the magnitude of what Pearse was about to do. Working in an isolated horse-and-gig farming community, without financial backing or technical training, and in the face of ridicule and indifference, he set out — possibly as early as 1899 — to build a piloted machine that could claw its way aloft through the insubstantial air.

The earliest recorded flight in New Zealand had taken place only ten years earlier, and that was by hot-air balloon. No one else would even attempt to build a heavier-than-air machine in the country until 1907, four years after the Wrights.

For Pearse it was to be a lonely endeavour. 'I don't think his parents were interested in what he was doing,' Jeffrey Pearse's father, Richard, nephew of the inventor, told me at Trewarlet. 'They thought flight was out of his reach. He didn't get any encouragement.' Richard, just a boy when his namesake was tinkering with flying machines, remembers his uncle as a tall, well-built man with a loud voice. 'He spoke of mechanical things. Weight-to-horsepower ratios — that was his obsession.'

As well it might have been. Unlike later pioneers, such as the French aviator Louis Blériot, the first to fly the English Channel, Pearse could not buy a purpose-built aero engine. When he began work at the turn of the century, most engines were massive coal-burners, driving steamships at sea and hefty traction engines on land.

So he set about making from scratch an aero version of the new, though still heavy, internal combustion engines that were then just beginning to power horseless carriages. He may have read of attempts by the American Samuel Langley to construct a suitable engine for his craft, the *Aerodrome*, but the only expert he could turn to locally was Timaru engineer Cecil Wood — in 1895 the first person in New Zealand to build an internal combustion engine. The unstoppable Wood went on to build the country's first motorcycle (1895) and its first car (1901).

He was invaluable to Pearse, showing him how to make spark-plugs and helping design surface carburettors. It is likely that the Pleasant Point blacksmith, Billy Hayes, also lent a hand, making Pearse's first crankshaft. Later crankshafts and some cylinder barrels were made by an engineering works in Timaru, but otherwise Pearse was on his own. He scavenged metal from tobacco tins and fashioned cylinders from cast-iron irrigation pipes, making them double-acting — firing at each end of the stroke — thus increasing efficiency by avoiding idle strokes. It was almost certainly an idea borrowed from steam engines.

For months, nothing much seemed to happen, then one evening sleepy Upper Waitohi was ripped apart by the sound of a dozen anvils being bashed by Titans, a noise like Judgement Day reverberating across the valley. It was Pearse firing up his first homemade engine and, inevitably, provoking the ire of local farmers. One thought the Boer War had come, another contended with frightened cattle.

But Pearse was pleased with the two-cylinder engine, a horizontally opposed air-cooled radial, claiming it developed 25 horsepower and weighed a mere 57 kilograms. It was, he said, the lightest engine in the world for its power. It is at least true that equivalent car engines of the day were four times heavier.

He tested the engine's pull by tethering it to a post and measuring the effect of changes to the propeller's pitch with a spring balance. After experiments with paraffin oil, he switched to benzene, which he found better for starting cold cylinders.

It is impossible, from Pearse's meagre references to his work and from the parts that remain, to piece together the exact development of his engines. No one knows which one was used on which flight attempt. And it does not really matter. They were reliable, if sometimes reluctant to start, and he was happy with them all — though he soon replaced the 25-horsepower engine with a more satisfactory one of 60 horsepower (the Wrights used a 32-horsepower one for their history-making flight).

There is less doubt over the actual aircraft. It consisted of a tubular steel frame on a tricycle undercarriage with pneumatic tyres and a steerable nosewheel. The pilot sat on a movable saddle under a rectangular bamboo-framed wing covered in fabric. A wooden propeller, 'finished with glass of a broken bottle and sandpaper', according to Warne, was fixed directly to the engine, which was mounted forward, above the pilot, on the wing's leading edge. Other innovations included a rear elevator (Pearse called it a 'horizontal rudder') to stop pitching, and horizontal wingtip rudders — elevons — to counteract rolling.

Endless trials followed. One Waitohi local reported seeing Pearse jogging after his machine, holding the wing's trailing edge. Another glimpsed him steering it around a paddock, using reins attached to the controls. A third witnessed the machine dragging a heavy sack about the place. And all the while Pearse continued to tinker with his design, rounding the wings a little and attaching a new iron-framed propeller which had blades cut from sheep dip drums.

He found it prudent to replace the calico behind the engine with a light-weight tin plate made from flattened golden syrup cans. The cloth had buckled up in the propeller slipstream and exhaust sparks threatened to set it on fire.

Then came the day that was to arouse so much controversy. Pearse wheeled his winged machine from its shelter and down to the school crossroads, watched by a few dozen locals who had got wind that 'Bamboo Dick' was up to something. He and a few helpers then tried several times to get the machine going, but no amount of revving and pushing seemed to help. Farmers began drifting back to their work, and the crowd thinned.

Late in the afternoon, Pearse mounted the saddle for one last attempt, signalling to his brother when he was ready. 'I had the pleasure of pulling the propeller for starting,' Warne later recalled. 'She was a wonderful engine and started with very little bother.'

The machine lumbered into the air with a sound 'rather like a giant chaffcutter' and almost immediately started to pitch badly. The climb, said another witness, was very slow.

Warne claimed his brother flew some 400 metres before veering into a gorse hedge. Others estimated the distance at 100 to 150 metres. Unlike the Wrights' flight at Kitty Hawk, no one in Waitohi wielded a camera or measured airspeed. They were, however, suitably impressed — 'goggle-eyed with amazement', in the words of Mrs Inwood, a neighbour.

Pearse (family motto *Cadent, porrigo dextram,* 'when I am fallen I stretch out my right arm') had injured himself in the attempt and was taken to Temuka cottage hospital to have his collarbone seen to. All was found to be well, and he returned home the following day.

Exasperatingly, for believers and sceptics alike, nothing now exists to pinpoint the day or offer proof of the flight. The hospital records were destroyed in a fire. And a photograph of the plane resting in the hedge, taken by a professional photographer the day after the flight, was later destroyed by flood.

Pearse's biographer, Gordon Ogilvie, assembled evidence for his 1973 book from 37 former Waitohi residents, including 21 who claimed to have seen Pearse flying. Another 22 offered information to him and fellow researchers about Pearse's activities at Waitohi. But attempts by some to push the date of the first flight back beyond 1903 worry Ogilvie. 'I've become increasingly cautious of what is said,' observes Ogilvie, onetime teacher at Pleasant Point, now living in Christchurch. 'All the witnesses are dead.'

Ogilvie, who will use only the terms 'powered take-offs', 'flight attempts' and 'tentative flights' — 'don't ever say "flights" when talking of Pearse', he told me — comes down on 31 March 1903 as the most likely date of the Waitohi inventor's farewell to the ground — fully eight months before Orville and Wilbur Wright flew.

The monument fronting Pearse's old fields opts for March 1904.

Muddying the waters are two letters Pearse later submitted for publication, in which he seems to deny his success. 'Preeminence will undoubtedly be given to the Wright brothers, of America, when the history of the aeroplane is written, as they were the first to actually make successful flights with a motor-driven aeroplane,' he wrote in a letter to Dunedin's *Evening Star* on 10 May 1915.

Most of the letter is taken up with the issue of the Wrights' patented system of wing warping — a method of bending either wingtip in flight to prevent tipping. Pearse pointed out that he himself had solved the problem using 'ailerons' — his wingtip rudders — which he patented in June 1906. Then comes the worrying sentence: 'After Langley's failure in 1903, I was still of [the] opinion that aerial navigation was possible, and I started out to solve the problem about March 1904.'

In a second letter, published in the *Christchurch Star* on 15 September 1928, he takes that date back to February 1904, saying that by 1906 his

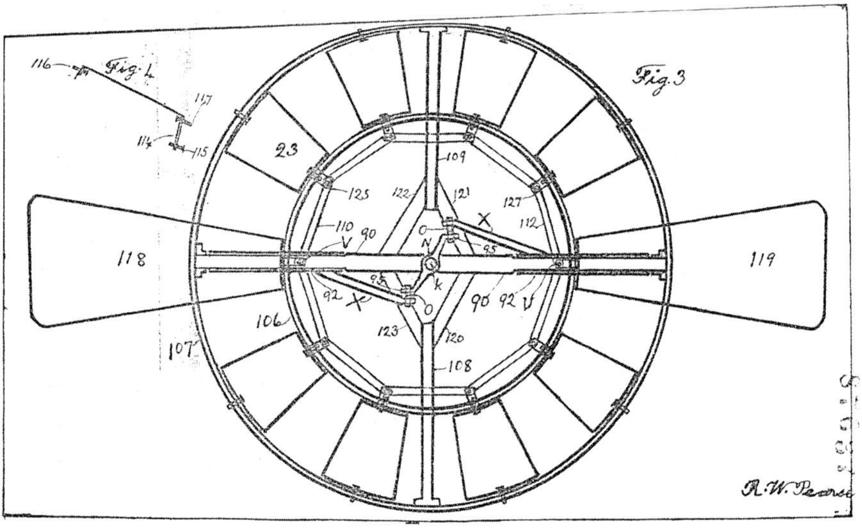

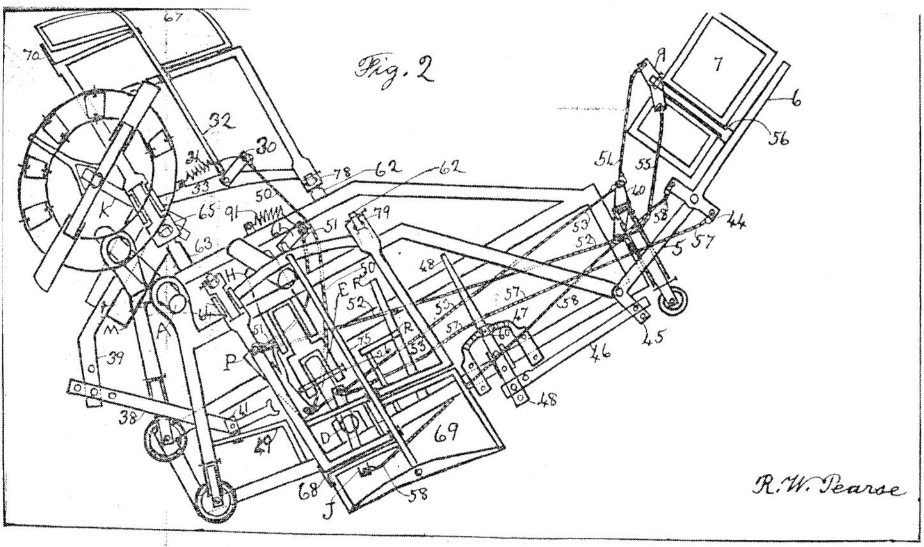

machine was sufficiently perfected to be patented. He argues that the Wrights gained a monopoly on world aviation because the ailerons later used by other designers were held to be variations of control by wing warping, and therefore infringed the Wrights' patent.

Pearse claimed to have invented what he called ailerons in 1904, and to have patented them at the same time as the Wrights patented wing warping. 'So ailerons would have given me a monopoly in New Zealand if I had kept the patent covered, but I let it lapse in 1910 because I did not know the Great War was coming, and I did not see much prospect of selling aircraft in New Zealand.'

He went on to say that the size and slowness of his own aircraft made it uncontrollable. It would lift off at 30 km/h, he recalled, an insufficient speed for the rudders to be effective, and would immediately begin to yaw. 'So I never flew with my experimental plane.' Pearse added, however, that, given his reliable motor, 'I had successful aerial navigation within my grasp . . . But I decided to give up the struggle, as it was useless to try to compete with men who had factories at their backs.'

There is a scrupulous even-handedness in Pearse's words, tinged with an undisguised regret at a chance lost for ever. However, the fact that Pearse dismissed his own early attempts should not be given undue weight. He did not think much of the Wrights' first efforts either, and was critical of their later use of a 'special catapult launching apparatus'.

For Pearse, 'aerial navigation' meant nothing less than a powered take-off followed by sustained and controlled flight. His attempts in the Waitohi valley did not fulfil those criteria; they were merely powered take-offs followed by erratic descents. But, given his definition, he could well have 'started out to solve the problem' of aerial navigation a year after his first flight attempt, when he set about building a bigger, more stable craft.

As it was, the Wrights managed 'aerial navigation' in the last of four flights, on 17 December 1903.

Former aviation engineer Geoff Rodliffe, cheerleader for the Pearse-as-first-aviator team, has argued in favour of an even earlier date — March 1902 — for his first take-off. But the evidence is unconvincing, and now, a century on from the event, proving the point looks like being a lost cause.

For the 'young, eccentric farmer engineer-inventor', as Auckland-born Michigan journalist Gordon Gapper later called Pearse, bitter disillusionment was to come with news of the Kitty Hawk flight. Oddly, the event was most extensively reported in a US beekeepers' journal, though *Scientific American*, which Pearse keenly devoured, carried accounts in early and mid-1904. The Wrights' achievement was for him, said Warne, 'a sad awakening'.

After Kitty Hawk, Pearse turned increasingly to theory, refining his aeroplane controls and getting everything down on paper. 'I, Richard Pearse, of Upper Waitohi, Temuka, in the Colony of New Zealand, Farmer, do hereby declare the nature of my invention . . .' he wrote in the preamble to his 1906 patent for his flying machine. They were the tones of a bequest, or the declaration of a fading dream.

Pearse sweetened his evenings at this time with the odd game of euchre or crib. He played draughts with one of the local lads, Jimmy Orr, or chess with Warne — even golf, on occasion, and table tennis. He holidayed in Christchurch, visiting the museum and going to concerts and the theatre. And, of course, there was the Pearse orchestra. It had such a reputation in South Canterbury that the family was kept busy performing at parties, concerts and musical soirées.

Perhaps, as Ogilvie suggests, it was a desire to preserve the sound of this unique ensemble that led Pearse to experiment with recording devices in these years. One machine used a clockwork mechanism, barbed wire and guitar strings to record and play back tunes. Another, a phonograph and trumpet using wax-coated discs, could be heard 400 metres away. Neighbours were treated not just to music but to the sound of the inventor reciting a piece called 'Professor Snuffles', which, according to a sister, 'had some tremendously big words, real jaw-breakers'. It is as close as the sober Pearse ever came to lightening up.

Then, in 1909, came glimpses of what Pearse had been up to since his first hair-raising attempts at flight a few years earlier. In November, the *Temuka Leader* reported that he was ready to trial his 'airship', made of steel-jointed bamboo and calico and powered by a 24-horsepower motor. The brief notice was picked up by several other provincial papers, and shortly afterwards an *Otago Witness* reporter beat a path to the inventor's workshop door, where he found the aircraft on which Pearse had 'toiled for five long years'. Its description is so unlike the earlier machine that it must have been something entirely new.

Not wanting to be outdone, the *Temuka Leader* reporter now also paid a visit, finding the machine to be 'nothing at all like what we expected . . . there was nothing to be seen but the skeleton framework and that looked much like an enormous spider's web, with the engine taking the place of the spider in the centre of it'. That four-cylinder opposed engine, now at

Auckland's Museum of Transport, Technology and Social History, was proving underpowered, however, and Pearse told the reporter he intended developing another. He also claimed to have made several short hops in the plane.

This sudden interest in Pearse — the only attention in relation to aviation that he was ever to get from the press — may have been a by-product of the great airship scare of 1909, when for some six weeks, beginning in mid-July, astounded witnesses in Dunedin, Geraldine, Temuka, Timaru and elsewhere reported strange aerial happenings. Having indulged in flights of fancy during the 'flap', provincial reporters with time on their hands may have followed any and every subsequent 'airship' lead.

Not that the attention did Pearse any good. The *Temuka Leader* reporter, in particular, seemed to know little about flight, or about Pearse's previous attempts, and filed a confusing story.

There was little excuse for such ignorance. By this time there had been well over 70 powered take-offs in the world, Loius Blériot had crossed the English Channel in July — his overheating engine cooled by a fortuitous shower — and the United States Government had awarded the Wrights $30,000 for breaking the 40 mph (64 km/h) barrier.

The accumulation of those successes, and the rapidity of the advances, must have bewildered Pearse. It is likely he realised by now that, having got off the ground in a shaky fashion in 1903 and then having worked for five years on something bigger and more stable, he had come to the end of what could be achieved.

It was useless to try to compete with men who had factories at their backs.

The young South Canterbury farmer of modest means — withdrawn, isolated, working with cheap materials and rubbish dump pickings, and limited to an airstrip of rough road or, when the crops had been harvested, uneven field — could have little impact.

I decided to give up the struggle.

Late in 1910, Pearse fell seriously ill with typhoid — the disease that was to kill Wilbur Wright two years later. Unlike the American, Pearse recovered. When he felt strong enough, he went south to Dunedin for a holiday, and on his return announced that he was leaving Waitohi. On impulse, he had bought a 75-hectare farm outside Milton, a sheep and dairying town 55 kilometres south-west of Dunedin.

He took a wagonload of things with him to the new Loudens Gully property: reference books, lathe, phonograph, tennis racket, golf clubs, bicycle. A few tools. His aeroplane. Earlier engines and bits of aeroplane he left at his Waitohi workshop.

As it turned out, Milton was to be an earthbound interlude. The land was less suited than Waitohi for launching or landing aircraft, and he had left behind the more satisfactory workshop. Perhaps Waitohi had become just too claustrophobic, too resonant with failure and hemmed about with parental rebuke. Loudens Gully may have been poor flying country, but it was good for the spirit.

Pearse may have tried once or twice to get airborne, but soon dismantled his plane and locked it away. Other projects vied for his attention. He bought a second bicycle and motorised it with the cylinder from an aero engine, using a greenhide belt to drive the rear wheel. The vertical exhaust pipe rose above his head and, without a muffler, the four-stroke engine made the indescribable din that was his signature tune. He was sometimes seen on country roads in the evenings, coat flapping, sparks scattering wildly from the high exhaust.

The power-cycle was useful for getting to the reading room of the Milton Athenaeum, where Pearse could often be seen on a Saturday evening lost in a book. It was also handy for getting to tennis, which he continued to play with relish, and to club dances. Pearse arrived at one knees-up wearing hobnail boots, but danced readily enough. The women liked this farmer with no gift for small talk, but early on seemed to have classed him as a career bachelor.

He also threw himself into golf, at one competition winning a pipe — he did not smoke — for his putting. Toward farmwork, however, Pearse continued to be indifferent. He retained his Waitohi habits, hiring others to plough the lower fields, sow turnips or harvest oats. As for the sheep, Loudens

Gully was a sentence of death. The pastures were overstocked and the animals underfed. Lambs rarely survived.

'He just didn't know any better,' said one local. 'He should never have touched animals.'

To the detriment of his farm stock, Pearse's attention was easily diverted by engineering projects that seemed to spring up about the farm unbidden. There was the device with angled discs that he contrived for making turnip ridges, and the fertiliser applicator with its steel worm. Then there was Pearse's crowning folly, an automatic potato planter with mechanical arms fixed to a plough. These arms were each induced, through an ingenious series of levers, sprockets, wires and plungers, to lower into a tray of potatoes as the plough went along, spike one, then swing out and knock it free.

It is hard to think of a more complicated way of putting a vegetable in the ground, though the attraction of the challenge to Pearse is obvious. The labour of untold workshop days to make, it lasted under an hour out in the world. Pearse did a few circuits of a paddock under the scrutiny of a neighbour, and the mighty contraption seized up. He abandoned it.

More successful was a motor plough he created using a modified oat cutter and the 16-cylinder engine taken from his forlorn aircraft. The engine had power enough to carry Pearse and a neighbour up a thirteen-metre ridge but he had skimped on materials and everything else was too flimsy. He was soon forced to replace a bicycle guide wheel with a more solid iron cutting blade. But when the shaft broke on a steep piece of ground, the machine's fate was sealed. Pearse removed the engine and left everything else on the hillside to rust. He lacked the money to persevere.

As it was, the shadow of war soon fell on Loudens Gully and put an end to all his activities. On 10 May 1917 the *Bruce Herald* announced that his name had been drawn for active service in Europe. Pearse pleaded for an exemption, explaining that there was no one to look after the farm while he was away — his inventions, he said, had been aimed at freeing him from the necessity of contracted labour.

The plea fell on deaf ears. So he sold off his stock, locked the place up and in August left for camp. No one farewelled him. It was a sad close to what were probably the most tranquil years of his life.

Private Pearse was overseas for a year, though recurring illness, possibly stemming from the earlier typhoid, left him unfit to fight. He arrived back at Milton in November 1918 aged 40, not particularly fit, his hair greying, and with few prospects. No one was at the station to meet him, and when he reached the farm he found his house and workshop had been broken into and many of his tools taken.

Pearse tried to settle back into his old farm routine but he was weary of the land. Wool prices were plummeting, and thistle and gorse had even more of a stranglehold on the property than when he had first bought it. A year after returning, he sold up and, without a word to anyone, quit Milton for good.

He went to Christchurch, where he bought a 1000-square-metre section to the east of the city at Wainoni, then a sparsely peopled stretch of dunes covered in lupin and broom. On it he built a house, carting the timber — mostly second-hand — to the site in typical fashion on his bicycle. He tenanted the house, and within four years had built two more in nearby

Woolston. These houses were better than the first, but still no works of art. The rooms were at best approximately square — Pearse had used neither ruler nor spirit-level — and the yards were without paths or garden of any sort.

He lived in the first house, in Dampier Street, where he became even more reclusive, accepting an occasional cup of tea from neighbours and returning the empty cup to their lawn, but otherwise shunning almost all social contact. And he neglected himself, subsisting largely on bread and cheese, and wearing a hotchpotch of clothing — long trousers tied at the ankles, shoes without socks and, in bad weather, a coat secured at the throat with a nail. It could not last, and in January 1927 he was hospitalised for three weeks, suffering from malnourishment and fatigue.

The following year he shifted back to the second house at Wildberry Street, where he lived for 23 years, until that ominous knock on the door on the last day of June 1951, and the journey that ended at Sunnyside. Sad to report, he had become even more isolated and obsessed by thrift in the Wildberry years, mixing together cheap house paint, which rain eventually washed off the weatherboards, chastising a tenant for buying a newspaper when one could be had at the library for nothing, and refusing to get his teeth seen to.

Yet, now and then, a touching thoughtfulness showed, as when during the Depression he dropped the rent for tenants unasked every time their wages were cut. 'Whatever the result of his labours,' declared one, 'I will always regard him as a gentleman and a credit to New Zealand.'

The Wildberry Street house no longer remembers Pearse. On its neat lawn, bordered with pinks, gladioli and nasturtiums, stands a child's swing. The garage, with its secretive high fence, has made way for a subdivision. On one boundary is a Montessori preschool.

After his death at Sunnyside in July 1953, an auction firm was instructed to sell Pearse's shedfull of junk and, if necessary, dump the 'aeroplane contraption'. This was the 'improvised autogyro' first sighted two years earlier by the Public Trust's property inspector.

Thankfully, another idea occurred to the thrift-conscious auctioneer, and Richard Pearse was rescued from certain oblivion. The auctioneer wondered whether the local aero club might be interested in a piece of machinery 'more like a windmill than an aeroplane' in a shed out at Woolston.

One member was, so Pearse's frail device was wired up to keep it together and carted to the club at Harewood. There it sat in the back of a hangar for

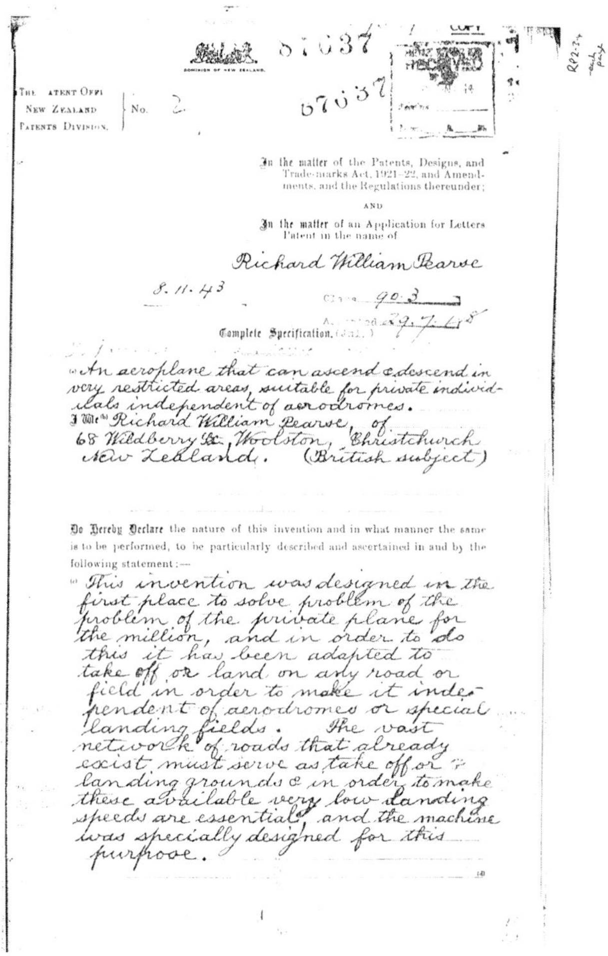

57037

The Patent Office
New Zealand
Patents Division.
No. 2

57037

In the matter of the Patents, Designs, and Trade-marks Act, 1921–22, and Amendments, and the Regulations thereunder;

AND

In the matter of an Application for Letters Patent in the name of

Richard William Pearse

8. 11. 43

Class 90.3

Accepted 29.7.48

Complete Specification.

An aeroplane that can ascend & descend in very restricted areas, suitable for private individuals independent of aerodromes.

I We Richard William Pearse, of 68 Wildberry St, Woolston, Christchurch New Zealand. (British subject)

Do Hereby Declare the nature of this invention and in what manner the same is to be performed, to be particularly described and ascertained in and by the following statement:—

This invention was designed in the first place to solve problem of the problem of the private plane for the million, and in order to do this it has been adapted to take off or land on any road or field in order to make it independent of aerodromes or special landing fields. The vast network of roads that already exist must serve as take off or landing grounds & in order to make these available very low landing speeds are essential, and the machine was specially designed for this purpose.

two years until March 1956, when an agent of history, in the form of George Bolt, turned up following a tip-off in Auckland. Bolt, Tasman Empire Airways' former chief engineer and a student of early flight, had himself been one of the country's pioneering aviators, setting several distance and altitude records and carrying the country's first airmail. His curiosity was instantly aroused by the odd relic, and he had it airlifted to Auckland, where it now resides, along with Pearse's power-cycle and other products of the inventor's restless imagination, in the Museum of Transport, Technology and Social History.

Encouraged by Pearse's surviving sisters, who had read of the find in a newspaper, the indefatigable Bolt set out on his trail, later followed by Ogilvie and others. There were bits and pieces of the first aircraft in a rubbish tip at

Waitohi, and any number of elderly witnesses to interview. The power-cycle was tracked down in Taitapu, south of Christchurch, and a handful of papers were found.

The formidable English aviation historian Charles Gibbs-Smith was unmoved by claims for Pearse pre-dating the Wrights, however, and, when Pearse's own letters to the press were found, seemingly, to assert that he did not start flight experiments until early 1904, Bolt lost heart.

That was a pity, as it seemed to suggest that Pearse was of interest only if he could be shown to have flown earlier than the Wrights. Yet what Bolt discovered about the last aircraft was truly astounding. Built of steel tubing and wood, it was a high-wing monoplane with a span of 10.5 metres and a tail that could fold back over the body for storage. Its wing fabric was calico, hand-stitched to the frame and treated with silver dope. Most unusually, the water-cooled engine pivoted, and by pulling a lever from inside the cockpit could be swung up from its normal position by some 80 degrees. The aircraft had obviously been designed to lift off and land vertically.

This was confirmed by the propeller, a curious arrangement of two blades superimposed over a ring of fans, creating what was in effect a hybrid propeller-rotor. A small tail rotor, fitted to counteract the torque, was driven from the engine via a steel rod connected with universal joints. Both main and tail rotors were variable-pitch, and the engine itself could, with a few adjustments, be run as either a two- or four-stroke. Carbon deposits showed the engine had done a great deal of experimental running, and Pearse seems to have decided that it worked most effectively as a two-stroke.

All up, the machine as it stands today is itself an appropriate monument to the man. Crudely finished and looking like an enormous baroque moth, it is more a sculptural sketch of his philosophy of aviation than a finished product. As such, it is a curious mix of the prophetic and the outmoded. He could not get anyone to fly it, not even experienced aviators (perhaps that should read 'especially' not experienced aviators). Yet at least one person saw the plane in a trial, tethered and with the engine running, its front wheels 30 centimetres off the ground. The engine, which more than once attracted the attention of the local council, at least had muscle.

It is likely that Pearse first began pencilling the design of what he was to call his Utility Plane in the late 1920s, but he could not have begun making it until 1932, when the garage at Wildberry Street was built. At first, he was not even going to roof the garage, which backed onto an earth-floored workshop. The machine was to take off vertically, after all. But he thought better of this, perhaps when the rains came.

Pearse had great hopes for his Utility Plane, which was to be the Model T of the air — compact enough, when folded, to fit in a suburban garage. The plane was to 'solve the problem of the private plane for the million', he wrote in his patent specification, by being able to take off and land 'vertically on rough ground or limited areas'. The spectre of his Waitohi experience lurks behind the words.

By now in his 60s, Pearse soldiered on, trying to get legal protection for his machine. Between 1943 and 1950 he wrote 24 letters to the patent office in Wellington and nineteen to Canberra, all in his big, round hand. He heroically battled official complaints about the size of the paper he used, his method of drawing, the width of margins, the colour of his ink. Finally, in June 1947, his patent was approved.

It was worthless.

In his eagerness to cover everything, Pearse had bundled all the Utility Plane's various innovations together in one patent. Anyone with a mind to copy his ideas had only to leave out a minor detail to avoid infringement. As it was, no one bothered. In the years Pearse had spent hunched over his machine behind closed garage doors, progress had marched past Wildberry Street. Helicopters were a fact and the jet engine had been developed. He wrote to leading aircraft companies, explaining his design. None was interested. Fifty years of devotion to flight had reaped . . . nothing.

Pearse had lived and worked for the most part in the remote valleys of a small country, seas away from the world's technology centres and outside the humming circles of scientific debate. He had no impact whatsoever on the development of aviation.

And yet, in some ways, Pearse led the pack. He was the first aviator in the British Empire to make a powered take-off and, if Oglivie's March 1903 date is right, the fifth to do so in the world. His Waitohi plane was far ahead of its time. In years to come, the world's aircraft would in almost every particular mirror its design in preference to that of the Wrights: single wing as opposed to biplane, wheels in preference to skids, propeller at the front not the back, movable wing panels rather than wing warping. The Wrights got the recognition, Pearse the legacy.

'There seemed to be an element of Greek tragedy in the man. Even the gods were against him,' says Oglivie. 'He was an inventive phenomenon in a small community where farming was everything. If you couldn't farm, you were an idiot. And yet he chose to do the unthinkable — to fly.'

Now, his descendant, Evan Gardiner, talks of importing a new aircraft into the country. A high-tech microlight, the Ban-Bi, built of space-age materials and with wings stressed to plus and minus 12 Gs — twelve times the pull of gravity. It is so new that he will have to test-fly it to get type approval from the Civil Aviation Authority.

Where will he test it? Just down the road at Timaru's Richard Pearse Airport.

September 1999

Illustrations

The Exploits of Herbert Pither, Engineer

Richard Pearse was not the only early New Zealand do-it-yourselfer to be bewitched by the possibilities of heavier-than-air flight. In 1909–11, Gore resident Francis Potter built a plane from Oregon pine in a woolshed on the family's Kelso farm. The wings were of unbleached calico waterproofed with gelatin and formalin, and the undercarriage consisted of two sprung wheels on castors and a third tailwheel fitted with a rim brake. Without its wings the machine was reported to have a ground speed of 43 km/h, but with wings fitted the speed dropped to around 16 km/h. Potter's 18-horsepower engine was just not up to the job. It was his second venture into the largely unexplored realms of aviation, and it seems to have broken his health. He died a young man in 1913. The engine was used to power a Bluff fishing boat.

Other try-hards included Napier's Bertram Ogilvie, who constructed three flying machines between 1907 and 1910, and Arthur Schaef of Wellington, who built a plane in 1909.

Most successful, however, was Invercargill engineer and former world champion cyclist Herbert Pither. Pither cut his teeth on marine engines and, in 1902, built a car. In late 1909, he began work on a tubular steel monoplane controlled by rudder and wing warping and fitted with an extraordinary engine of his own design: a four-cylinder 40-horsepower motor weighing a mere 72 kilograms and powering a two-metre two-blade aluminium propeller. Remarkably, Pither had not the slightest knowledge of 'aeroplaning' before beginning work on his machine, and had seen nothing more advanced in the air than a balloon.

Eight months later, the job was finished. In order to conduct his flight trials in private, Pither secretly towed the machine from his garage out over sandhills to a remote part of Oreti Beach, where he set up camp. While waiting for the right weather and tides, he occupied himself testing the engine and taxiing about the beach.

Then, on Tuesday, 4 July 1910, Pither wheeled his plane down to the level sand and fired up the engine. He set off along the beach, applied the elevator, and suddenly found himself rising gracefully into the air. The aircraft carried on along the beach at a height of nine to ten metres for more than a kilometre, before a combination of headwind and curving beach threatened to drive him into the sandhills and lagoons. Realising that over-correction would take him out over the breakers, Pither shut down the engine and glided onto the beach.

'As he had never had a flight before, his feelings during the landing were somewhat mixed,' the *Southland Daily News* reported with admirable understatement. Pither was left feeling thankful that he had substituted motorcycle wheels for the less substantial bicycle wheels.

In 1969 several witnesses belatedly came forward to confirm the flight. One, locomotive fireman Gordon Whiting, said he saw a lattice-framed aircraft 'like a flying ironmongery' out near Waikiwi in 1909 or 1910. 'We just laughed at it.'

Invercargill barber Mick Barr claimed to have seen the plane over West Plains when out cycling with his stepfather one day in 1909 or 1910. 'We got such a fright we nearly fell off our bikes,' he said. 'There was a great noise, and I can remember seeing this thing like a huge bird roaring over us. It was rattling and making an awful noise.' Barr had never seen a plane before, and was unaware there were any in the country.

Pither's untrumpeted feat was the first sustained powered flight by an all-metal framed aircraft in the world. As far as New Zealand was concerned, the other crucial element, control, would have to await the Walsh brothers of Auckland, who on 5 February 1911 flew their imported kitset biplane *Manurewa* — a far less elegant craft than Pither's — at Papakura.

After the Oreti Beach flight, Pither exhibited his machine in Dunedin's Caledonian sports grounds — where Pearse probably missed seeing it by six months — then shipped it to Victoria. There, it made a permanent mark in Australian legal files when the aviator was, with no small irony, fined £15 by a magistrate for falsely undervaluing it.

Sister of Compassion: The Miraculous Life of Suzanne Aubert

Having lingered over-long at Pipiriki getting the measure of the old tunnel-screw steamer *Ongarue*, now permanently cradled ashore after a lifetime of toil on the Whanganui river, we were late reaching Jerusalem.

Dusk had settled over the forested hills and metalled river road by the time Theo and I reached the old valley settlement, the car's headlights picking out a small wooden sign announcing it by its Maori name: Hiruharama.

Turning up a gated gravel driveway, we made for the courtyard of a two-storeyed weatherboard building, the silent evening flooding in as I cut the engine. Sister Sue Cosgrove appeared out of inky shadow to greet us, the shingled spire of nearby St Joseph's church needling the night sky at her back.

With a word of welcome, she led us past a craft studio and in through the old convent's side door, snapping on the lights in one room after another. A big kitchen with tables and long benches. Dining room. Toilets. A cosy fire nook with assorted armchairs. A chapel. Up steep stairs, the dormitory.

We climbed to take a look at where we were to rest and found fifteen or 20 iron-framed beds ranged through several rooms, each covered with a patchwork quilt. Above them the ceiling peaked and splayed as it followed the shell of the roof. Crucifixes hung from the matchboard walls.

'Sleep anywhere,' Sister Sue told us with a smile. 'No one else is expected.'

With a last glance at the empty rooms, she turned and was gone, retracing her steps down the narrow stairs and out past the church to the modern

house which is home to her and two other Sisters of Compassion. They are the kai tiaki, the guardians, of this place. Keepers of the faith, custodians of a singular outpost of Christian mission.

Later, as my son slept, I lay in darkness thinking about Jerusalem. Not much had changed here since the photograph that I had come across, reproduced on a franked turn-of-the-century postcard, had recorded it in the early 1890s. The card shows a monochrome Jerusalem nestled on the river bank, foregrounded by ponga and facing an amphitheatre of forested ridges. On a broad plinth of land linked to the water by clay tracks lies the Maori kainga, while above it rises the diadem of St Joseph's church, newly built after the destruction by fire of the first house of worship in 1888.

From the start the settlement, founded by Church Missionary Society priest Richard Taylor, had attracted men and women animated by a deep religious conviction. It was one of these that I had come here to learn more about. One who, following the example of saints, had devoted her life to helping society's downtrodden, ministering to outcasts, misfits and the poor. A remarkable woman who, in this often mist-shrouded encampment, founded New Zealand's only indigenous religious order, the Daughters of Our Lady of Compassion, and who made homes here and elsewhere for illegitimate children and for the aged and the unwell, dispensing home-made herbal medicines and aroha in equal measure to all.

She was Suzanne Aubert, born Marie Henriette Suzanne, later known variously as Sister Mary Joseph, Mother Joseph, Mother Mary Aubert, and then, crowningly, as Mother Aubert. Maori called her simply 'Meri', a 'wahine tino whakapono' — a very holy woman.

Born into an affluent middle-class family near the French city of Lyon in June 1835, Suzanne Aubert soon found her life gathering a powerful symbolism, her experiences in retrospect seemingly shaped by divine hands to prepare her for a lifelong labour among the needy. The diminutive nun, whose rock-solid stance in early photographs suggests a supreme fixity of purpose, was to prove more than capable of holding her own against parental disapproval, church intransigence, business malpractice and the barbs of ill fortune.

At the age of two she fell through the ice skin of a frozen pond and, according to her own later account, was pulled from the water almost dead. The accident left her blind and crippled and she was diagnosed incurable. Her parents, both devout Catholics, refused to accept the verdict. They prayed for a miracle and subjected their daughter to a succession of therapeutic treatments. At length the damage was repaired, though she was left with a permanent cast in one eye.

That, at least, was the reality Suzanne patched together from the recollections, the stories, of others. In later life she often evoked the calamity as a morality tale, a spur to compassion. The woman who was to show such devotion to helpless and disfigured children had herself been a 'freak', *un monstre*, as a child. Such things were mere externals. Surfaces. We must learn to look inward, as God does, and search the human heart.

While Suzanne was still shaking off the lingering effects of her brush with death, her mother was diagnosed with cancer. That case, too, was considered hopeless, and on 15 August 1845 Madame Aubert was given extreme unction, the last of the seven sacramental rites of the Catholic Church. Inexplicably, within hours her health began to improve. She recovered to live a further 40 years.

Suzanne put the sudden change in her mother's condition down to the novenas, the special masses, which had been held for her sake. 'Prayer is the greatest of powers,' she later wrote. 'We cannot do anything without prayer, and we can do everything with it.'

Throughout Suzanne's life, prayer was to be the armature of faith.

If such personal experiences attuned her thinking to matters spiritual, the very geography of Suzanne's childhood provided a religious framework, a map of action. Lyon in the mid-nineteenth century was a mission city, headquarters of the Society for the Propagation of the Faith and home town of Jean-Baptiste François Pompallier, the first Catholic bishop of Auckland.

In 1860, Pompallier returned to Lyon to raise money and recruits for his work in New Zealand. Thousands packed the city's big churches, eager to hear the bishop's report of progress among the 'noble savages', *les naturels*, of Oceania.

Suzanne, for one, was won over — not that the message was new to her. She was to claim that years earlier, when he called on the family, Pompallier had promised one day to take her with him. Indeed, it seems that most Marist missionaries to the South Seas were acquainted with her parents. One who knew them well, Father Peter Chanel, had been killed on Futuna and later canonised. Others wrote regularly to people in the city. The mission field was no mere intellectual construct to the faithful of Lyon.

Thanks to her father, Suzanne was forced to leave France by stealth. He did not approve of the church as a career choice for his daughter and had refused her request, at eighteen, to join a religious order. She marked time by training as a nurse with the Sisters of Charity, later tending soldiers on the Crimean peninsula and cholera victims in France.

She also deepened her contact with a man who was to guide her undeviatingly towards New Zealand. Jean-Marie-Baptiste Vianney, parish priest of Curé of Ars on the outskirts of Lyon, was an unusual if prominent manifestation of Catholic France — an ascetic and charismatic sage who lived on meagre rations and frequently scourged himself with chains. The curé's advice was sought by men and women throughout the country. So great had his reputation grown that between 1857 and 1859 some 80,000 made the pilgrimage to Ars. Madame Aubert herself had done so years earlier in a futile attempt to persuade Suzanne to accept an arranged marriage.

In 1858, at the height of his fame, the curé made a series of uncanny predictions about the future course of Suzanne's life. Among them, that she would go to the missions within two years accompanied by a relative of someone she knew, and that the curé himself would help her 'more by my death than by my life'.

Within a year the curé was dead and it was on the pretext of attending a ceremony to mark the anniversary of his passing that she left home, catching the train not for Ars but for Le Havre and Pompallier's vessel, a whaling ship bound for New Zealand. She sailed in company with the bishop's niece Lucie Pompallier. His nephew Antoine was also on board.

Knowing that her father would take legal action to have her returned from any French territory, the British colony seemed to Suzanne the safest destination. As it happened, Monsieur Aubert — who once threatened to shoot Pompallier — was to make brief replies to only two of his daughter's letters and did not forgive her until hours before his death, eleven years later.

On Sunday, 30 December 1860, after a four-month voyage, the 25-year-old Suzanne stepped off the *Général Teste* in Auckland with the bishop's party. Ahead lay 66 years of toil in the service of God.

Through the panes of the window I could see Theo at a batten fence, attempting with a young boy's enthusiasm to photograph a large sow. The sow, pregnant and irascible, had ploughed up large chunks of her paddock and now through the wire was making short work of a carrot.

I was in the convent kitchen listening to Sister Josefa Tikoisolomone as she recalled her own path to service. Born in Fiji, she grew up with a desire to care for old people. Being the twelfth child of a stately old father may have had a bearing on that impulse, Josefa admitted. She became interested

in the work that went on in a Home of Compassion which the sisters have run in Fiji for more than 50 years.

'There was something about the name "Compassion",' she said. 'I didn't even speak English. I had to look it up.'

(When Suzanne Aubert named her order, she may have had in mind the words of the medieval German mystic Johannes Eckhart: 'You may call God Love, you may call God Goodness, but the best name for God is Compassion.')

In 1964 Josefa began working in the order's orphanage in Wellington, but the chance to help the elderly soon lured her back to Fiji, where she lived for twelve years. After a further long spell in Wellington, she fetched up three years ago at Jerusalem.

Once a week she drives to Ranana, downriver, to study Christian living. Every other month a priest from Whanganui celebrates mass at Jerusalem for the faithful. There are not many. The settlement has a population of 20 or so. Fifty in the school holidays.

'The early sisters were teachers and nurses. The big question is: what do we do here now?'

Josefa's gaze fell on the sow. Nearby, Sister Sue was tending plants in the rosary. White roses for the joyful mysteries. Blood red for the sorrowful ones.

Gold for the glorious. The well-dug soil crumbled under the trowel. Above the sister were images of the descent of the Holy Spirit. Of Jesus. The crowning of Mary in Heaven.

'The order was founded for Maori people,' said Josefa. 'Our very presence at Jerusalem is important.'

Suzanne Aubert was fond of saying that on landing in New Zealand the first hand to reach out to her, as she clambered from ship's boat to wharf, was Maori. Bishop Pompallier, who himself had begun to teach her Maori on board ship, showed a remarkably enlightened attitude towards other races, and his influence was clear in Suzanne's instructions to her charges: 'Christianise the Maori, educate them too, but do not aim at making second-rate Europeans out of them.'

Much had changed since Pompallier witnessed the signing of the Treaty of Waitangi 20 years earlier, however, including the nature of the Catholic mission in the colony. A steady tide of European migrants — soon to be strengthened by the discovery of gold in Otago and on the West Coast — turned what had been a mission to indigenous people into a settler church.

Suzanne found that, far from ministering exclusively to Maori, she was expected to attend to the needs of colonial families. She was placed in the Wyndham Street convent of the Sisters of Mercy, Irish nuns who constituted New Zealand's first female congregation. There she taught French and embroidery to the daughters of Auckland merchants and wrestled with language study.

Within six months Suzanne was received as a novice, becoming Sister Mary Joseph. She worked determinedly and contributed to the social life of the convent — a skilled pianist, she claimed to have had tuition from the Hungarian composer and musician Franz Liszt. However, tensions soon developed between the French novices and Irish sisters, and in 1862 Pompallier founded a new diocesan community, the Congregation of the Holy Family, for the French women. They took over a school and boarding establishment for Maori girls in Ponsonby which was renamed the Nazareth Institute.

Suzanne sensed it was a move in the right direction, away from the teaching of European salon skills and towards true mission work. The day she received her habit she wrote with relish in her red notebook: 'There are five of us in all, three French and two Maori, Peata and Ateraita. We break our fast at eight in the evening, the feast consisting of a sheep's head that we hack into with an axe.'

Peata was to be a mentor to the new sister. Well connected with many tribal groups, she accompanied the French women to outlying kainga. There Suzanne, 'Meri Hohepa', learned Maori whakapapa and lore from village elders.

Undaunted by distance, rough ground or bad weather, Suzanne began to follow the example of the colony's itinerant Catholic priests and brothers, journeying further afield on foot to 'prospect for souls' among tribes as far away as the Waikato and Bay of Plenty.

Not every encounter was peaceful, though. At a gathering of tribal chiefs on the outskirts of Auckland, she and another sister were forced to match their faith against the terrifying powers of assembled tohunga.

The men stood in a large semicircle, grimacing and shouting.'I was not afraid for I had taken care to carry my relic of the True Cross and I knew they could not harm me by occult powers,' wrote Suzanne. 'We advanced, making a large Sign of the Cross over and over again as we went . . . When we came close to the Tohungas, they redoubled their efforts and they looked like demons. If I had known there would be so many of them, and what it would be like to confront them, I would not have wished to face them.'

The sisters weathered the spiritual storm. From then on, their pupils were left to practise their Christian religion unhindered.

For Suzanne, activity of any sort almost came to a premature end when disaster struck in 1866. While preparing a liniment for Pompallier's rheumatism, she splashed her face with neat ammonia, swallowing a mouthful. Over the next few days she was violently ill, and eventually lapsed into a coma. As Suzanne herself tells it, even the bishop was convinced she had died. A grave was dug and she was measured for a coffin. Only the presence of mind of a newly arrived nurse saved her, at the last moment, from being buried alive.

She slowly recovered, but her stomach had been permanently damaged. Never again could she eat beef, potatoes or cabbage without feeling nauseous.

The Congregation of the Holy Family was to suffer a far worse fate. The ageing Pompallier, more noted for his missionary zeal than for any business sense, had allowed the affairs of his Auckland diocese to fall into a parlous state. In February 1868, frail, indebted and beset by anxieties, he sailed for France — courtesy of a French naval vessel — to attempt yet another financial rescue.

This time, however, he met with a tepid reception in Europe, the old magic failing to win him much in the way of funds. In March 1869 he resigned his bishopric, effectively sealing the fate of the sisters in Auckland.

Pompallier's personal effects — 'harmonuim, hair-seated chairs, cheval glass, hat stand . . .' — were auctioned off to settle a debt, but the shortage of funds continued to bite.

Left in charge of the Nazareth Institute, Suzanne had enjoyed a liberating, if short-lived, period of control. By various unorthodox stratagems she managed to settle most of the institute's debt and even to find backing for a new building elsewhere.

Pompallier's replacement soon put a stop to such wilful behaviour. Bishop Croke, a confirmed Irish nationalist with a dislike for French Marists, arrived in December 1870 and, having reluctantly heard Suzanne out, ordered her back to France.

She had no mind to go.

By taking away both her veil and her pupils, Croke had inadvertently freed her hand. 'I came here for the Maoris; I'll die here among them. Nobody can stop me doing that,' she told him.

Instead of taking passage to France, Suzanne boarded the Napier-bound *Lord Ashby* in February 1871 with '2 cases pianos, 6 packages luggage'. At the age of 35 she was taking up a long-standing invitation from a Marist priest, Father Euloge Reignier, to join him and run a mission school at Meeanee.

As it was, poor health reduced her on arrival to working in the kitchen of the boy's orphanage rather than running the school. Reignier, struck by her accomplished singing voice and 'sunny nature', did his best to safeguard her failing eyesight and restore her health.

Suzanne was to remember her twelve years at Meeanee as the happiest of her life. As a lay sister, she slipped easily into the daily routine, helping the brothers work their farm and raise funds for charitable work. Soon she was once more covering vast distances to visit Maori kainga, mostly on foot, often in the company of a white fox terrier called Prince. For such treks, she wore a pleated grey frock and cape and straw sunhat, and carried in two detachable pockets under her skirt small devotional books in French and Latin as well as bread and cheese for the journey. Often she held a flax kit or on her back wore a rucksack filled with medicines.

A priest accompanying Suzanne on a visit to Pakipaki captured something of her approach:

> The Sister's intention was to see an old woman who was ill. She was a Protestant married to a Catholic. The Sister sat down alongside her in the tent, next to the mat which served as a bed and got her talking. She said all manner of bad things about her husband. He was a drunk who mistreated her . . . He wasn't there to give her any protection . . . When we were about to leave the husband of the sick woman arrived. The Sister took my walking stick and made a show of hitting him. He scratched his ear with a doleful look . . . and started saying how sorry he was. He was such a funny sight, enough to make you burst out laughing. Finally the Sister relented and ended up making peace with him on the grounds he promised to take good care of his wife and not drink any more.

Increasingly, Suzanne took on the role of nurse, travelling some 160 kilometres a week throughout Hawke's Bay and the Wairarapa to minister to settlers and Maori alike. She baptised the dying — especially the young

— and when smallpox broke out at Omahu she was kept busy vaccinating the nervous locals.

Building on medical skills acquired in France and a knowledge of botany and Maori herbal lore garnered in New Zealand, she began experimenting in her 'red shed' in Meeanee, incorporating native plants into her medicinal cures and using one end of the presbytery as her dispensary.

Concocting the remedies often involved an early morning start. This, for asthma: 'Gather the snails while the dew is still on the plants in the morning; crush and put equal parts of vinegar and water; stand twenty-four hours, drain off liquid and drink.'

At a time when medical practice was largely unregulated, patent medicines flourished. Suzanne vied with a cornucopia of cure-alls, including Weston's Wizard Oil, Dr Bright's Phosphodyne, Dinneford's Solution of Magnesia and Hitchen's Blood Restorer. She had two advantages, however. Her remedies incorporated Maori ingredients, and they were free. As a bonus, they also appeared to work.

Often the lawn in front of the mission building was crowded with patients waiting to consult 'Meri' — in 1873 alone more than 1300 of them sought her out. She even claimed success in curing leprosy: her treatment was written up by a Hastings doctor and sent to London, where it was published in the medical journal *Lancet*.

When she heard, 48 years later, that the leper station on Quail Island in Lyttelton harbour was to be closed, Suzanne offered to staff the station with her sisters. The government thanked her but declined the offer. The patients were instead shipped out to Fiji.

Early in 1878 Francis Redwood, Bishop of Wellington, gave Suzanne the job of revising the Maori prayer-book, *Ko te Ako me te Karakia o te Hahi Katorika Romana*, originally published by Pompallier in 1847. She did so, and had it printed in Napier the following year, subsidising the cost with family money, but was clearly frustrated at the shortage of labourers in God's vineyard. 'Bishop Redwood is doing what he can,' she told a friend, 'but what can the book do without the priest?'

Much enlarged by the addition of Old Testament stories — included to satisfy the Maori thirst for the epic — the prayer-book was not a great success. Whereas by then Protestants were giving away a fully translated Bible, the cash-strapped Catholic Maori mission was forced, in the midst of a looming depression, to sell its prayer-book. To lessen the disadvantage, a cheaper selected edition was quickly produced.

When a lively new priest arrived at Meeanee fresh from France in 1879, Suzanne again applied her language skills, this time compiling a Maori–French phrase book. Father Christophe Soulas spoke no English and the book — of which only a draft remnant, written in Suzanne's clear hand, survives — was one way of easing him into the work of the mission.

Soulas, a stubborn Breton missioner with a mystical streak and a yearning to make an impact — he was to become known as Pa Hoani Papita (John the Baptist) — was to find the going hard. For four years the zealous but prickly Father Soulas toiled for his faith, encouraged by Suzanne.

In February 1883 he travelled up the Whanganui river, meeting in its wild and isolated middle reaches a group of Maori who for the most part still clung to the teachings of Catholic priests they had befriended 20 or 30 years earlier.

The story was even told that in 1862 the Marist Father Jean Lampila had won Hiruharama for the church by flamboyantly challenging his opponent, the Reverend Richard Taylor, to walk through fire. Taylor had too much Protestant sobriety for such outlandish showmanship, and Lampila was pulled from the flames by the Ngati Hau chief Te Kere. Impressed by Lampila's boldness, Hiruharama adopted Catholicism.

During his own stay, Soulas baptised 58 people and celebrated ten marriages. He was also given a petition asking Redwood for a resident priest.

The idea of rekindling the Maori mission on the Whanganui found little favour among church leaders in Wellington. Nevertheless, Redwood decided to go ahead. It was to be a turning point in Suzanne's life.

The bishop's scheme was to found a convent of the Sisters of St Joseph there to teach Maori children. Suzanne was to accompany the sisters as a nurse and to instruct them in Maori.

The final entry in Suzanne's *Aide Mémoire* for 24 June 1883 reads simply: 'I am leaving Meeanee.' Aged 48 and in poor health — the swampy flats of coastal Hawke's Bay had not been kind to her — she was hardly up to the rigours of life in a remote settlement. 'A premature old age is dragging me towards the grave,' she had written two years earlier. Now she was ill with what she thought might be angina. A local doctor gave her six months to live.

Nevertheless, she packed, and caught the train south.

The *Hawke's Bay Herald* expressed a heart-felt sorrow at her departure, and praised her 'practical Christianity', which it said 'has never been hampered by questions as to creed or belief'. Merely to be in need was sufficient claim on 'her kindly offices'.

On 4 July Suzanne stepped aboard one of the waka waiting to take supplies from Wanganui 95 kilometres upriver to Jerusalem. Thanks to Soulas, she contributed not a little to the cargo. While still in Hawke's Bay she had received from him a typically expansive letter in which he listed what she ought to bring. There were 'cauldrons, pots, distilling apparatus, evaporator . . . bottles, jars, drugs, herbs . . . ' and, from Pakipaki, 'blankets, sheets, linen, clothes . . . your little harmonium . . . slates, school books . . . board games and my alphabet letters'. Also, Soulas's best whip, his cassocks and assorted crosses, statuettes and rosary beads.

The three-day journey by canoe to Jerusalem was an ordeal. Midwinter mornings on the river can be bone-chillingly cold and, although the weather held, the going was hard. Suzanne and her fellow passengers clambered over muddy paths and through thick bush whenever the vessels were poled up rapids, and at night the sisters made do with minimal shelter.

At Atene, they used a deserted whare which had been taken over by wild pigs. The animals were evicted and manuka laid on the floor as bedding, but the women were kept awake all night by the numbing cold and by the persistent efforts of the pigs to rejoin them. The second night, at Parikino, was equally cold but pig-free.

On the third day, they at last reached Jerusalem.

The river journey — which Suzanne later retraced many times — transported her into a new realm, one which would enlarge her experience and burnish her faith.

For months she lived on pumpkins and maize until her own garden grew, learning how to build an oven from clay, river stones and cow dung.

Gradually, a rhythm of daily life developed. They taught the children of local Maori in the old schoolhouse, using *Willie's First English Book*, a primer written by William Colenso. On Sundays the schoolroom was converted into a church. The sisters lived in the attic and adjoining rooms, while Soulas stayed in a whare down at the pa.

The women endured the isolation as best they could for month after month, but they suffered increasingly from poor health. Before a year was up it became clear that the Sisters of St Joseph were better suited to their Pacific Island ministry and that there could be no future for them in the raw river settlement.

On 20 May 1884 Redwood wrote to Soulas, telling him of the decision to establish the Sisters of the Third Order of Mary at Hiruharama, with Suzanne as Superior and postulants recruited from colonial families. Under her guidance, religious life in the settlement flourished. A church was built and soon she could write: 'nearly a thousand are now praying where there were not 50 doing so before'.

The sisters made coffee from tawa berries, which they dried, burned and ground, and tea from scented manuka. Later they switched to a brew made from a mix of dried sage, penny-royal and verbena from the garden. In 1888, with inheritance money, Suzanne bought a 120-hectare farm nearby, planting thousands of trees, including cherries, pears, apples, chestnuts and walnuts. When steamers began pushing up the river to Pipiriki and beyond, the fruit became a much-needed source of income for the cash-strapped sisters.

In 1883 Suzanne took to writing once more, this time compiling a bilingual phrase book. Its aim, as she noted on the title page, was to gather for the benefit of the reader 'phrases and dialogues on a variety of useful and interesting topics'. Soulas encouraged her, no doubt seeing the project as yet another potential money-earner.

The *New and Complete Manual of Maori Conversation*, published in 1885, was a lively work, which encouraged cultural exchange and assumed a desire among Pakeha and Maori to get along. Her readers were expected to want to talk about sea travel, natural disasters, inclement weather and politics. There were sections on horse racing and fishing, on children's games and on trade.

Though the book had a long life, Suzanne's name soon faded from its pages. A second enlarged edition, printed in 1901, gave editorial credit to Apirana Ngata, 'MA, LLB (Barrister at Law)'. All references to Suzanne as author had been removed. The 1964 edition went even further, claiming it to have been 'originally prepared under the guidance of the late Sir Apirana Ngata, the notable Maori scholar'.

Such literary hijacking may have cheated Suzanne of deserved recognition, but her real worth was forged in day-to-day encounters with other people. Visiting Hiruharama in May 1885, the photographer Alfred Burton was taken with the apparent religious zeal of the place. His travelling companion Edward Payton warmed to Suzanne, finding her 'a very accomplished physician', and 'most un-nunlike, being very chatty, and in every way a most kind and sensible "sister superior"'.

The life at Hiruharama suited Suzanne, and her resourcefulness there reached new heights. The old hand found, for example, that boots could be blackened with iron acetate got from soaking old iron in beer, and that they could then be softened with turpentine and waterproofed with a mixture of tallow, lard, beeswax and olive oil dissolved together.

Attending to the feet was important for someone who spent so much time on the move. Rising early to tend her garden in the weak light between morning prayers and mass — under a waterproof cape in bad weather — Suzanne set a tireless example to her charges. Not content to let Soulas and other priests do all the travelling, she also ventured far into the surrounding bush with her healing medicines.

Five years after Suzanne's arrival, an unforeseen disaster spurred her to go much further. The church was razed by fire — blame fell on a disgruntled Pakeha — and, accompanied by a novice, she took to the road for twelve months, revisiting Hawke's Bay and touring the South Island to raise funds for a new church and a convent. It was harder than she had anticipated, but the task prepared her for difficult times to come in Wellington and it introduced the order to a broader public.

In what had been the convent's sitting room, where Soulas took his meals, remnants of those early years now form a modest museum. Looking around, it is not hard to evoke that distant time when the early morning angelus rang out over the dewy paddocks to mark each day's beginning, the sisters a familiar sight as they shepherded children or worked in the fields.

There is the chair where Suzanne sat to press the starched white ruffle of her veil with goffering irons. The louvred shutter from her herbal drying-house in the orchard. Dairy cans, which were hung from the horse's saddle to bring milk and cream from the top farm. Wooden dumb-bells, for children's drill. In a cabinet, her famed medicine bottles and devotional books in Maori.

The pattern of life was to persist for many years. The delightful Sister Anna-Maria Shortall, now 84, told me of her time at Hiruharama in the 1950s. Up at 5.30 am — even earlier when she first arrived — for the 6.30 mass. Then, if the farmhand was away, off to milk the cows. That task, at least, was familiar to Sister Anna-Maria, who had been raised on a Colyton farm.

The sisters were the first on the river to use a Landrover. 'We used to take suckling pigs to the Wanganui market.' Sister Anna-Maria laughed, shaking her white curls. 'I wasn't so good on reversing with the trailer.'

The room where Theo and I slept was for seniors, she said, glancing at our hastily made beds. The infants were next door. And in those days they had not curtain rails around the beds, but wheeled screens. On Saturday nights a film projector was set up for local families. There were raffles, anything to raise money. Downstairs, in the grate where we had enjoyed a blazing fire the previous night, was 'the very place where Mother Aubert burned her medicinal recipes'.

Startling news, but sadly it was true. In 1913, before leaving on a trip to Rome, she set fire to most of her personal papers (as well as her skirt) and

destroyed the priceless formulas.

Suzanne had begun producing her remedies — her 'rongoa' — in commercial quantities at Hiruharama. In 1886 one of them, Karana, had been sent to a Lyon chemist for analysis and found to be 'superior to quinine in the treatment of atonic stomach ailments'.

Suzanne registered her trademarks in August 1891 and signed a contract for distribution with Dunedin-based Kempthorne and Prosser. Backed by testimonials from Lord Onslow, a former governor, from (by then Archbishop) Redwood, from the late chief commissioner of taxes, from surgeons and respected actors, and supported by heavy advertising, the formulas were an instant success. In the first three months of 1892, 10,000 bottles were sold in Wellington alone.

Mother Aubert, 'New Zealand Vegetatist', 'celebrated herbalist', became a celebrity. The country could not get enough of the cures, blazoned with her image: Marupa to fight asthma and whooping cough, Paramo to cure liver complaints, heartburn and indigestion, Wanena for cuts and bruises, Natanata to banish scrofula, the tonic Karana . . . They had become, claimed Wellington's *Evening Post*, 'the chief proprietary medicine of New Zealand'.

MOTHER MARY JOSEPH AUBERT'S

Remedies.

Exclusively Manufactured and Bottled by herself, and under her own personal supervision.

MARUPA for Influenza, Bronchitis, Cough, Asthma, &c. ... 2/6

PARAMO for Liver and Kidney Complaints, &c. 2/6

WANENA for Deep Wounds, Cuts, Bruises, and Internal Injury 2/6

NATANATA for Chronic Diarrhœa and Vomiting, Scrofula, &c. 2/6

KARANA a powerful Tonic, restores vigour and strength after Influenza, &c.... ... ... 2/6

No Packet is genuine unless bearing the Signature of Mother Mary Joseph on both ends.

KEKAKO Plasters for Lumbago, &c. ... ... 1/- a packet

ROMINO Ointment for Sprains, Rheumatic, Pains, &c. 1/6, 2/6, 3/6 a pot

WANENA Ointment for Contusions, Bruises, &c. 1/6, 2/6, 3/6 a pot

NATANATA Ointment for Scrofula, Lumps, Tumours, &c. 1/6, 2/6, 3/6 a pot

THESE PREPARATIONS ARE PURELY VEGETABLE.

A Trial will speak for itself.

It was not to last.

In 1893, after complaints about the contents fermenting, bottles were found to have been diluted by Kempthorne and Prosser. The company had tried to cut costs to cover its advertising bills. Suzanne was paid damages and freed from the contract.

For a time she continued production on a small scale, but eventually stopped entirely. Very likely Suzanne sensed worldly business getting in the way of her spiritual mission. It was she, after all, who had admonished the sisters to 'study medicine with care, not from any desire for recognition but from a pure spirit of charity for the suffering'.

In 1892 Redwood had formed the sisters into a new congregation, the Daughters of Our Lady of Compassion, appointing Suzanne, the Very Reverend Mother Mary Joseph Aubert, as its first Superior. By then, a new dimension had been added to her work.

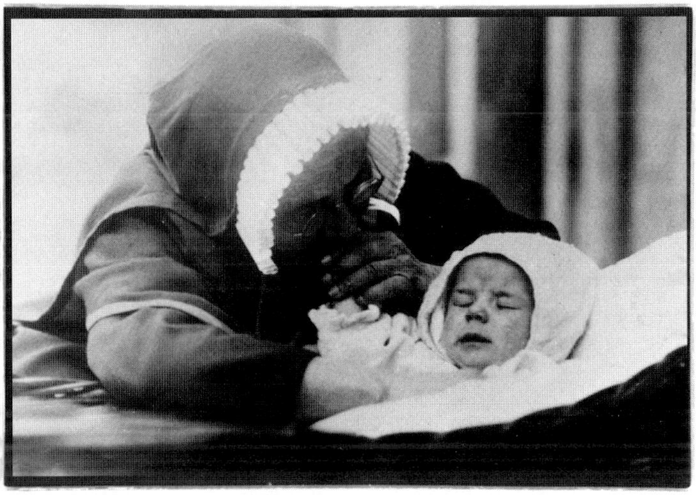

Perhaps as a result of her chance meeting with a desperate Pakeha widow in Hawke's Bay, who was contemplating a life of prostitution to support her children, Suzanne embarked on something new when she returned to Hiruharama from her fund-raising mission — she began taking in foundling children. Nor would she ever divulge the names of their parents, despite mounting pressure to do so to avoid hiding what her critics called 'the consequences of vice'.

The influence of Suzanne's mother is clear. In Suzanne's youth Madame Aubert had often helped young pregnant women, finding them work once they had given birth and sometimes even covering the cost of a child's schooling.

The number of foundlings in the sisters' care at Hiruharama — many just months old — grew rapidly. Nineteenth-century New Zealand was not tolerant of working mothers with children, or of illegitimacy, and the sisters refused no one in need.

The surviving register tells the story. Twenty-four were 'given unconditionally' by the mother, one by the father. Six were 'committed by

the judge in Wanganui'. Aunts brought two. Two more were left on the Wanganui steamer. Two were given to the captain 'for delivery to Mother Aubert'. One was 'received at the Wellington Railway Station from an unknown elderly lady' . . .

Most were illegitimate, many were Protestant. All were Pakeha.

Despite the best efforts of the sisters, it became obvious that remote Hiruharama was poorly located for the job of childcare on such a scale — a conclusion reinforced by a spate of deaths at the mission in 1898. The following year Suzanne gladly took up an invitation from priests and doctors to start a foundation in Wellington, and along with three sisters she shifted to the capital.

On our last evening at Hiruharama, the sisters invited us to dinner. It was a convivial meal. Venison and vegetables. A little wine. Lemon meringue. Suzanne would have approved of the gathering, no doubt, but frowned at the meringue. She once instructed her sisters to eat 'neither sweets nor pastry delicacies nor custards or fancy puddings, these things being good only for pandering to one's sense of taste at the expense of religious restraint'. It could have been the Curé of Ars talking. But, ever the motivator, she had allowed the occasional 'scorns or buns' with their cups of tea.

Sister Anna-Maria spoke of the school, which closed in 1968. Sister Sue, who had joined the order that year, told how she travelled to Jerusalem every Christmas. That is how she got to know the poet James K. Baxter, then experimenting with communal living no more than a field or two away. 'If I hadn't been a novice I would have been a sixties hippie, so I got the best of both worlds.'

The next morning, as the sun burned mist off the paddocks, we took our leave of the sisters — there was a parting of sorts, too, with the sow — and traced Suzanne's journey downriver to Wanganui and on to her final home at Island Bay, in Wellington.

In some ways, the Island Bay years were the most important ones for Suzanne Aubert. It was there that her vision solidified into concrete and steel of impressive proportions, there that she guided the order to the full expression of its healing ministry, and there too that she became a truly national figure.

Yet, in leaving Hiruharama, she also lessened her ties with the very people she had crossed half the world to help. Years later, while in Rome, she wrote to Sister Cecilia: 'So you are at Jerusalem! In the middle of my dear Maoris who I always loved so much and amongst whom I would be so happy to live again . . . For the last 55 years they have had the softest corner in my heart . . .'

The sisters rented an unfurnished cottage in Buckle Street and began their work as *de facto* district nurses amongst the city's poor and destitute. They collected unused food from hotels and cast-off clothing to redistribute, using large, purpose-built wicker prams. The squeal of pram wheels and the crunch of the sisters' sturdy boots were to become familiar sounds in the city's winding streets.

Faced with so many chronically ill outcasts, Suzanne soon bought a nearby house in Buckle Street which she opened in early 1900 as St Joseph's Home for Incurables. The first institution of its kind in New Zealand, it was followed a year later by a soup kitchen and in 1902 by another novelty, a crèche, which allowed mothers in need to take on daytime work.

The sisters' care embraced the infirm and the unfortunate, the young and the old alike. Their mission, as the *Evening Post* of 23 October 1903 reported, was 'to lift humanity from the slough of the world, no matter how they got there'.

An increasing number of their clientèle were ageing men, unattached, unemployed and unloved by the state. They were the drifters and the outcasts, the front-line workers turned vagrants of the colonial dream, and they queued thankfully at Suzanne's slide window for ladled soup and the warmth of a smile.

Edwin Arnold, maker of Suzanne's prams, described a visit to the Home for Incurables: 'I found some stone blind and stone deaf as well; others paralysed; some with rheumatics. Many of them as helpless as they were when they first came into the world, unable to feed themselves or to attend to the calls of nature . . . The work you are engaged in I believe the angels of heaven would like to participate in . . .'

Thanks to Suzanne's unstoppable drive, the citizens of Wellington, if not the angels of heaven, had repeated opportunities to help — and, to their credit, they often seized them.

The most spectacular of her ambitions was to build a Home of Compassion in Island Bay as a replacement for the cramped Buckle Street buildings. She began buying land in Island Bay for the purpose just six months after opening the Home for Incurables, and by 1909 had accumulated a total of fourteen hectares there.

Her building project was unveiled to the world in 1906. It proposed a grand structure 106 metres in length, containing dormitories, refectory, surgical and clinical wards and all the other trappings of institutional care. Very French in its feel, it was to be sited on a hillside to keep it before the public. Visibility, familiarity, were important, given Suzanne's reliance on donations. 'Providence is my bank', she was fond of saying, and her confident belief in divine assistance — what Redwood called her 'holy audacity of faith' — prompted her to courses of action which even seasoned entrepreneurs might have thought reckless.

She set construction in train without having the full sum to hand, though some additional money was promised and she expected to raise more as work proceeded. Even financial specialists, however, were won over by the force of her personality and by what was by then a well-honed skill at lobbying and cajoling.

Stories of that ability abound.

Once, when the merchant Alexander Turnbull banished the 'begging sisters' from his house under the impression that they had taken something of his, Suzanne immediately took issue with him, saying: 'They took nothing but what was given to them. My sisters are not thieves.' Having declared that she would no longer allow her sisters to call at his house, she then confounded Turnbull by placing with his firm a valuable order for cradles and iron bed frames. Chastised, he arranged for a monthly supply of tea for the sisters, and his firm remained an unswerving benefactor.

On another occasion, Suzanne was camped outside the office of Joseph Ward, then Minister of Public Health, waiting to see him about the plight of a woman with tuberculosis. Hearing a secretary tell the evasive minister that Mother Aubert was getting angry, she thundered: 'Mother Aubert is not *getting* angry. She *is* angry! And what is more, if something is not done for that woman immediately, she will take a cab to the *Evening Post* and have it published in tonight's paper!'

With admirable speed, something was done.

The Home of Compassion was opened with much pomp and goodwill in April 1907. Several thousand people listened to stirring declarations of support and gratitude from civic leaders before making their way to the building's flat roof, where beneath fluttering flags they weighed the scale of the undertaking and admired the view.

Just four months later Sister Baptista, writing of the new home's spacious hall and its walls of 'a lovely white plaster', added: 'it is such a pity after all the expence to see how they have been spoiled by the rain coming in everywhere'.

The vision had quickly descended into nightmare, thanks to defective asphalting of the roof and to serious design faults, which included girders of inadequate strength. At great cost the damage was repaired and load-bearing columns inserted to support the upper storey. Suzanne, in her seventies, was bowed by the calamity. Before the building's opening she had been laid low by nervous strain, and it was in a weakened state that she was forced to oversee the remedial work.

The hardship was to some extent of her own making. Suzanne's conduct often flew in the face of wise leadership. For all her energy and focus, she was autocratic, poor at delegating and seemingly careless of the need to train a successor.

These were natural extensions, perhaps, of her grasp of Christianity's big picture at the expense of individuals. Sister Clotilde Webber, who knew her through these years, confessed that, although she had a spontaneous tenderness, 'Mother Aubert appeared to have little natural attachment to persons, places or things . . . Her sole interest, almost, was their eternal salvation.'

Notwithstanding that, Sister Clotilde was impressed with Mother Aubert's ability to 'pray, work, fight, in sacrifice of every description for any of the causes she had at heart'. This she undoubtedly did for her Home of Compassion — though, perhaps from a sense of guilt or embarrassment at how horribly wrong things had gone, she refused to seek additional public funds for the repairs. Late in 1907, Suzanne tackled another of the difficulties that Island Bay threw at her with such spirit and determination that it seemed all of Wellington was galvanised into action on her behalf.

The sisters found themselves beset by a water shortage, and the logical solution — constructing a reservoir — involved an expensive bill for carting gravel and concrete up to the proposed site on the hill behind the home. Whether Suzanne told Lady Plunket, the wife of the Governor, of her plan to pack the materials up the steep track with the aid of the sisters, or whether Lady Plunket saw the loaded sugar bags for herself during a visit — with Suzanne Aubert, truth often splinters and kaleidoscopes — His Excellency the Governor soon found himself at Island Bay, attired for hard labour.

The public willingly colluded with Suzanne's overt manipulations. As the *Evening Post* declared: 'She is the apostle of optimism. She does not worry about whether people will help her sufficiently to realise her dreams for good; she knows they will.'

Wellington did not let her down. Over the next few weeks the press tirelessly reported the doings of Suzanne's working bees, which in total moved some 200 tonnes of building materials to the elevated site. The Governor was joined by boys from St Patrick's College and their rector, Father Keogh. By 81 boys from Wellington College and their principal, the strapping Joseph Firth, who hoisted two bags of shingle at a time onto his broad shoulders. By lads from the Marist Brothers' school, a party from the Post and Telegraph Department, medical doctors. The Mayor, 'with the perspiration of toil bathing his alabaster brow', stood on the slopes, heaving sand. Some 220 men, including off-duty tram workers and pupils of the Wellington gymnasium, formed a chain to relay bags up the hill. Women too pitched in, shouldering sacks of gravel up the rough track in the heat of the day.

It was a triumphant display of the high regard in which Suzanne Aubert and the blue-robed Sisters of Compassion were held by the people of Wellington. Their relationship with ecclesiastical authorities, however, was less smooth. Suzanne was increasingly frustrated in her plans by conservatives within the Catholic Church and in 1913, at the age of 78, she left for Rome, hoping to gain papal recognition for her congregation and so win freedom from local diocesan control.

In a basement archive room at the Home of Compassion in Island Bay I came across reminders of that European journey — a journey which, due to travel restrictions following the outbreak of war, lengthened into a seven-year sojourn. On a wooden stand was the robust Gladstone bag that accompanied her everywhere. Under glass, lay a bodice handsewn in Italy to fit the diminutive nun, and beside it her underskirt with pockets the size of small saddlebags. In a cabinet, a tray of pottery shards and other fragments picked up from the Roman catacombs. Acorns, dried roses, a sprig of leaves from St Paul's Outside the Walls.

'She was a real magpie,' assistant archivist Sister Josephine Gorman confessed with a flicker of amused pride.

There were other things too. Iron nails made by the Marist brothers for her red shed in Meeanee. A Berlin wool tapestry embroidered for Bishop Redwood's silver jubilee. An escritoire. Shelves of leatherbound books — among the mostly religious texts a goodly number of medical and botanical works, grammars, the novels of Charles Dickens. Shelves, too, of her medicines, some still corked. Her narrow wrought-iron bed with its unforgiving horsehair mattress. Part of the headstone from her grave. A neatly bound album of funeral photographs . . .

Suzanne arrived back in New Zealand in January 1920 a weakened woman. The years were beginning to take their toll. She endured minor heart attacks, a stroke that left her partly paralysed, a cataract operation that went wrong.

For the last three years of her life, Suzanne did not venture much from her room at Island Bay. However, appointed by Rome as Superior-General at last, she remained the guiding hand of the Daughters of Our Lady of Compassion; a thing almost of legend.

Journalist Nelle Scanlan visited the 90-year-old Suzanne in 1925, picturing her to readers of the *NZ Free Lance*:

> The sunshine picked out the high-lights on the bare polished floor. A small fire glowed in the grate in one corner of the room. By the window, seated in a deep chair, was the frail figure of Mother Mary Aubert . . .
>
> Papers and books lay on the table before her; she has recently been engaged in some translation work. Her active mind is alert, although her frail body, worn with an excess of zeal, a long life of labour for others, is now confined to a chair.
>
> 'I cannot work now — only this hand can write,' and she lifted the thin, trembling right hand from the folds of her dark blue habit.
>
> 'But you still direct,' I suggested. 'They know what you would have done.'

Sixteen months later, on 1 October 1926, Suzanne died. Thousands of people, close friends and strangers alike, came to pay their respects at Island Bay. Thousands more filled St Mary of the Angels in Boulcott Street for her funeral. It was the most impressive public farewell to a woman that the country had seen. The mile-long cortège brought traffic in the capital to a standstill, Willis Street and the Quay becoming 'as silent as unpeopled lands'.

The album's carefully annotated photographs capture the occasion. The sisters, framed by columns, forming a guard of honour at the Home of Compassion. The lead-lined casket being lifted reverently into the polished hearse. A line of motorcars passing a throng of onlookers. And on the album's last leaf, a bespectacled Mother Aubert at her desk, hands resting on her lap. She is leaning back into an armchair, her face framed by the frill of her coif, gazing out with longing as if trying to bring eternity into focus.

Some years earlier, she had written from Rome: 'I must be thankful for

the strength God leaves me. I can do and I do a good day's work. I wish to die in harness at the service of my Divine Master, though I think that my old bones would rest more happily in Maoriland.'

Rest in peace.

July 2002

Illustrations

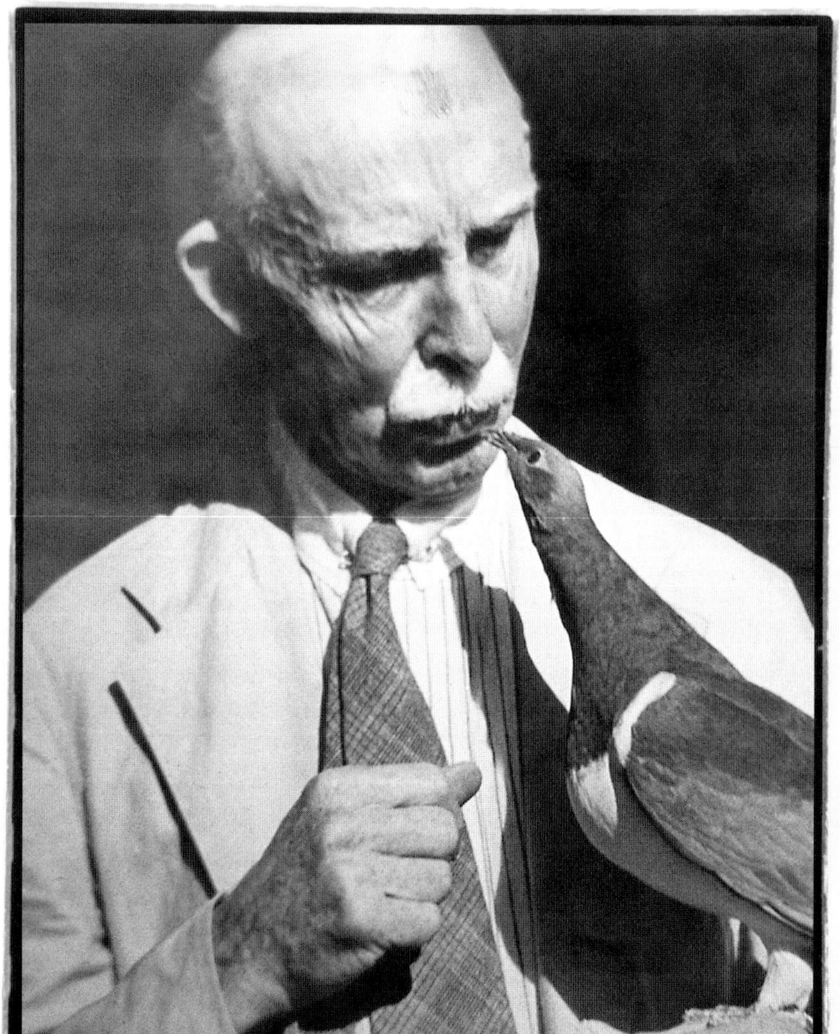

The Man Who Spoke for the Land: Guthrie-Smith of Tutira

South of Te Pohue on State Highway 5 the downpour strikes, driving rain hard against the windscreen and masking the plantation forest on either side; reducing the Napier road to an indistinct ribbon of grey gauze.

The deluge is insistent but brief, a mere foretaste of what is to come. By the time I reach Lake Tutira, 45 kilometres north of Napier, following what once had been the Wairoa coach road, I am again in clear weather. Black swans and mallards ply untroubled waters fringed with willows. The cradling hills, rugged and timeworn, soften in the evening light.

The lake, declared a wildlife refuge in 1957 and a domain in 1964, is now known for boating, picnicking and year-round fishing, and is a haven for bitterns, dabchicks, pied stilts and spur-winged plovers. Indirectly, it is the birds that have brought me here.

Since 1882, Tutira and the sheep station of which the lake forms the liquid heart have been synonymous with one person, William Herbert Guthrie-Smith. A farmer, philosopher, gifted writer and pre-eminent naturalist, Guthrie-Smith made Tutira his home for almost 60 years — until his death in 1940 — wrestling the unyielding land and creating through his books and essays a vivid picture of the workings of nature.

The homestead where in later years he laboured on his writings still stands on a rise overlooking the lake. Behind it, ringed by a newly painted picket fence and shaded by a favourite cherry tree, lies his unadorned grave.

The airy weatherboard house is now home to station manager Steve

Reiri and his partner Margaret, who run the property on behalf of a trust set up, in accordance with the wishes of Guthrie-Smith and his late daughter Barbara Absolom, for the benefit of the country's youth.

Over dinner, talk turns to the workings of the farm, now much reduced from its height when Guthrie-Smith grazed upward of 30,000 sheep on 61,000 acres. The stock-count these days seldom exceeds 4600 sheep and 440 cattle on an 810-hectare (2000-acre) rump of land. It is enough, says Steve, to subsidise the trust's Outdoor Education Centre, whose newish building is visible through the kitchen window. As the evening wears on, we all note the rising wind which intrudes increasingly on the conversation. At ten o'clock Steve, with a farmer's tired vigilance, goes out to check the roof. It is in the process of being replaced, and by the light of a temperamental torch I help him hammer leadheads through loose iron, our words snatched and broken by the storm.

During the night I hear Steve on the roof again, attending to ridge iron, while the wind tosses things noisily about the yard and threatens to stave in doors and windows.

The next morning, the work of what Guthrie-Smith called Hawke's Bay's 'emotional climate' becomes evident. Gale-force nor'-westers have snapped

power poles, ripped out trees and closed roads throughout the district. Tutira station is badly hit. Phone and power lines are down. Twenty-metre poplars uprooted by the 100 km/h winds lie across the drive, blocking our exit. A shed has collapsed onto the vegetable garden.

'It's going to be busy round here for a while,' Steve declares over breakfast. 'I'll sharpen the chainsaw.'

The damage is heavy but not unprecedented. The close-cropped hills around the lake still carry the scars from slips caused when Cyclone Bola came through in 1988. The rainstorm of 1938, when Guthrie-Smith ran the station, was even worse. On slopes weakened by earthquakes, the ground seemed to weep mud. Saturated subsoils erupted, tearing out turf and leaving gaping chasms. Floodwater washed out Lake Ngatapa, formed seven years earlier by earthquake, taking with it the Mohaka bridge. Other bridges went too, severing the link between Napier and Wairoa. Lake Tutira rose three metres, and waist-deep silt covered 700 hectares of the nearby Esk Valley.

A onetime neighbour of Guthrie-Smith, Beatrice Heays — still formidably alert just a year short of her 100th birthday — recounted the effect on her station, Te Rangi. Stock losses were high, the telephone stayed out for months and, with bridges swept away, supplies were airlifted in. Thinking the access road through the gorge would never be rebuilt, she and her husband made the final act of surrender to isolation: they jacked their Buick off its wheels.

Concern for the well-being of the Land — often spelt with the capital — whether from flood, fire or animal hooves, was as characteristic a part of Guthrie-Smith as his lanky frame or his public reticence. Out moving sheep when the 1931 Napier earthquake struck, the 70-year-old could not help speculating on its pastoral possibilities: whether the jolts would revitalise the fields, stimulating cocksfoot, ryegrass and white clover; whether, in fact, the tremors would perform 'at no cost to the station the work of a titanic rotary plough'.

Typically, he refrained from commenting in his later writing on the human suffering caused by the Napier earthquake — New Zealand's worst disaster — even when its scale had become known. Often he masked his true feelings with a smokescreen of pragmatism, as when in later life he gifted farmland to war veterans with the excuse that he could no longer manage such an acreage, or when he arranged anonymous delivery of a book he wished to give to a close friend.

Occasionally, he let an impish humour show. Lured to the home of his future biographer, Airini Woodhouse, to see her stuffed laughing owl —

a species he had pursued in vain for years — he was indignant to find the bird gathering dust in an upstairs room. He carried it ceremoniously downstairs and set it prominently on the hall table. The next day, on leaving, he turned to his hosts. 'Remember,' he said sternly, 'if the house catches fire, before you save anything, before the piano, save the laughing owl. And *then* go back for the children.'

This fierce attachment to wildlife began on the moors in the Scottish county of Stirlingshire under the tutelage of his father, John Guthrie Smith, a man he admired throughout his life — the son's hyphenated surname was itself a token of respect. After an undistinguished education at Rugby, Herbert (as he preferred to be known) emigrated to New Zealand in 1880 in the company of a distant cousin, Arthur Cuningham. The two men took up apprenticeships on a relative's South Canterbury station for two years before moving briefly to a Hawke's Bay run. The plan was to make money from sheep farming, as had English writer Samuel Butler 20 years earlier, before retiring to a comfortable life in Scotland.

Tutira was to change all that.

Its infertile skin of bracken-covered hills, seamed with gullies and ravines,

had broken the fortunes of a string of farmers since Europeans first tried their hand on the 8100-hectare run in 1873. The early years of settlement coalesced into a painful collage of adversity: crippling stock losses of up to 30 per cent a year, sinking wool prices, nagging debt and the demoralising battle against fern. The fact was that, unlike the rich farmland of southern Hawke's Bay, the land bordering the Esk River marked the fringes of the agricultural badlands: unproductive country covered in a fine silty clay and worthless pumice. From a sheepfarmer's perspective, said Guthrie-Smith, New Zealand had been discovered and Tutira taken up hundreds of thousands of years too soon — more time was needed for a deep organic topsoil to form. Once covered in forest, Tutira had been burned but not broken in, and so languished under a reign of bracken. Its Maori owners were content to sacrifice the dubious prospect of riches derived from working the land themselves for the certainty of income as absentee landlords.

They had not always been so aloof. In pre-European times Lake Tutira bristled with pa, its waters heavy with canoe traffic. The lake and the nearby rivers yielded freshwater mussels, crayfish and eels whose flavour was renowned, as well as flax prized for its strength. Saltwater fish were got

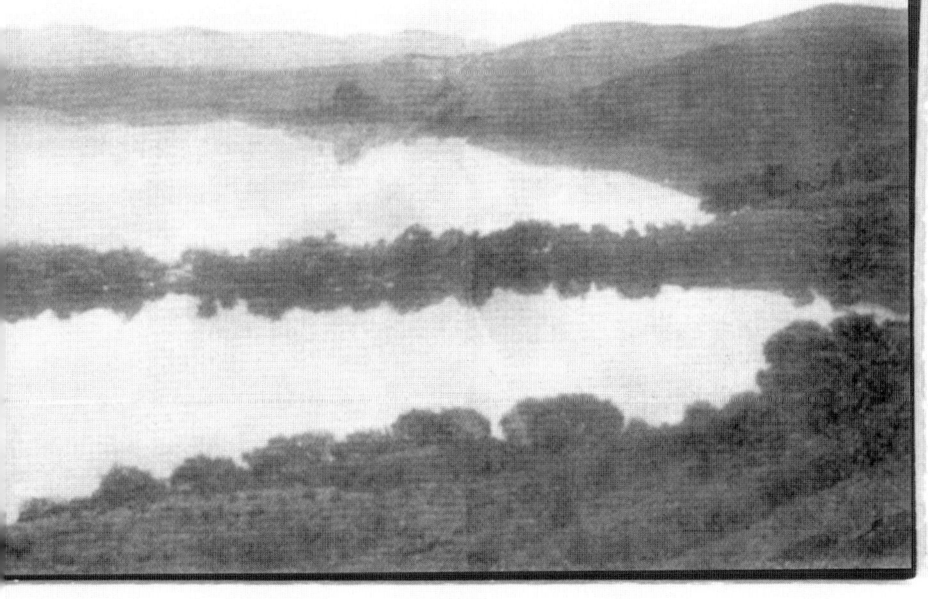

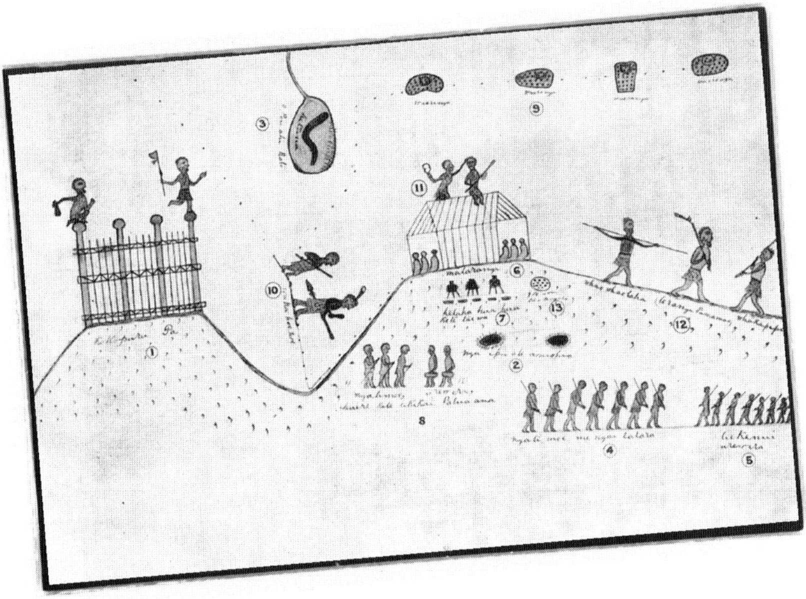

from the Hawke's Bay coast, while further inland forests held pigeons, tui and kaka. The local peoples, the Ngai Tatara and the Ngati Moe, joined to defend their rich harvest grounds against envious neighbours, and, after the arrival of missionaries, peach groves and patches of thyme marked their kainga. However, the region was too wet and cold and the land too poor for widespread cultivation of taro or kumara, and to the Maori the wealth of Tutira's waters far exceeded the value of its arable land.

Europeans were less interested in the area's liquid assets, and tried to play down the high rainfall. One runholder was pressured by neighbours to stop filing official rainfall statistics, which, they claimed, were hampering settlement. It was a view Guthrie-Smith could sympathise with. Heavy rain was, in his opinion, the bane of Tutira. Not that it was constant, or uniform. Once he measured seventeen inches (about 430 mm) of rain in 48 hours on the homestead lawn, while on Image Hill, less than five kilometres off, not enough fell to wash dust from the trampled stock paths.

All such knowledge lay in the future, however, when on 4 September 1882, having freed a previous tenant from a large debt to the New Zealand Loan and Mercantile Company, Cuningham and Guthrie-Smith, both barely out of their teens, rode through the sleeping town of Napier, crossed the Esk River and turned inland toward the distant ranges of Tutira.

'Shortly afterwards we . . . splashed across the unsung ford of the Waikoau. We trod Tutira soil. We viewed for the first time our own sheep. They were merino ewes — skin and bone, scrags, their wool peeling off — anxious to escape yet balked by the river, the kind of stock always in the very worst of condition,' Guthrie-Smith wrote years later. 'Such was our fatuous folly, that we believed against the evidence of our senses that they were not so very, very, very wretched, that not every single solitary bone in their lank frames was visible.'

If the sight of his scruffy herd had stirred a proprietorial pride, the sudden vision of the glittering lake, embraced by silky willows and flax spears, richly flowering kowhai and delicate drifts of peach blossom, began an attachment to the land which was to pin Guthrie-Smith for ever to Tutira.

For many years, his chief pleasure was in physical toil: draining swamps, hewing tracks, fencing, sowing seed; delighting in body sweat and the raw work of hands. He wrote rapturously of rising in the early dawn, stars framed by the whare's open door, and rekindling fire in the glowing heart of the fireplace's ash cone. 'In those times to think of an improvement to the station was to be in love,' he confessed.

Even recreation entailed hard work. Periodically, Guthrie-Smith would ford the river and ride the 48 kilometres of tracks to Napier, play rugby in the afternoon, dance until midnight, then ride back to Tutira to be ready for work at daybreak.

The daily ebb and flow of money held no attraction, and the partners were astonishingly naive in matters of finance. Accounts were attended to only in the depths of storms, when the 'proper business' of improving the run had to be suspended.

Somehow, in the midst of all this activity, Guthrie-Smith found time to make the occasional trip back to Scotland, and on one of these trips, in 1901, he married Georgina Dennistoun-Brown of Balloch Castle, Dumbartonshire. She was somewhat taken aback by the remoteness and roughness of Tutira, but soon put her stamp on the house and grounds. Barbara, their only child, was born two years later.

Guthrie-Smith acknowledged that, though eventually he managed to see his way to a debt-free tenure of Tutira, it was because he stood on the shoulders — the labours — of the many who went before. Under Guthrie-Smith the station began to prosper, but even then only after decades of backbreaking work. Wool slumps led almost to financial ruin, as did floods, lungworm, footrot, barren soils, the constant attrition of stock, and that unstoppable plant demon, bracken.

When the first farmer took up the Tutira lease, there was not 40 hectares of sheep feed on the run. Apart from a scattering of forest, marsh and upland meadow, it was an almost unbroken sheet of fern. The animals had to create their own pasture by a process Guthrie-Smith called 'fern-crushing' — simple enough on good land, but in marginal country full of snags. It began with an autumn burn-off of bracken followed by sowing grass of whatever quality could be afforded, often little more than floor sweepings. The moment young

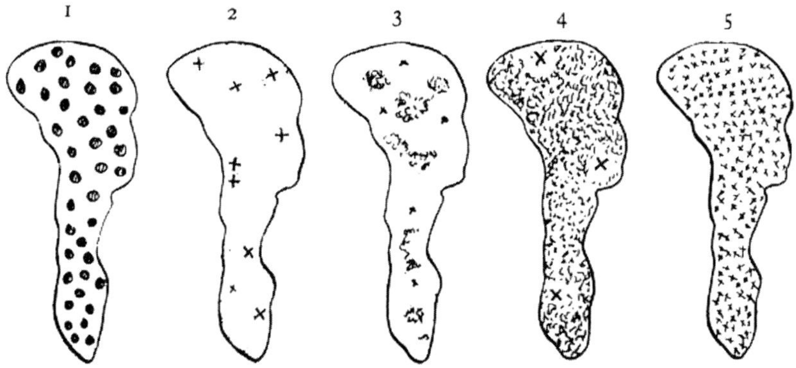

fern shoots appeared sheep were driven into the paddock, the number determined by weather and land fertility. If the calculations were right and fate kind, the sheep would subsist on the shoots and keep them in check until the grass took over, permanently banishing the scourge.

But Tutira land was poor, and the animals detested the stubborn, unpalatable fern which flourished in the wet climate. 'The old sheep died, the young refused to live,' Guthrie-Smith noted bleakly. Fresh sheep were introduced to bolster numbers and the process was repeated, the land, in effect, being 'stamped, jammed, hauled, murdered into grass'. Sheep mustered for shearing were often found to have bellies and even flanks worn bare of wool through constant abrasion by fern and scrub. The fleece of merino wethers, stunted through poor diet, became blackened by sand and grit. It was not uncommon to see the backs of sheep drafted in a hot, wet autumn turn green through the sprouting of trapped grass seed.

Success was slow in coming, and Guthrie-Smith learned an expensive lesson: sheep taken from a good environment and introduced onto inferior land would never thrive. Nor were merinos suited to the conditions. They preferred dry ground, short grass and room to move, and were replaced for a time by Lincolns. Eventually sheep of several breeds subdued the land, remodelling its contours through the wear of their habitual wanderings.

This unending press of stock, both sheep and cattle, compacted the soil and hardened what was once an absorbent sponge into a crust of slate. Heavy rain flushed surface dirt and dust into rivers and caused flooding, while the turf deteriorated into a mass of tough native grasses. Especially after times of drought, rain ran from uplands and hills as though from paved roads, gouging out the land in slips which became ever larger and more frequent. Guthrie-Smith called it 'the melting of the highlands into the sea' and, as anyone knows who has flown over the northern Hawke's Bay, the melting is with us still.

Yet Guthrie-Smith did not condemn fellow runholders for what they were doing to the land. He had sympathy for the farmer who 'for five extra blades of cocksfoot would scalp his parents'. He recognised that he was implicated in the wholesale alteration of an ecosystem — the transformation, as he put it, of stately woodland into prosaic turf. In his defence, and theirs, he invoked an old-world sense of destiny. 'It is impossible for any individual to withstand the stream of tendency,' he wrote. 'Like the lady in Sheridan's translation, they "fell, but unwillingly fell".'

The fall was not without its pleasures. His account of the torching of the land, for example, is compelling and seductive: 'Towards noon, then, the fateful match is struck, the smoke curls upwards blue and thin, the clear flame, steady at first but soon lengthening and stretching itself, arises like a snake from its cold coils. Then, as often seems to happen, the draught of the fire summons at once the waiting wind; out of the hot calm bursts forth the new-born storm . . . As a lover wraps his mistress in his arms, so the flames wrap the stately cabbage-trees, stripping them naked of their matted mantles of brown, devouring their tall stems with kisses of fire, crackling like musketry amongst the spluttering flax, hissing and spitting in the tutu-groves, pouring in black smoke from thickets of scrub.'

Alas that Tutira could not again be broken in nor past years relived, lamented Guthrie-Smith the incendiarist, the man who had perfected the art of striking matches on his breeches and from the saddle tossing them into the dry grass before fully ignited. 'A fire on a dry day in a dry season was worth a ride of a thousand miles.'

Guthrie-Smith was a stew of seeming contradictions: he mourned the loss of natural sheep tracks caused by the 'abominable utilitarian necessity' of running fence lines through farmland, yet claimed a fence could be erected to the glory of God as surely as could a cathedral pile. He despised manuka for the way it resisted efforts to break in pasture, while praising it as a necessary nursery crop for forest regenerating on the station. Above all, he rose to the challenges of farming while begrudging the limits it imposed on his life as a field naturalist — shearing, for example, occurred in months when birds were nesting, and kept him from sallying forth with his photographic gear. With the passage of time, he became even more interested in the original flora and fauna of the Land — life that was being annihilated as the ground was cleared and grassed for farming.

From his first days at Tutira he had noted the habits of its wildlife, and in 1895 read a paper on its birds — awkwardly and self-consciously penned — to the Hawke's Bay Philosophical Institute.

Earlier, in 1882, to test his belief that land damage could be reversed if protected from fire and cropping, Guthrie-Smith began noting the changes on an unused ten-hectare hillside at his back door. Later he fenced off what had come to be known as the 'Hanger' and, until 1938, faithfully recorded its tapestry of renewal. No seeds were sown, no saplings planted, no unwanted aliens grubbed out or misted with herbicide. Yet, seemingly to an ineluctable timetable, bracken gave way to manuka, which in turn yielded to softwoods and finally to totara, matai, rimu and other hardwoods. As if to humour the old man, tui, bellbirds, native pigeons and other long-

departed birds returned and bred.

To walk among the thick tangle of the Hanger today is to experience a dream unfurled, a wound healed. Yet it was not only through his living monument that Guthrie-Smith inspired future generations. He was a talented writer who developed an engaging, highly confessional style which won over generations of readers to his conservationist cause. Alive with the insights of tireless fieldwork, his books from *Birds of the Water, Wood and Waste* (1910) to *Sorrows and Joys of a New Zealand Naturalist* (1936) painted an unsentimental picture of animal behaviour and habitat destruction.

His eloquence was often warmly empathic, as in this account of snipe that were quite unafraid of humans on a remote southern island: 'I could have lingered for weeks in the company of these fascinating birds, wondering over their loss of flight, large eggs and contracted range, watching the little creatures, brown like Autumn, harmless as Autumn's fallen leaves. There was something extraordinarily attractive in their trustfulness, an irresistible appeal in their absence of fear, of even the shadow of suspicion of fear. We were back in the days of our first parents to the golden dawn of the world, to that delectable garden where fear and pain and anger and sorrow were all unnamed, unknown . . . We could not but grieve that a few field naturalists on one lone isle should be in sole enjoyment of what should have been a happiness to hundreds the world over.'

As Tutira prospered, Guthrie-Smith could afford to spend more time as a naturalist, pursuing vestiges of old New Zealand, generally in its last refuges: out-of-the-way places. Seizing chances — as, for example, when a berth became available on the government steamer *Tutanekai* — Guthrie-Smith left Tutira in the hands of a manager and reached for a camera. Laden with tripod and cumbersome glass plates, and often in the company of his adventurous daughter, he stalked birds from the Kermadecs to Campbell Island.

No stranger to uninhabited shores, forsaken islands and desolate riverbeds, he spent much time 'under canvas, in shepherds' huts, in grimy gold-washers' shanties, in the oily wigwams of muttonbirders'. His labours were often attended by epic discomfort. On Big South Cape Island off Stewart Island, for example, in the worst hut he had ever struck, he improvised a darkroom: an assistant sitting on the floor while he anxiously paced about, throwing over her whatever was to hand — blankets, rags, musty abandoned clothes — to seal out light. Once developed, the glass plates were carried carefully over rough country to the nearest source of fresh water, a stream almost two kilometres away.

Even on Tutira photography was arduous, each image often needing days of preparation. He scorned binoculars and, later, telephoto lenses, claiming that with patience it was always possible to get close to birds. Getting close was, for Guthrie-Smith, the only way to understand wildlife. His method was to build a screen of raupo or branches near a nest and set up a dummy camera. Days later, once the birds had accepted the oddity, he would replace it with a real camera and crouch motionless for long hours until the right shot presented itself.

Sometimes, more elaborate methods were called for, as in 1926 when Guthrie-Smith photographed yellowheads in Nelson. These birds, known as bush canaries for their colouring and musical trill, are canopy dwellers, living in the trunks of rotting trees up to 20 metres off the ground. Having discovered one of their nests, he had no option but to construct a tree platform at the same height, with the help of a friend, John Morel. The two men then took turns to sit aloft in the buffeting wind, 'serene, refrigerated, cold as stone, content'. Before any photographs could be taken, however, the yellowheads abandoned their nest. With the season drawing to a close, Guthrie-Smith and Morel searched for twelve days in relentless rain before another nest was found. Within two weeks they had built a new platform and over the next nine days took two usable photographs.

Efforts to photograph the yellowheads paled alongside the experience of recording rock wrens in the Southern Alps. The second day on the job grew so bleak that Guthrie-Smith lost all feeling in his fingers and could not work the shutter. The third day, 'in weather such as no man ever did bird-nest in before, or, I should imagine, ever will again', he persisted for a few hours, before giving in to gale-force winds and icy rain. Despite the conditions, he came away with printable photographs and, as he comfortingly noted, it was thanks to such a climate that the rock wren survived human destruction at all.

Guthrie-Smith downplayed the images he printed from what he called his 'vicious brood of negatives', though others applauded them. Indeed, he was one of the country's pioneering natural history photographers, taking the first (and, in some cases, probably the last) good photographs of many rare and elusive birds. Despite these achievements, he had little trust in his own technical competence. To guard against overconfidence, he printed in large letters above a set of clear instructions on one of his cameras the words:

IDIOT

Fool! Fool!! FOOL!!!

Nevertheless, he did not skimp on equipment, and ended up with an array of cameras — seven or eight in all. During one of his trips to the northern hemisphere, he was bewitched by an Akley camera in New York. It was almost as pricey as the car Georgina wanted, and for a time the two machines tussled for his attention. In light of the fact that service cars now passed Tutira regularly, Guthrie-Smith concluded that a private car was an unnecessary luxury; the camera was duly purchased.

Domestic comforts were not, however, entirely banished from his mind. On the same trip, he dined at the home of the assistant director of the New York Botanical Garden, and while there searched out unfamiliar electrical gadgets with the enthusiasm of a cargo cultist. Among the objects of desire: a vacuum cleaner, an iron, a coffee percolator and a washing machine. The dignified and knowledgeable antipodean endeared himself to the American scientist, who later wrote: 'I have always considered this brief contact as one of the more pleasant experiences of my long botanical career.' The two stayed in touch, Guthrie-Smith regularly sending letters written in his cramped, almost illegible hand.

Staying in touch was one of Guthrie-Smith's strong suits. Throughout his long life he developed deep friendships with a number of kindred spirits

— some unlikely, such as that which blossomed with Captain Bollons, the charming and well-read skipper of the *Tutanekai*, and a seafarer of formidable bearing and rich experience. Guthrie-Smith was so taken with the man that he offered to help work on his reminiscences, and was devastated by the captain's unexpected death.

To others he could appear cold and aloof. Beatrice Heays hints at a snobbish disdain of those he felt to be his intellectual inferiors, and recounts with disapproval that once, travelling across the United States, Guthrie-Smith demanded — and paid for — an entire railway carriage to himself in order to avoid fellow passengers. John Haliburton, now retired to Napier, knew Guthrie-Smith from the age of ten and remembers him as 'one of nature's gentlemen'. Haliburton, who became a stockman as soon as he had a couple of dogs, recalls the local dog trials and dance nights in the woolshed which stood between Lake Tutira and Lake Waikapiro. Some revellers, arriving in gigs and on horseback, would stay overnight at the homestead. 'Guthrie-Smith and his wife were great hosts,' he says. 'People helped each other in those days and Tutira was a warm spot.'

Guthrie-Smith was less accommodating to those he suspected of artifice. Woodhouse, his biographer, recounts the fate of a stranger who rode up late one day, assuming lodging would be offered, and feigned an interest in botany. The woman, whose name Woodhouse tactfully surrenders to the mists of time, cajoled Guthrie-Smith into showing her his pressed fern specimens. After much persuasion he relented. Courteously, patiently, he set each page before her, not moving to the next until she had made a suitable comment. It was almost midnight when Guthrie-Smith put the last dried plant away, and the guest finally could stagger off to bed. 'Well,' he said when he found himself once more alone with his wife, '*she*'ll never trouble us again.'

It would be wrong to portray Guthrie-Smith merely as a farmer who happened to be a bird and plant enthusiast. He was alert to the nuances of nature, and particularly to the changes brought about by colonisation — what he called 'the minutiae of the grafting of one civilisation upon another'. Self-taught, he became a leading authority on New Zealand plants — not in the arcane world of classification, which he left to ardent specialists, but in what might be called the sociology of plants. His was one of the early voices calling for conservation of New Zealand's native flora and fauna. When the first society for forest and bird protection was founded about 1915, Guthrie-Smith was a leading member. In 1923, when the precursor to the Royal Forest and Bird Protection Society was set up, he was one of the three inaugural vice-presidents.

While many academic zoologists were studying bones and skins from the comfort of their offices, Guthrie-Smith was enduring the rigours of the field, painstakingly piecing together natural history based on the observations of living organisms.

His crowning achievement came in 1921 with the publication of *Tutira*. Subtitled 'the Story of a New Zealand Sheep Station', the book is an unlikely amalgam of, among other things, geology, geography, history, meteorology, animal husbandry and botany. It has insights akin to those found in Thoreau's *Walden*, and mirrors the stylistic audacity and inclusiveness of *Moby Dick*. Totalling more than 440 pages in its third edition, and replete with photographs, line drawings, maps, tables, lists, swelling footnotes and even the results of a bathymetric survey of the lake taken by the future Bishop of Waiapu, it is unique in New Zealand writing — in world literature. Hailed as a classic on publication, *Tutira* is, above all, an intricately layered biography of the station. It is as though Guthrie-Smith had sunk walls of

glass into the earth along the boundaries of his land, divining the history of New Zealand's settlement, its economy, its distant geological past, its culture, from a close scrutiny of nothing more than what he had contained.

'From the moment a strange sail bosoms towards a new country, that country's transformation is inevitable,' he wrote. *Tutira* charted those changes. Guthrie-Smith was fortunate to have settled in Hawke's Bay at a time when the effects of European colonisation were accelerating, and to witness what he called 'a later and greater trek of living things'. He marked the waves of animal and plant migration, his 60-year vigil giving them the quality of fleeting clouds in time-lapse photography. Alien predators such as stoats and ferrets darkened the landscape with the shadow of their destruction, dislodging native species and altering the web of life for ever. Ironically, weasels arrived in Hawke's Bay before rabbits — the cure, as Guthrie-Smith quipped, before the disease — and moved on without trace.

Meanwhile, farmers grew anxious to detect the anticipated invasion of rabbits. 'There wasn't a sheep-farmer in the province who could not produce rabbit-droppings from his waistcoat pocket, who would not tremblingly request his friends to smell 'em and affirm they were hares' or lambs' or sheep — anything, in fact, but what they were.'

Immigrant birds such as thrushes, mynahs and magpies, freshly released in New Zealand cities, found their way to the station by following coastal routes, the ridges of ranges, river valleys or road cuttings, according to their habits and needs. Plants arrived and, under the watchful eyes of Guthrie-Smith, revealed the changing pattern of the country's commerce: Chili grass registered the flourishing trade with South America, Bermuda grass the transfer of troops from India, Californian stinkweed denoted dealings with the United States, Cape barley the exchange of goods with South Africa.

He described the spread — the 'pedestrianism', he called it — of wayfaring plants as they advanced in stages across the countryside, seeding then re-establishing themselves, hitching a short ride on a roadworker's shovel here, the wheel of a dray there, taking advantage of an accommodating mane or hoof, a warm, sheltering stomach. Instinctively, his gaze fell on the things others ignored or trampled underfoot, elevating the striving of mere weeds to heroic proportions: 'To my backwoodsman's heart there is indeed something austere, distinguished even, in the brotherhood of weeds. They are the MacGregors of our artificial highlands seizing as of right . . . conditions they must yet despise.'

Guthrie-Smith was well placed to mark the changes. When he arrived,

Tutira was home to 35 species of bird and more than half of New Zealand's native ferns. Thanks to accidents of geology, the station, at the centre of a narrow funnel between one fertile belt of land running up from the Wairarapa and another leading down from Waiapu and Poverty Bay, lay in the path of a double current of migration.

Prefacing *Tutira*, he wrote: 'Should its pages be found to contain matter of permanent interest, it will be owing to the fact that the life portrayed has for ever vanished, the conditions sketched passed away beyond recall.' Reading it afresh, I marvel at its brimming footnotes, its spirit of enquiry, its monumental scope.

By the third, and much enlarged, edition, Guthrie-Smith was well known. His writing, increasingly outspoken in defence of conservation, had helped sound the wake-up call over New Zealand's declining wildlife. The Minister of Internal Affairs even came to Tutira to discuss Guthrie-Smith's plans for forest preservation. Yet he did not live to see the new edition published. Just short of his 80th birthday, Herbert Guthrie-Smith had a heart attack and was confined to bed. He had been tending rhododendrons when it happened, and shifting heavy stones about in what had become a favoured spot: the rock garden.

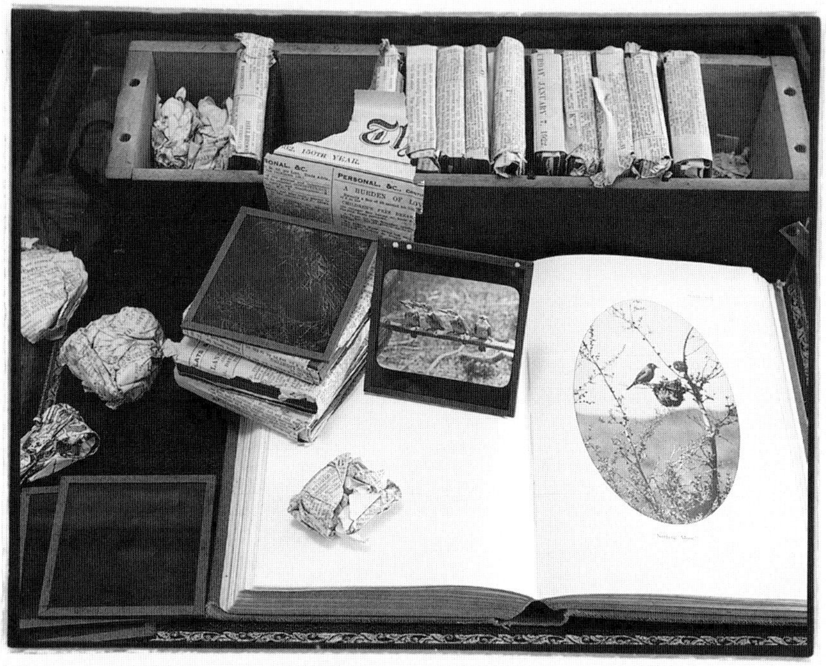

Three days later, on the afternoon of 4 July 1940, he died. The way we would all like to go: untroubled and pain-free, laughing. In the company of his daughter. 'I always dreaded the failings of old age for him,' she confessed. 'But he never grew old.'

Oliver Duff, editor of the *Listener*, described his death as a public calamity, and Guthrie-Smith himself as 'not so much a man as a voice — a voice expressing the sorrows and joys of the earth that we in New Zealand know . . . His field was one small patch of land on which *Homo sapiens* was no more and no less interesting than the weasel or the rabbit, so that *Tutira* is literally New Zealand speaking . . . He noted things as Darwin and Fabre noted them — looked at them, examined them, brooded over them; looked below, above, and around them; got them into focus; established their connection with other things; found what they meant, and still would mean to himself and to generations who would come after him; and not till he really knew what he was saying did he put his knowledge into print.' Eulogies appeared in the British papers, including *The Times* and *Daily Telegraph*, and the world's pre-eminent scientific journal, *Nature*.

Driving back from Tutira, I take State Highway 2 through the Urewera ranges toward Opotiki, imagining newly arrived chaffinches coming at me above the road, following recently cleared farmland and the thread of rivers — Guthrie-Smith's 'lines of sight'. Seeing the landscape come alive with these lattices, these networks of creaturely migration, I realise his enduring gift. Like all true artists, Guthrie-Smith had the ability to make new things familiar, and turn what we so long have taken for granted into something rich and strange.

April 1995

Illustrations

Poet of All His Tribe: James K. Baxter

As the inland scenery slid past the curtained window of seat 6a, CAR U, I leaned back absently, watching and not watching trees, scrub, a distant jawline of alps. The pinned hover of a hawk under sullen cloud. Having attended to some business in Picton, I had caught the afternoon train south. Now, around me, CAR U and the coupled carriages fore and aft yielded little more than a whispering turbine hum as they followed the double steel of the rails, imposing on the act of travel an insulated comfort.

Upon the upland road
Ride easy, stranger

On the broad table before me, resting with the unadorned utility of a clay vase, was a hefty 656-page *Collected Poems* — the poet's name branded on its jacket in chunky letters the colour of rouge: James K. Baxter.

For years Baxter has been a travelling companion of mine. No, not quite. Since my student flatting days Baxter the poet, the outcast, the straggle-bearded, bare-footed instrument of God, has formed part of the fabric of my world. His poems — or rather the flavour of his poetry, its take on life — added to the sleepless Greek chorus in my head, the chorus that at times of emotional salience weighed in (and still does) with quips, admonitions and advice.

Surrender to the sky
Your heart of anger.

That is part of the pull. Then there is Baxter's fidelity to what is out there. More than any other New Zealand poet he nailed the startling physicality of nature, its raw high-revving immediacy: 'Groper with throats like buckets'; 'Quartz-eyed barracouta'; 'The iron legs of the kina'; walnuts 'Round and hard, the shape of a man's scrotum'; 'Fat flesh of the terakihi'.

And all that in the space of twenty lines.

Such attention to the world's wiring may be the flip-side of Baxter's mythologising impulse. When everything is seen in terms of an *über*-reality, and when the field of God is extruded unexpectedly into the everyday — a guiding star, a burning bush — it pays to attend to detail. Such habitual awareness came easily, instinctively, to Baxter. It gave the poetry tang and reach. Later in his writing there came to be an almost constant traffic or interchange between the mundane and the informing world of the spirit.

What would Baxter have seen out there in the spooling landscape beyond the carriage glass? A raptor, perhaps, at the moment of stooping. The vee of its wings frozen as the imagined eye of the beholder sweeps around it (I borrow from *The Matrix*). Then a flash of angel as the bird sweeps down, its talons those of the bitch-goddess.

That's how it is with Baxter. The profane and the sacred mixed. He is all aggregate — in life as in art. It is no more possible to leave the man out of the poems than to hold back salt from a tear.

Approaching Kaikoura, CAR U's speakers announce the prospect of spotting seals on the sea margins to our left. A few passengers who are not reluctant to show an interest in such things peer out at the hard-edged rocks. There, a sleek black body. Two . . . three. Someone on the far side of the carriage catches my eye. A smile flickers.

Mermen and merwomen
Ruled by the moon.
Some forty lay
Like boulders on the boulders. Others played
Through seaweed corridors, beyond the surf,
And a strong smell was in the air

That is what Baxter had to say on the subject after a family outing to the seal colony on Otago Peninsula (he carried pencil and notebook everywhere). From an early age poetry began to shape his life and it was never to desert him. Even through the self-imposed poverty of his sojourn at Jerusalem on the Whanganui river late in his life, poetry kept him rich (the very fact of that richness he found at once frustrating and inescapable). At a time of renunciation and privation, it was the one thing he could never leave alone.

Baxter was prolific. Prodigious. Everything went into the poems — he counted it a poor week when he hadn't written three or four — and, unlike many poets, the 'I' of the text was always close to Baxter himself. In that sense, the poetry was confessional. But then, Baxter was also overtly a player of roles. He continually recast himself: as maker of ballads, romantic rebel, man of the people, prophet, outcast, 'hairy nuisance'. Jokerman. Holy fool. He was New Zealand's Bob Dylan.

We still have Dylan. Regrettably, perhaps inevitably, for a good many years we have not had James K. Baxter.

Born in Dunedin on 29 June 1926, Baxter inherited from his father an indomitable moral courage — Archibald, a conscientious objector in World War I, wrote a harrowing yet surprisingly restrained account of his suffering, *We Shall Not Cease*, published when James was thirteen. Archibald's ability to recite swathes of the output of his literary hero, Robert Burns, also surfaced in his son. Through his life, Baxter astounded friends and acquaintances with his effortless recall of other people's poetry.

Then there were the clan connections. His paternal forebears were

Highlanders from Rothesay on the Isle of Bute in the west of Scotland. His grandfather's family arrived at Port Chalmers in 1861 — the Otago settlement having been established by the Presbyterian Free Church of Scotland — and with strong, honest hands they set about building a new life. They were Baxter's true tribe: 'Those Gaelic-speaking men and women, descending with their bullock drays and baggage to cross the mouth of what is now the Brighton river; near to sunset, when the black and red of the sky intimated a new thing, a radical loss and a radical beginning.'

Having such an attractive and ready-made myth to hand made Baxter's job easier, or at least supplied his path towards a poet's vocation with a useful gradient. The earliest bards — the reciters of the Bible, the Veda, the Homeric epics, the Icelandic sagas — occupied themselves with the great theme of tribal identity. They recalled past struggles, celebrated warrior valour, told why the tribe believed what it did and acted the way it did. In the words of writer John Updike, they were 'part of the living tribal fabric, the part that voices what all know, or should know, and need to hear again'.

Baxter willingly shouldered that burden; he seemed born to it. But his tribe grew to include those on the perimeter of society: alcoholics, the homeless, drifting youth, Maori. His staff was to be Christianity, his destination the Holy City, Jerusalem.

During the long, tortuous journey, he would cut and stitch the myth to suit his purposes. He moved in a parallel world, ignoring much that went on around him and inflating the rest to overwhelming significance. 'What happens is either meaningless to me, or else it is mythology,' he once said.

It was a demanding, often damaging, course to take, one that relocated heroism (of sorts) in the present, giving it a new face and a hard adversary.

Father, is it easier to fight
The military machine, or the maggots of one's own heart?

Baxter's struggle against those maggots — alcoholism, infidelity, religious doubt — distilled his best poems.

There was, too, the social heart. Archie had named his eldest son Terence after Terence McSwiney, the martyred Lord Mayor of Cork. James carried the 'K.' in token of the British socialist leader Keir Hardie, the first working-class member of the House of Commons.

Archie's disobedient pacifism got the family a hard time from neighbours in the post-war Dunedin suburb of Brighton, but that same pacifism had brought James K. Baxter's parents together — literally. Millicent Amiel Brown was given a copy of a letter Archie had written as a conscientious objector. It was a letter of such profound integrity that Millicent was immediately won over by it, and when she came to New Zealand after the war she made a point of searching him out.

Millicent was an extraordinary woman in her own right, the daughter of John Macmillan Brown, a founding professor of Canterbury University College, and Helen Connon, the first female graduate with honours in the British Empire.

Baxter had little use for the patrician inheritance that she represented — much of his life was spent rebelling against it — but it was from her that he derived the self-assured manner, and the poetic tone, that so readily marked him out. It was from her father, the inexhaustible lecturer John Macmillan Brown, that he acquired (or was inspired to hone) the capacity for sustained eloquence.

Baxter had the usual sort of childhood. He was perhaps more serious and distracted than most, though open, amiable and mischievous. He got on well enough with other children but developed a deep distaste for school. He later recalled the punishment for poor spelling meted out by 'a tough young lass with a black moustache'. Baxter passed muster, thanks to his avid reading, but the farm boys, deprived of books and obliged to milk the cows before school, fared badly.

'I remember one big mother's boy with a running nose going up for his dose of leather morning after morning . . . This early initiation into the rites of sadism gave me an insight into myself and others.'

In the essay where he recorded that memory, 'Notes on the Education of a New Zealand Poet', he confessed that 'the sense of having been pounded all over with a club by invisible adversaries is generally with me, and has been with me as long as I can remember'. As a five-year-old, he had felt as if he were 'a young calf being trodden underfoot in the infant school stockyard'.

So what, for Baxter, was the ideal education?

'Perhaps — till ten years old, on a farm in the South Island mountains or the Urewera country, learning to handle a horse and a dog and a gun; then for a year or two, during puberty, in a Maori pa; then perhaps on the coastal boats.' Better that, to his mind, than transformation into a peon for the 'dreary empires of economic liberalism'.

It was an impractical vision with a breath of Highland romanticism blowing through it, but no less appealing for all that. And, as ever, there was a lurking fear of eroded freedom. He was to recommend heartily the novelist Samuel Butler's rallying call to filial independence, *The Way of All Flesh*.

Throughout his life — even when, as a teacher, he did a spell at the chalk-face himself — Baxter disliked institutions. The reaction against authority, stoked by the suffering of his father, eventually swelled to the proportions of a phobia, producing immoderate outbursts and the occasional bitter doggerel against what he regarded as tools of oppression.

Nor was the intellectual life of the university exempt. Rather unfairly, Baxter saw that too as closing up the mind — unfairly because at one time or another he studied, taught or held fellowships at most of New Zealand's universities, and they were unfailingly supportive of him.

Baxter drifted through a succession of schools — Brighton primary, of course, and a school in Wanganui run by the Society of Friends. An interlude at Sibford, a Quaker boarding-school in the Cotswolds, during a trip 'Home' where the family soaked up European culture (lost on Baxter) and traced its Highland roots. King's High School in Dunedin.

All the while he read and wrote, made the usual clumsy adolescent forays into sexual territory, and dwelt darkly on death. Several poems from this time find their way into the collected edition of 1979, but the real work began in 1944 when he enrolled at Otago University College.

Baxter soon became known as a poet, his work appearing in the student newspaper, *Critic*. He won the Macmillan Brown prize for poetry with a long piece called 'Convoys', which was liked by some — the *Otago Daily Times* printed it in full — but criticised by one reviewer for its tendency to 'lapse into philosophy'.

During his first year at university Millicent, ever energetic and ever mindful of her son, took Baxter to the Caxton Press in Christchurch. They had travelled up to see Terence, who had been interned at a camp for conscientious objectors in Shannon — how parents influence — and they made time to call on Lawrence Baigent at Caxton. Baigent was filling in for Denis Glover, then serving in the Royal Navy, and like Glover he was to become a good friend. More, he became for Baxter a gateway to the larger literary world. Surprised at the quality of Baxter's poems, Baigent immediately accepted them. The collection was published early in 1945 as *Beyond the Palisade*.

Even before they were out, fellow poet and anthologist Allen Curnow was after them for his *Book of New Zealand Verse 1923–1945*. The

discriminating Curnow was full of praise. 'It seems to me that since Mason in 1923, no New Zealand poet has proved so early his power to say and his right to speak', he wrote in his introduction.

At one bound Baxter had joined the front rank of New Zealand writers. Poets R.A.K. Mason, A.R.D. Fairburn and Curnow and writer Frank Sargeson had all been published by Caxton, which was building a reputation for showcasing artists with important things to say about New Zealand society.

Soon enough, Baxter began to 'flow like a river into the gulf of Bohemia'. He got casual work at a foundry, on a dairy farm and as a labourer on Wanaka station. He frequented pubs and grills and the rooms of girlfriends. He wrote. He spent time at a freezing works.

Such jobs, physically demanding but easy on the spirit, suited him. His reckless way with women didn't. The day came when he got badly burned, branded, by love. More than once over the next few years he returned to the memory of the young woman, Jane Aylmer, trying to work through the hurt, dissolve the pain of his torn relationship.

In the 1966 sequence 'Words to Lay a Strong Ghost', he wrote:

They've bricked up the arch, Pyrrha,
That used to lead into
Your flat on Castle Street — Lord, how
I'd pound the kerb for hours,

Turning this way and that
Outside it, like a hooked fish
Wanting the bait but not the barb —

Baxter the leviathan was wary of hooks.

In his forties Baxter was still mulling over the adolescent wound. 'When a woman I loved youthfully and ineptly, with my head and heart and prick, went away with somebody else, the poems, the real poems, grew like a bunch of grapes inside the hole where my guts had been severed,' he wrote at Jerusalem.

It was an enduring motif: woman as muse and temptress, bitch-goddess and destroyer.

Another motif, another destroyer, was the bottle. Several times Baxter was found rolling drunk at the back of the Brighton bus. More than once he spent the night at a bus shelter within walking (or rather lurching) distance of his house. His parents encouraged the distant rural labouring jobs as a way of drying him out.

From Wanaka station he told his mother that he thought he could do without women (he was at the time doing without drink). They didn't attract him as persons. 'So I stand back with a nice smile and my heart in the highlands . . . Good for poetry. Not so good for marriage; [but] the split between wife and art comes to all artists.'

Who knows what his rock-steady mother made of that. His father, a man in thrall to a great cause, might have got closer to what came next: 'The gentle and intricate music of the normal social pattern is not the music at the heart of poetry, which is the wind, pollen-bearing, infinitely desolate and all-embracing.'

As always, Baxter was being unflinchingly honest. In this case, he was also flagging the difficult road ahead.

Even as he nursed the loss of Jane, he had befriended the woman who was to become the most important person in his life: Jacquie Sturm, a Taranaki Maori with an interest in psychology, then studying at Otago. For 20 years or more the none-too-steady poet was to try dancing with her to society's 'gentle and intricate music'.

A house. Children (Hilary and John). A day job. Respectable friends.

All that lay ahead when Baxter celebrated his 21st birthday in fine style, and much after the manner of his drink-besotted Welsh hero Dylan Thomas, by entering the Prince of Wales hotel 'on my hands and knees, dead sober, and barking at the ulcerous Scots barman'. He was thrown out on the street.

In Christchurch, where Baxter and Sturm had separately gone (one ostensibly, the other primarily, to attend university), he fell in with Glover, Fairburn, Curnow, the editor Charles Brasch and others.

He had taken his bad habits with him. Glover recalled arriving at the Caxton Press some mornings to find Baxter 'sitting on the doorstep in a very good severe Anglican frost . . . wearing some sort of hugger-mugger coat, no doubt stolen from the St Vincent de Paul's Society, and eating a crayfish'. The old salt found the 'cherubic, innocent-faced, baby boy from Otago' utterly addicted to alcohol and easily the most troublesome friend he had ever known. Baxter was a shameless borrower of money and often gave the Caxton printers a hard time, badgering them to get his books off the press faster.

A friend, visiting his Merivale flat one day, found him asleep between filthy mattresses, surrounded by empty cans and a half-finished tin of baked beans. The poverty, which was becoming second nature, also counterpointed his relationship with Sturm. They lived off milkshakes, pies and soup. When the money was not there, they did without.

It was a lifestyle that couldn't last.

Salvation of sorts came in the shape of something Baxter had been prodding with a stick for a while: formal religion. His 1948 collection, *Blow, Wind of Fruitfulness*, introduced a new element into his iconography — the betrayal of Paradise. The loss of Eden.

In 'The Bay', an idealised past is established in memory: a quintessential New Zealand location of sandstone cliffs and Maori ovens. A place to race boats and swim in amber water.

So now I remember the bay and the little spiders
On driftwood, so poisonous and quick.
The carved cliffs and the great outcrying surf
With currents round the rocks and the birds rising.
. . . I remember the bay that never was
And stand like stone and cannot turn away.

The poem signalled a surrender to, or at least an embrace of, mythopoeic Christianity. Characteristically, it was the Fall, not the device of redemption, that struck a chord, the conviction that man was 'a moral being whose suffering proceeds from his denial of the light of conscience within him'.

One day in 1948, Baxter turned up at Baigent's house wanting shoe polish. He was off to St Michael's, an Anglo-Catholic church, to be baptised. A photograph of the time shows him standing outside the church, cigarette in mouth, hair swept back from his youthful face. Symbolically, he wears his trademark greatcoat back to front. Baxter the 'turncoat'. He was on the path to Catholicism.

In December 1948 he and Sturm married.

He genuinely seems to have thought it could work, that love papered over the cracks could shore up his life. Two decades of heartache followed as he stumbled aimlessly in a 'Cretan labyrinth/Of money, conscience, work, glum dreams'. For a time the keen edge went from his poetry. He ricocheted from job to job: teaching, subbing on a newspaper, editing at the Department

W. McKaskell

of Education's School Publications branch. Treading the streets as a postie — or arguing some point in a Wellington bar, while the disregarded mail floated in beer. By his own account, he was relieved of that particular job after being found asleep dead-drunk with his head on a bag of undelivered letters in the Karori post office.

On occasion he would travel to Auckland, hanging out with his printer mate Bob Lowry. Once, they got drunk for a fortnight, 'stuck at the bar like two octopuses in an aquarium'.

'To want to be a good man is one thing; to want to be a good poet is another,' he wrote to his parents. 'I hope they are not incompatible, for if so I may well not make the grade.'

It was not, however, a time of unmitigated darkness. In 1954 Baxter joined Alcoholics Anonymous and two years later he began taking instruction from a Marist priest at St Mary of the Angels in Wellington. They were significant conversions. He warmed to AA's belief that alcoholism was a disease not a moral failing, and from the organisation got his first taste of the healing power of community. From Catholicism — Baxter wryly called it his 'fire insurance' — he drew the comfort of certainty, a ladder across the void. The austere Trappist monks at Kopua taught him that prayer, poverty and sharing were the best antidotes to the failures of modern life.

There were outward successes with his art, too. Baxter had by now built a solid reputation as an orator and critic, whether ranting to revellers at a dissolute party or addressing a gathering of literati (which sometimes amounted to the same thing).

Pat Lawlor, a later confidant of Baxter's, noted their first meeting, at the New Zealand Writers' Conference at Canterbury University in 1951. Baxter was clean-shaven in those days, his profile smooth as a cameo. With some awe, Lawlor wrote in his diary: 'His voice had a violin quality and . . . he revealed a lambent, percipient mind. When he finished speaking there was a palpable hush, and then the applause sounded out strongly and continued undiminished for nearly a minute.'

The occasion was Baxter's landmark address on 'Recent trends in New Zealand Poetry' — delivered with impressive eloquence to academics and writers — in which he hammered out old Macmillan Brown's theme that a writer's job was to speak the truth to a society gone astray.

By 1968, however, he had done with trying to reconcile his dual life: that of the family man and what he called the 'convict self'. The failure was prefigured in the poem 'Tomcat', where the Baxter of home and hearth observes his wild twin, the tough, mad scrapper, source of scars and poetry:

> *the old fool*
> *stood, body hard as a board,*
> *heart thudding, hair on end, at*
> *the house corner, terrible,*
> *yelling at something. They said,*
> *'Get him doctored.' I think not.*

Baxter thought not. Instead, the man who had applied for, and got, the prestigious Burns Fellowship at Otago University (and the next year renewed it), the man with eleven books of poetry and criticism under his belt, much of it groundbreaking, a man with wife and family, friends and work, walked out of his tidy life. Baxter, who in 40 years hadn't 'found a cure/For being human', went north.

He went alone. Since their marriage he and Sturm had not always lived together. Now the separation was to be more or less permanent. Fleeing from a domestic 'pattern of death', one which he sensed was slowly rubbing him to 'an armless legless headless stump', the newly bearded poet steered towards the Whanganui river, hoping — willing — the direction to have been God-given.

It was this later Baxter, the author of *Jerusalem Sonnets*, *Jerusalem Daybook* and *Autumn Testament* — three broadcasts from the frayed outer edge of life — that I had come to Christchurch to learn more about.

The Picton train reached its terminus after dark, and I caught a shuttle to a friend's house overlooking the Avon river. Having unloaded my gear, I stepped out into the crisp night air and walked a few blocks through suburban streets to a place called 'Under the Red Verandah'. It was a two-storeyed weatherboard building on a quiet street corner, the lower half taken up by the café that gave the place its name.

From the side street, a wooden gate opened onto a yard framed at one end by an old, weather-beaten shed, once a butcher's, that now earned its keep as an artist's studio. Towards the rear of the main building, in the closed café's kitchen, I found the owner, Roger Hickin.

Tall and trim, pared almost to an ascetic alertness, Hickin greeted me warmly and showed me up a flight of stairs to a big wooden-floored room lightly furnished with desk, bookcases and a clutch of sofas. The walls were hung with articulate, muscular art — some of it Hickin's own. I was lucky to catch him, as it turned out. He was due to leave the next day for Auckland, where an exhibition of his work was about to open at a dealer gallery.

Settling down, we started talking about Baxter straight off, as though he had just then left our company, as though any minute he might swing that unmistakable head of his back around the door jamb to dispute, to encourage or merely to throw in a shard of snappy metaphor.

Hickin had grown up in Dunedin and Otago, the part of the world Baxter came from. The poet's early writing was all about the places Hickin loved, and as a teenager, had seen them largely through the eyes of the older man.

The two met in April 1970, when Baxter returned to Dunedin for the première at the Globe theatre of a play he had written, *The Temptations of Oedipus*. The nineteen-year-old Hickin had earlier journeyed to Jerusalem ('Hiruharama' to Maori) to unburden himself to Baxter about military service and to get advice (he was approaching the age of call-up). Finding Baxter absent, he had stayed briefly at the nearby pa.

At the Globe, Baxter was receptive and encouraging. 'He said, "Well, if you decide to get out of the concrete shithouse [university], come up and see me,"' Hickin told me. 'So I did.'

For two months Hickin lived with Baxter and two others in a two-room farm cottage owned by the neighbouring Sisters of Compassion. Visitors drifted in and out during those two months, but no one else stayed. It was early days. Baxter was still setting the trap to catch his community of lost souls, his tribe: Ngati Hiruharama.

For a while few people even knew what Baxter was up to. News was slow to filter out. When Hickin first tried to hunt him out he had called Jim Henderson, only to be given the vague information that Baxter was sleeping 'under a bridge somewhere' on the Whanganui river.

Hickin bedded down in the same room as Baxter, an arrangement that he often found exhausting. 'He used to go to sleep talking and wake up talking.' Then there were the dreams. Baxter's head was home to the most surreal nightlife, which he made a point of sharing the next morning with anyone who would listen.

Even more extraordinary, to those who knew him, was Baxter's openness. 'Young people in the 1960s found it incredible to come into contact with someone like that. As a schoolboy you were regarded as a species of vermin. So to meet an adult who understood what you were going through . . .' Hickin shook his head. 'He had this uncanny ability to pick up on what was happening inside you.'

Hickin was frustrated, though, by the way Baxter could articulate so well what he himself was fumbling to express. 'He recognised it as a fault he had. Sometimes the realisation would strike him and he would just stop mid-sentence and say "glub, glub, glub". Then he'd hop around the room on one leg and flap his arms.'

Baxter often delighted in the ridiculous spectacle of himself.

The days at Jerusalem were often spent doing small jobs. Fitful gardening. Improvising something about the house or working on a makeshift repair. Baxter padding up the road in bare feet with a shovel to help a road gang. Playing cards.

'He seemed to divide up his day quite consciously. A lot of time was spent writing — he was always writing letters.' Typically, Baxter preferred corresponding with strangers who had problems to keeping in touch with friends.

He was often in the company of the local Marist priest, Father Wiremu Te Awhitu. A remarkable old man — Baxter called him 'the Maori angel' — Father Te Awhitu had been shunted off to the backblocks after suffering a stroke which impaired his speech. When the community at Jerusalem grew, the priest set aside a room in the presbytery where Baxter could write undisturbed. In return the poet often preached the homily.

Baxter had renounced material things on the road to Jerusalem and that included books. His motto: 'Kaore nga pukapuka.' No books.

'I thought, it's all right for you, you bugger. You've read them all,' said Hickin.

That was no doubt true. Baxter was well read and had a retentive memory, so he had less use for texts — one of the few things he brought with him to the river was a Maori Bible. There was also vanity in such an extravagant gesture of denial — as he well knew. In a consummate sonnet to an old friend, he wrote:

Colin, you can tell my words are crippled now;
The bright coat of art He has taken away from me

The art of this poem, and of the entire sequence published in 1970 as *Jerusalem Sonnets: Poems for Colin Durning*, gives the lie to such a notion. Baxter's attempts to staunch the flow of his own words were doomed.

Elsewhere, he wrote: 'The man called James K. Baxter, who is like a dead body in the ground, swells up and gives off a stink of words. I suppose he does it for the money and kudos. It is absurd to say I am really a poor man while I keep on putting words together . . .' Baxter then indulged in a piece of wistful doublethink worthy of a commissar: 'best for me to write my words, and then forget what I have written. Dead leaves do not clog a stream for ever.'

He may have tried earnestly to forget, but he nevertheless despatched the poems with due care to Durning, who saw them through the press.

Hickin remembers the printed copies of *Jerusalem Sonnets* arriving at the cottage, and Baxter handing him one. The 39 sonnets (Baxter had hoped for 50) marked something new in the poet's work. Rhyme was no more — it had been on the way out for a while — and, though the poems kept to the fourteen-line sonnet form, the line length varied almost casually. There were no more attempts at a clever twist of meaning, no concluding 'thump' to turn a piece on its end. No convoluted abstractions. Instead, the poems relied for their power on the cadences of ordinary speech, on closely observed detail and on the sudden starbursts of vivid imagery. They represented the culmination of his determination to build poems using 'many stones but not much mortar'.

As Vincent O'Sullivan noted, they had about them 'the very qualities of Baxter's own talk . . . the same tone of personal address . . . of a man chatting, reminiscing, explaining'.

What he was explaining, in not much more than 500 lines all up, was

Jerusalem before the flood — before the deluge of disciples, bludgers, drop-ins; before the unstoppable tide of friends, health inspectors, the police and the pressing ranks of the plain curious.

In the cottage, Baxter slept with a picture of the Curé of Ars — the French priest and prophet — on the wall.

Gently he smiles at me when I undo my belt

And begin to hit my back with the two brass rings
On the end of it

Penance, worship, the endless struggle to climb out of 'the ditch of ownership'. He waged a war against spiders, employed disinfectant against small fiery tormentors:

'Do You or don't You expect me to put up with lice?'

He made his way barefoot across thick wet grass at two in the morning to kneel in prayer at St Joseph's church. Dug a lavatory, hidden from the eyes of the nuns by 'a great fort of bracken'. Lost the struggle to give up tobacco — 'I confess that I need a smoke/More than I need a woman!' Harvested watercress and ripped out couch grass to plant garlic, sunflowers. Said his rosary.

And over it all hung the leaden apocalyptic sky of Judgement.

Baxter's response was submission.

Let the Maker of rainbows and mountains do what He wishes
With this poor idiot, this crab in His beard

Who will not be dislodged — becoming, as it were,
Available is all my science

Jerusalem's attraction for Baxter lay in the fact that it was Maori, Catholic and rural. All three were at the core of what he considered fundamental to establishing a community of neighbours — as opposed to what was widespread elsewhere: a society of strangers.

In particular, Baxter was drawn to Maori spirituality. He shed his own name, signing himself 'Hemi', the Maori equivalent of James. His thirteen-year-old son John became Hoani.

'God, give me a Maori heart,' he prayed.

The glue for Hemi's tribe was to be love of the many. Aroha.

A drawing by Baxter survives which shows the five principles he thought

should underpin his community. They are inscribed on the five fingers of a sketched hand: to share goods; to speak truth; to love one another and express it by the embrace (the famous Jerusalem hug); to take no job 'where one has to lick the boss's arse'; to learn from 'the Maori side of the fence'.

These principles, which amount to a social manifesto, have their roots in a trip Baxter made to India on a Unesco Fellowship in 1958. Undertaken while he was an editor at School Publications, the visit threw him into collision with subcontinent-sized inequalities and injustices that profoundly affected him and which, years later, were to haunt the pages of *Autumn Testament*. Both the scale and the intensity of the suffering Baxter witnessed pushed him towards an increasingly engaged social activism. It was the spur for, among other things, his rescue work with junkies in Auckland, and his attempt to set up Narcotics Anonymous there, before being drawn south to experience a new kind of vulnerability on the banks of the Whanganui.

After two months, Hickin left Jerusalem for Dunedin to be with his girlfriend. In December they both returned briefly. By then Baxter's tribe had grown to eleven and over the summer the numbers mushroomed. In May, 40 people were living there, and on one memorable evening some 80 sat down to eat. Most were young — between seventeen and 25 years old. Baxter was tolerant even of those with dubious motives — 'jewels hidden in a ball of mud'.

Baxter by then had use of a semi-derelict building he called the top house, which Father Te Awhitu had earlier busied himself with by putting up new posts for the collapsed verandah, and another called middle house. All were strewn with sleeping bags, clothing and the carry-in trappings of rootless youth.

The late 1960s were a time of social experiment, but a commune headed by a bohemian poet with a penchant for the shock effect of lewd poetry, who saw swearing as necessary 'salt' and whose stand on promiscuity was ambiguous, was bound to attract attention.

'In early 1971 one of the Wanganui newspapers, a redneck rag, gave Baxter a hard time, printing things about hygiene and underage girls,' said Hickin. 'Baxter was very careful about who he let stay. Underage girls he would pat on the knee and tell them to bugger off. There were no drugs. No alcohol.'

Nor were there the people with the skills or determination, the vision, to make the commune sustainable. Work was unevenly shouldered. There was much talk, much idleness as the sun arced across the sky. Winters were cold. Food was often meagre and poorly cooked.

Gradually Baxter's brave new world collapsed. Imploded. Finally he was asked by locals to leave. Perhaps it was for the best. He made abortive plans for a new commune in Auckland's Takapuna. Stayed with Sturm in Ngaio for a time. Camped in a three-storey Wellington squat.

In February 1972, however, he was back at Jerusalem, having voluntarily restricted the numbers to ten or fifteen to appease the locals. In this more cohesive group he found the energy for a new collection, *Autumn Testament*.

As with his other Jerusalem books, *Autumn Testament* presents a carefully edited take on his time there. Baxter's groove was myth, after all. Nevertheless, in its mix of poetry and prose it manages a deeper authenticity. The collection was intended for Sturm, and early on she enters the heart of it:

I have seen at evening
Two ducks fly down
To a pond together.

The whirring of their wings
Reminded me of you.

Reminded Baxter of the woman he loved, evoked her as a scent evokes. But also paraded unity of purpose, a togetherness, that he had failed to achieve.

The rest is largely an elaboration of the daily ordeal of 'overcoming the hard rind of the ego' in order to serve God, 'the dark Master'. 'I would not advise any man to follow him. He comes like the sandstorm out of the desert, or the avalanche on a mountain village, or tons of black water from the depths of the sea,' Baxter wrote in *Jerusalem Daybook*.

And in *Autumn Testament*:

Our life is the one
We make in darkness for ourselves.

'The feeling he had in late adolescence of standing on the edge of the abyss never left him,' said Hickin. He was quick, though, to correct the distortions of zealous disciples and of Baxter's own authorised version. 'He had an enormous appetite for life and a wonderful sense of humour. Always, with Baxter, you find yourself saying "He was one of the most . . . I've ever met" because he was larger than life in so many ways.'

Before I left Under the Red Verandah, Hickin told me of his journey from Wanganui to Jerusalem in the winter of 1970. For one reason or another — transport is infrequent on the river road — he ended up walking almost all the way. 'It was one of the most significant experiences in my life,' he said. 'It plays into my artwork even now.'

Baxter had also covered barefoot miles. Once when he returned to Jerusalem his feet were badly blistered from the hot asphalt: 'The life of the streets dug in,/Taking charge. I thought my feet were rotting.'

He healed himself by boiling bark and soaking in the water. But he couldn't heal the commune, even in its lean reincarnation. A lifetime of poor food and physical hardship had left him weak. The failures at Jerusalem had knocked his spirit.

'In a sense Baxter was one of those who were always old. He was talking of being an old man even when he was in his thirties. He went on long fasts. He offered himself up to people,' said Hickin. 'The poetry he wrote in those last three years — that would have been a vocation in itself. He wore himself out.'

Days later, I drove up Cashmere's winding roads to the roof of Christchurch to talk to someone who had enjoyed a long, close friendship with Baxter, who had witnessed the slow descent of his last days. Jennifer Barrer was at her small cottage surrounded by vibrant flower gardens and a sizeable pond — the remnants of a three-hectare family estate.

The day we met a fire was burning in the hearth. Outside and far below,Christchurch sprawled across its plain, bordered by a distant string of snow- frosted mountains.

Between Barrer's family and Baxter's there were old connections and associations. Her father, Brian Amhurst Barrer, had been a pallbearer at

the funeral of John Macmillan Brown. Millicent's sister Viola went to art school with Barrer's grandmother, Grace Butler. In fact, the Barrers were part of a community of artists, writers and academics on the Cashmere Hills. Her mother once went out with writer John Mulgan, author of *Man Alone*. Barrer herself knew the poet R. A. K. Mason and spent time with Mervyn Thompson before he became a theatre director. The two had talked of starting a theatre group in Christchurch.

Barrer, who had studied drama under Ngaio Marsh, in those days balanced school teaching and acting. When he was a teacher, Baxter had mailed his children's poems for her to try out on her primary class.

Barrer was playing the role of Sonya in the Globe's production of Chekhov's *Uncle Vanya* years later when she got the first intimations that all was not well with Baxter at Jerusalem. He was due to lecture at the Globe the following day and wanted desperately to talk. He had got into bad habits that he couldn't escape from. He talked of hallucinations and wondered if he were going mad. In a subsequent letter he wrote of a 'fear of real and imaginary demons when I put the light out'. He spoke of 'a sense of one's utter useless absurdity'.

Baxter's relationship with Barrer was characterised by honesty and unwavering commitment. At one low point in her life, when she hit emotional heavy weather, he had written: 'It's no good blaming oneself for having been born. Perhaps you have to know and suffer out what other members of your tribe have failed to know. It will look like falling down to them. But it need not to you.'

When Barrer became pregnant in 1964, he encouraged her to leave Christchurch to have the baby (he became godfather) and start afresh. 'Jim described it as a "Flight into Egypt",' said Barrer. 'He was very supportive and it was wonderful getting his letters.'

Baxter's generosity to so many individuals over so many years came at a price. 'I felt there was an element of abuse in what happened,' said Barrer. 'He was famous and a lot of people took advantage of him.'

In one of his last poems, 'The Tiredness of Me and Herakles', Baxter wrote:

Today I smashed a green hydrangea bush
With a walking stick
At the edge of somebody's private lawn.
Every leaf was the head of a friend.

He had moved to Auckland, where he was living in a Mount Eden commune run by an old friend. Wracked by self-doubt, he inhabited a hall of shifting mirrors. For weeks he saw a psychiatrist every day, doggedly returning to the unfinished business of his youth.

On 21 October 1972 Baxter went to a friend's place in Birkdale, and asked if he could stay for a few days. That afternoon he worked in the garden. The next day, a Sunday, he complained of chest pains and the friend, Jean Tuwhare, took him to a doctor's surgery. After a consultation, and while the doctor was attending a call-out, Baxter had a heart attack outside. He died later that evening, in the house of strangers across the road. One of the last things Tuwhare heard him say was: 'I have a wife and children in Wellington.'

He was 46.

In the short section 'Te Whiore o te Kuri' (the tail of the dog) which completes *Autumn Testament*, Baxter quotes Thomas Merton:

'At the end of life God presses down a seal
On the wax of the soul. If the wax is warm

'It receives the mark; if not, it is crushed to powder'

'His outward poverty personified the poverty he felt in his own spirit,' Barrer said as I was about to leave. 'In the end maybe the performance became a hanging rope and he couldn't get out of it.'

No doubt.

Yet Baxter seemed compelled to remake in flesh the words that draw *Autumn Testament* to a close:

A man's body is a meeting house,

Ribs, arms, for the tribe to gather under,
And the heart must be their spring of water.

September 2002

Illustrations

Poems

Claudia Orange

Bill Oliver

Makin' Them Dry Bones Dance: *The Dictionary of New Zealand Biography*

Since this piece was written, volume five of The Dictionary of New Zealand Biography *has been published, along with its Maori language companion volume, and dictionary staff have moved to a new home at the Ministry of Culture and Heritage. In December 2001, after two years of development work, another watershed was reached when the dictionary went online. Its website address www.dnzb.govt.nz contains all 3042 biographies from the published volumes, all fully searchable, along with more than 1800 images.*

Tairongo Amoamo rises, pushing back his chair with one foot, and fixes me with a steady gaze.

'Let's talk about a Stone Age man. Born . . . who knows when? Died 1954.' His lips purse. 'How did he travel to a tangi?'

I hesitate.

'He came on a horse,' says Amoamo. 'Rode right up to the marae. He was completely naked apart from a wreath of petipeti leaves on his head. In his hand was his taiaha, his weapon. He entered the marae creeping and writhing like an eel.' Amoamo imitates a snake. 'Now and then he stopped to strike the ground with the taiaha.

'When he reached the body he sat down, and for nine days he stayed there, eating nothing. With each passing day he seemed to those watching more and more to resemble a ngarara — a reptile. Finally, when the wreath on his head was dry and withered, he took it off and cut his hair, laying the leaves and hair in the coffin. The women sitting with the body did the same.

'Those were the actions of your ancestor. His name was Te Pairi Tuterangi, chief of the Tuhoe. He was one of the last links between the old world and the new.'

After a pause Amoamo, assistant editor of *The Dictionary of New Zealand Biography*, reaches behind for the chair and sits once more, his impassioned speech-making at an end. He has done with the story, told for my benefit to demonstrate how the lives that pack the pages of the dictionary can be used in a classroom to draw young Maori closer to their heritage.

It is all there in volume three. The story of Te Pairi, child of the rugged Urewera ranges, a boy dedicated to the war god Tumatauenga at the age of seven, who grew skilled in the warrior's art and who, during the unrest of the 1860s, set aside the traditional taiaha and the toki poutangata (greenstone adze) and embraced the gun.

When the embattled chief Te Kooti retreated to Urewera in 1868, Te Pairi became a fervent supporter, waging war on his behalf as far away as Taupo. During lulls in the fighting he took up woodcarving and horse-racing, his lean build making him a favoured jockey — so much so that songs were composed about him and his horses.

A devout follower of the Ringatu faith, he became a charismatic orator with a style all his own. An imposing figure with his white hair, the beard of a sage and long greenstone ear pendants, he used the marae as a stage, gesturing with his adze, strutting, running with clipped steps and leaping in the air to emphasise his words. On landing, he would nimbly flick one foot back and set off in the opposite direction.

'He never stood in one place, reasoning that it was more difficult for opposing tohunga to direct makutu [harmful supernatural powers] at him,' states the dictionary. 'He usually wore a rapaki (kilt) when speaking, and if he was wearing European clothes he would deliberately remove his shoes, socks and trousers and wrap a blanket around his waist before starting.'

He was fastidious in his daily life, and a strict observer of tapu — to the extent that, if his or someone else's shadow fell across his food, he would immediately stop eating. Partial to an occasional whisky and fond of suits and top hats, he was a fine weaver of feather cloaks and, again wary of makutu, never wore a Maori garment unless he himself had made it.

A firm believer in the old ways, Te Pairi never learned to speak English. In 1927, when in his 80s, he was persuaded to take the part of Te Kooti in the silent film *The Te Kooti Trail*. The following year he played a minor

character in *Under the Southern Cross*, at one point rescuing the film by reciting an appropriate karakia so that other Maori actors would act out the tapu ceremonies demanded by the script.

Reading the dictionary's account of Te Pairi 'The Leaper' Tuterangi, it becomes clear that this is no ordinary work of biography. The tale of the Tuhoe chief, and others like it among the 2500 or so entries published to date, sing with anecdote, with the remembered details that amplify the past until it seems to shimmer before us, the reconstituted slivers of experience becoming so many stepping-stones back to the lives of our forebears.

This mark of lively authenticity stems in part from the decision of the dictionary's editors to move away from what now seems, in previous works of national biography, a misplaced emphasis on public life and the recording of 'worthy' achievements — the commemorative instinct that gave rise in their pages to a seemingly inexhaustible parade of minor politicians, mayors, bankers, headmasters, lawyers and others whose doings for generations swelled the columns of the national and provincial press.

What we have here is a celebration of New Zealand life in all its rich diversity and effervescence.

The person largely responsible for casting the net wider, former editor Bill Oliver, wrote in his introduction to *The Dictionary of New Zealand Biography*'s first volume in 1990 of a determination 'to draw in common soldiers as well as their officers, community leaders as well as politicians, matriarchs as well as patriarchs, followers as well as leaders, entertainers as well as painters, bullock drivers as well as engineers, missionary wives as well as their husbands'. In other words, to add to the familiar mix of dead famous people others who, if not imposing presences in their lifetimes, might at least become 'memorable historical presences'.

A start in this direction had been signalled in England in the late nineteenth century by the work most historians today think of as the blueprint for all such endeavours — the 66-volume *Dictionary of National Biography*. Its visionary first editor, Leslie Stephen, best remembered now as the father of Virginia Woolf, emphasised the importance of 'minute names, the mere rank and file of the great army', and made a claim for the importance of 'amusement' as well as factual fidelity. Among the subjects tackled by Stephen's surprisingly (for the times) broadminded dictionary were sportspeople, murderers, actresses, deviant clergy, agnostics, journalists and transvestites.

The latest instalment of the ongoing New Zealand project, volume four, put together under the watchful eye of general editor Claudia Orange and focusing on the years 1921 to 1940, continues that early favouring of utility, variety, individuality and reader appeal. Between its marbled salmon-pink covers can be found essays on runner Jack Lovelock, prime minister Michael Joseph Savage, rugby great George Nepia and aviator Jean Batten, but also entries on others who would have fallen through the cracks of more sober histories: endurance swimmer Katerina Nehua, for instance, and swagger Russian Jack.

Katerina Nehua's is a moving tale. Born in the Bay of Islands, she fell on hard times early in life and moved to Sydney with her husband and young family in the Depression years. They became destitute when he lost his job and, lured by big prize money, she entered one of the endurance swimming contests then in vogue. The aim was to stay afloat in a pool for as long as

possible without touching the bottom or sides.

To conserve energy, Nehua spent the last of her money taking a tram to the venue, the tidal baths at Manly. Unable to pay for the special grease used by other competitors (including famous English Channel swimmer Mercedes Gleitze), she was coated with a mixture of olive oil and axle grease and entered the water determined to 'stay until they carry me out'.

After more than 47 hours in the choppy water, and showing signs of distress, she was helped out ahead of the only remaining swimmer, Gleitze, who was so taken by Nehua's courage that she shared her prize money. Nehua went on to set new world endurance records, including one of 72 hours 21 minutes in Brisbane.

Barrett Crumen, one of the last of the old swaggers, remains something of a mystery to this day, despite the determined attentions of the dictionary.

Reportedly born in Latvia, and later known to all as Russian Jack, he made a dramatic arrival in New Zealand in 1912 aboard the steamer *Star of Canada*, which encountered a violent gale off the East Coast and was blown ashore at Gisborne. Nothing is known of his family, and doubt surrounds even his name. 'Crumen', says the dictionary, may merely have referred to his shipboard occupation, while 'Barrett' apparently had no meaning to him.

It appears that, having narrowly survived the shipwreck, he decided to save money by walking to Wellington, where, presumably, he intended signing on with another ship. He never got there. At some point on the journey he heard the siren call of the road and spent the next 53 years obeying it, tramping through much of the North Island — though avoiding Hawke's Bay after experiencing its 1931 earthquake.

Squat and tanned and sporting a sagging moustache and wide-brimmed felt hat, Crumen was a familiar traveller on country roads, with sugarbags and kerosene tin billy over his shoulders, and his patched clothes stuffed with paper. He took to wadding his ears with brown paper soaked in mutton fat as protection against the cold and 'to keep the bugs out'. In the early days he had removed his boots when leaving a town, walking through the countryside barefoot to save leather. In later life, however, he let the habit slip, lining worn boots with cardboard and patching them with leather and car-tyre rubber. At the height of his artistic make-do his boots together weighed more than eight pounds (3.6 kilograms). Life under the southern stars did Russian Jack surprisingly little harm. He died after a short illness in 1968 at the age of 90.

Biographical nuggets abound among the almost 13,000 biographical files which have accumulated in the dictionary's downtown Wellington offices. 'We have a gold-mine here,' says Orange, who is also acting chief historian at the Historical Branch of the Department of Internal Affairs, which runs the project. 'We just hope it doesn't develop into a quartz-crushing exercise.'

It is unlikely that even such an unhappy turn of events would slow things much at the dictionary. From her orange-walled office — well, the colour just happens to be her favourite — she runs a tight ship. The marshalling of facts (and of people) is second nature to the former university lecturer, thanks to skills honed on a doctorate which, published as *The Treaty of Waitangi*, went on to win the 1988 Goodman Fielder Wattie Book Award (as did volume one of the dictionary in 1991).

'If we publish on time,' one staffer later confides, 'that is entirely Claudia's doing. It is almost unheard of with national dictionaries.' The Italian effort, the *Dizionario Biografico degli Italiani*, as I am reminded more than once, took 35 years and one supplement to reach the letter F.

Orange, who starting work at the dictionary in 1984, becoming general editor six years later, lives and breathes the project. For the first fourteen years she commuted weekly from Auckland, putting an end to the air-miles only in October 1997 when she and her husband Rod, a school principal, finally surrendered to geography and moved south. Often, while he heads for the bush or takes to the water, she stays put, making sure history turns out the way she likes it — accurate and accessible.

A latecomer to higher education herself, having been a school dental nurse and mother of three children before starting university at 30, and one

of the first professional historians to learn Maori, she has an in-built drive to democratise history.

This is reflected in the process as well as the product. An enormous number of people have become caught up in the dictionary — more than 1000 writers alone. And not just academics, but music specialists, radio people, engineers. Anyone and everyone.

She and her team are determinedly telling history like it is. Among the surprises: the significant contributions amateur New Zealand astronomers have made to the world of science; the way plastic surgeon Cecily Pickerill often withheld her gender from distrustful patients until after an operation; the fact that radio presenter Aunt Daisy (Maud Basham) — mother to a nation — was also a singer, once performing as contralto soloist in *Messiah*.

The scope for things to go wrong with the dictionary juggernaut is enough to crack the strongest constitution. With seventeen regional and specialist working parties to co-ordinate, in-house workflows to juggle and, in the case of the newly published volume four, the labours of 417 writers to check and hone meticulously, an intricate organisational structure has evolved — one Oliver called 'more complicated than the Vatican'.

By the time the fifth volume appears in 2000, one of New Zealand's largest publishing ventures, and the most substantial work of history yet undertaken here, will have been going for seventeen years. At that point, and in obedience to an implacable law of nature, the project will drastically scale down. The simple reason for this can be found in the answer to a query by Robert Muldoon when the dictionary was first mooted. 'What do I have to do to get in?' he wanted to know. 'Die,' was the frank reply.

The former prime minister will, of course, 'get in', but it may take time. With the dictionary entering the 1940s and 50s — 'snapping at our heels', in the words of the publicists — a problem has arisen, thanks to the way subjects are selected. A candidate's place in the chronological series is determined by when they first 'flourished', by which dictionary folk mean the date they first made their mark. It is conceivable that someone — a potter, say, or a trade unionist — who did significant work at an early age in the 1950s will be hale and possibly even hearty well into the new millennium. The natural buffer of these long-lived early achievers gives the dictionary a built-in lag.

'We have all become hearse-chasers,' says assistant editor Ross Somerville with an amused grin. For Somerville and his colleagues, each fresh obituary brings with it the possibility of introducing a new candidate to the lengthening subject list or giving a previously favoured one the green light for a write-up.

The prospect of the brakes coming on as the dictionary catches up with history in the making does not faze him. Publication of the fifth volume is, he says, the obvious point at which to go electronic. Somerville, who joined the project ten years ago as a researcher, soon gravitated towards editing, and one day woke to find himself responsible for computer operations. Since then he has overseen the transfer of all data to a sophisticated searchable database that holds out the possibility of accessing the dictionary's data in ways undreamed of by the nib-wielding Leslie Stephen.

CD-Roms are one possibility. Another, with more lasting potential, is Internet access to the data, which may come to include newly discovered material and currently unpublished biographical files as well as video, sound and still images. Given that people tend not to read at length on-screen, says Somerville, the information could be presented in summary, with details layered underneath, the whole being searchable by keyword. The trick, he says, is to future-proof the data by anticipating new needs and emerging technologies.

Meanwhile, the quiet, machine-like hum of a dictionary under way continues. Assistant editor Nancy Swarbrick, who functions as a sort of literary chief engineer, introduces me to the repositories of the project's real wealth: its banks of filing cabinets, locked against earthquake, each of which is jammed with files. She opens a drawer and lifts out a worn manila folder, leafing through it to reveal photographs, correspondence and a 1000-word draft typescript, heavily marked with blue pencil. I note that the author, a professor known for his well-turned phrases, has not escaped lightly.

Contributors often assume that only one editor sees their work. In reality each essay is read by up to twelve staff, culminating in a read-through by Bill Oliver, now retired and acting as consulting editor. He likens the process to chain slaughtering as opposed to solo butchery. 'I think his father was a freezing worker,' says Swarbrick helpfully.

No fact is free from scrutiny. As if to underscore the point, I am told of a staffer who once leaned out of an office window to confirm the number of storeys in a nearby building. 'Normally our research is a little more rigorous,' Swarbrick says, apologetically. Sometimes, however, the survival of one 'fact' over another comes down to a judgement call over conflicting sources.

One useful innovation, forged in the white heat of research, has been a device called the NAF, the Name Authority File. Introduced after volume one, and the result of impressive labour, it is an assemblage of index cards charting the changing identity of New Zealand organisations. Invited to test-drive it, I pick something I had trouble with recently — the name in 1919 of what is now New Zealand Post. A quick flick through the cards and there it is: 'Post & Telegraph Dept 1890–1959. Fr 1959 Post Office.' Never, as I had read somewhere, Postal Department. Anticipating argument, the NAF cites New Zealand Statutes, the *Appendices to the Journals of the House of Representatives* and Post & Telegraph Dept reports.

Such exactitude can test the mettle of those in the field. 'Some die for their country,' veteran contributor Frances Porter told me, only half in jest, 'others work for the dictionary.'

On a wall at Dictionary HQ is a whiteboard marking the progress of the essays through the various edits, rewrites and proofs — Maori subjects in green, others in red. Maori memoirs are tracked separately because they are destined for a further stage, translation into Maori. From the beginning, a parallel Maori-language publication, *Nga Tangata Taumata Rau,* has been issued, which collects together all the Maori subjects from the main dictionary. The Maori biographies from the first and second volumes have also been published in English as *The People of Many Peaks* and *The Turbulent Years,* and selected essays from the first Maori volume as *Mapihi Kahurangi.*

Given the dictionary's aim of bringing the information to the broadest possible range of readers, the whole thing has become something of a micro-industry, with an illustrated *People's History* derived from volume one appearing in 1992, selected essays from the first two volumes emerging as *The Suffragists: women who worked for the vote* in 1993, and *Te Kingitanga,* a book on the King movement, hitting the shelves in late 1996.

Tairongo Amoamo's preoccupation, since joining the dictionary in 1988, has been with piecing together the Maori biographies and getting them out in Maori. It has not been easy. Maori lives are not well documented, with births, deaths and marriages often going unrecorded. Then there is the difficulty of finding the people with the knowledge. The dictionary relies heavily on family writers — people knowledgeable about their whakapapa and able to work confidently with senior members of a whanau.

Nevertheless, for a culture where mana is often held collectively rather than being associated with individuals, sensitivities have sometimes meant switching off the light of scholarship. This was the case with an essay commissioned for volume two which revealed that a prominent community leader was the natural child of a rival group leader. It was felt that public revelation of this would have undermined the leadership of the current generation and possibly torn their community apart. The essay was dropped.

A Maori working party chaired by Tipene O'Regan has lent important support to the work of the dictionary. Faced with calls from descendants to suppress information because it denigrated the mana of ancestors, the working party's response has usually been to say, 'We are writing history, not accolades.'

More often than not, however, oral evidence gathered by the dictionary has unearthed treasures absent from earlier written records. Tuhoe writer Pou Temara's essay on Te Pairi Tuterangi reveals how warriors were trained to use the taiaha. Another from Ngai Tahu describes the methods of southern muttonbirders and the traditional uses of river and sea resources. Amoamo himself gives a fresh account of the methods of a Ringatu tohunga.

Even more important for Amoamo has been the role of the dictionary in fostering the Maori language. The most substantial publication in Maori since the Bible was translated in the nineteenth century, the dictionary draws on the skills of editorial staff including Angela Ballara — fluent in Maori and the author of some 22 essays in volume four alone — and outside advisors such as Timoti Karetu of the Maori Language Commission.

Thanks to the broad reach of its subjects, the dictionary has even helped extend the language. Assisted by the Maori Language Commission, staff have coined Maori words for 'thermosphere', 'cardiovascular disease', 'carbon monoxide' and many others.

Nga Tangata Taumata Rau is now used as a source for University Bursary exam papers. 'We are writing for a new generation,' says Amoamo with pride.

Stepping outside, I notice the dictionary's address — Waring Taylor Street — and on a whim look it up in a Wellington library. (Once you get in the groove, everything reduces — or should that be enlarges? — to biography.)

The *Dictionary of New Zealand Biography* (not the present work, but a two-volume compilation dating from 1940) has him covered: Taylor, William Waring (1819–1903). Born in Yorkshire, arrived in New Zealand 1848, became a Wellington merchant. 'Rather retiring in disposition, but a useful citizen and highly respected.' He was deputy-superintendent for the province, a member of the waste lands board, and a capable sheepfarmer who, in the entry's concluding words: 'retired from public life in the eighties, and died on 11 Oct 1903.' No mention that the retirement was occasioned by his being indicted for fraud.

Underscoring the half-century gap between the two radically different publications, the *DNZB* passes over the retiring Waring in favour of his sister, Mary Taylor — feminist, music teacher, businesswoman, writer. Two years older than Waring, she was a close friend of Charlotte Brontë — though not above rebuking the writer for attitudes she considered insufficiently progressive. For example, when Brontë asserted in a novel that work was for some women only, Taylor called her 'a coward and a traitor'. To Taylor, a woman who did not wish to work was 'guilty of a great fault — almost a crime'.

Taylor emigrated to New Zealand in 1845 and opened a drapery and clothing shop. The venture was a success, and in 1853 the shop was listed as one of Wellington's principal stores. According to the *DNZB* entry, Taylor

may have been the first to import a sewing machine to Wellington.

On her return to England, she began publishing articles which developed the feminist ideas she had mulled over in Wellington — that marrying for money was degrading, that women were not duty-bound to sacrifice themselves for others, and that women should earn their own living — and went on to write several books expanding on these views. The independent and forthright Taylor, whom the *DNZB* describes as having a hatred of hypocrisy and a coolness towards religious dogma, certainly appears a more interesting person than 'useful citizen' Waring, after whom the street in the capital is named.

It is perhaps harsh to make too much of the shortcomings of Guy Scholefield's 1940 *Dictionary*. A labour of love, and reverential in tone, it reflects the obituary source of much of the material and was, like all dictionaries, a child of its times. Scholefield never intended the work to be representative of the people of New Zealand. It was to be a record of the country's (mainly political and military) men of note, along with Maori leaders and a smattering of women 'of particular prominence'. Nor did he attempt to evaluate his subjects, reasoning in his introductory 'On the Practice of Biography' that 'Estimates of the significance of a man in the history of the country must inevitably change with the passage of the years; but the facts of his life, once they are accurately ascertained and recorded, cannot change.'

He might have said with Dickens's Thomas Gradgrind: 'Facts alone are wanted in life. Plant nothing else, and root out everything else.' Except that Scholefield himself rooted out a little too energetically. His entry on Dunedin businessman and politician William Larnach skims over much of the financial misfortune that plagued the man and neglects to mention that he ended by killing himself in Parliament Buildings. The account of Presbyterian minister and lobbyist James Gibb fails to note that he was accused of heresy in 1890, and it plays down the intensity of his pacifist convictions after World War I.

'I didn't have much time for Scholefield,' admits historian Frances Porter. When Orange asked her to write him up for the *DNZB*, she was reluctant, arguing that 'it is easier to work with the absolutely, positively dead'. Scholefield, the parliamentary librarian, was too close. As a young graduate she had often seen him in the General Assembly Library, and, with his eyesight failing, was brought in to help work on his massive two-volume *Richmond–Atkinson Papers*.

'I was appalled by the way he had edited them,' she says. 'I was trained that primary sources were sacrosanct, but he had added comments in ink and put indelible crayon through sections he didn't want.' Porter later came across a letter in which he explained that, thanks to his work, students no longer needed to 'grub through' the original letters, as they would be available in libraries. 'He thought he'd done a good job in his defacement, but what he called the "discards" were women saying that they didn't want another pregnancy, that husbands shouldn't spend so much time at the General Assembly. History for him was political, it wasn't about tea parties or women slaving away.'

I recollect a passage in his 'Practice of Biography' where Scholefield trusts readers to recognise the efforts he has made to rescue from oblivion people who may appear insignificant, 'particularly those whose activities were confined to the halls of some of the provincial councils, those quaint little parliaments round which the hopes and passions of average New Zealanders centred'.

Like Te Pairi, he stood at the crossroads. 'To a degree, history is a matter of fashion and Scholefield spanned a watershed,' explains Porter. 'He was definitely on the side of the generals. Now the generals have been moved aside and the housewives brought in.'

Almost a third of the entries in the *DNZB* are about women. Among them are people such as Agnes Harrold, manager of the Travellers' Rest boarding house on Stewart Island and unofficial 'bush surgeon' and midwife to the island's few-hundred-strong population during the latter years of the nineteenth century. From the dictionary we learn not only of her medical competence, but also of her forceful character and sympathetic heart. 'She listened to troubles, never spread them and kept her own to herself,' writes contributor Maida Barlow, concluding, 'If anyone deserves a monument on this island, it's Granny Harrold.'

Grace Hood joined the School Dental Service in 1922, when dental decay among school children was common and dentists in short supply. Women trainees were selected 'on the basis of their academic achievement, sound health and pleasing personality'. Appointed school dental nurse in charge of the Waipukurau area, Hood was conducting a clinic at the very moment the 1931 Napier earthquake struck. Still clutching her basin, her young patient took off — with more justification than perhaps she could have hoped for.

In achieving a balance between the sexes, the New Zealand dictionary is doing better than its British counterpart, the *New Dictionary of National Biography* — a monumental revision of a dictionary that has its origins in the 1880s. Editor Colin Matthew and a legion of helpers are working against the clock to revise or rewrite the *Dictionary of National Biography*'s 36,000 entries and add a further 14,000, for a staggering total of some 50 million words in 50 or so volumes, all to be published in 2004.

The old *DNB*, even with its voluminous supplements of 'missing persons' unintentionally omitted from the main work and ten-yearly (later five-yearly) 'interim notices' on the recently dead, was notoriously short of female subjects — around three percent of the total. Matthew admits that his revision is unlikely to reach the *DNZB*'s target of at least 20 percent women. Even addressing the domestic circumstances of male subjects is proving difficult.

'To integrate fully the home and sexual life of a person who is, as most are, in a DNB for "public" reasons, requires space, and space equals money and time,' he has written. 'But this incorporation is perhaps *the* central challenge for DNBs of our time.'

When I visited the *New DNB*'s offices in Oxford — an elegant eighteenth-century building in St Giles — Matthew was full of praise for the New Zealand project, and not just because of its inclusiveness. 'They are doing fundamental primary biography there,' he said. 'Carving a trail through the woods.'

Gratifying as the commendation may be, Claudia Orange complains that the British editors are 'pretty mingy about who they let in from down here'. Apart from editing the homegrown product, she is the *New DNB*'s associate editor for twentieth-century New Zealanders, and finds herself arguing hard for the inclusion of even major figures.

But Matthew is philosophical, envisaging a time when, with the click of a button, a reader of the online *New DNB* can switch from its entry on, say, Sir George Grey, to Grey's entry in the New Zealand dictionary. 'Perhaps it will be the final act of Her Majesty to link up the dictionaries of national biography in all her realms past and present,' he says with mock grandiosity. If so, he adds, they may collectively come to embody *DNB* founder George Smith's original vision of a comprehensive *Universal Biography*.

Sheila Robinson's mind is focused on matters closer to home. She is one of the New Zealand dictionary's seventeen working party convenors, charged with seeing that her region is accurately and adequately represented in its pages. Dunedin-born but having called Gisborne home for 28 years, she writes from a house surrounded by nearly a hectare of tranquil gardens and decorated with images of the countries she and husband Robbie once sojourned in as Colombo Plan workers.

Gisborne is one of the smallest and most isolated areas covered by the dictionary — two hours of hill-country driving to Opotiki and six, as Robinson is quick to point out, to the university libraries in Hamilton or Palmerston North. Appointed convenor for the East Coast because of her work as historian and archivist at the Gisborne museum, she overcame the meagre supply of local academics by recruiting researchers through subsidised labour schemes, donating her own fee (from volume three on, convenors received a modest honorarium) to the museum.

The group's job was eased by several published local histories and an enthusiastic local newspaper which printed requests for information. 'The main difficulty here was often what generation to settle on. Take the Williams family, for instance. I did an entry on four cousins, all descendants of Bay of Islands missionaries Henry and William Williams, who each had twelve children. Who do you choose? In the end I decided on one who became Minister of Works, because of his national prominence.'

Which brings Robinson to the fate of regional centres in this country. 'What tended to happen here is that we had outstanding early pioneers, but as the population grew and travel got easier we lost a lot of our top achievers. Gisborne became a service centre for a district that relies on farming and horticulture. People tend just to be good citizens.' Dictionary folk in Hawke's Bay and Nelson agree, she says. 'Look at my own family. Four sons with degrees and not one of them ever likely to work here.'

Keen to salute the pioneers, Robinson wrote *Gisborne Exposed*, a celebration of local photographer William Crawford (1874–1913), for the 1990 sesquicentennial. Crawford, a hearty, fun-loving bear of a man, captured provincial life exquisitely on hundreds of fragile glass plates, two-thirds of which are now in the local museum collection — and, yes, Robinson helped him into volume two of the dictionary.

Her great-great-grandfather, James Hamlin, however, has not made the cut. 'He came out in 1826, and almost always worked alone, in the Manukau and the Waikato. In 1835 he became the first permanent missionary in Wairoa.' And there it is again: a reminder of all those files in Wellington, waiting for something more inclusive even than the print dictionary — Somerville's microprocessor wizardry, perhaps — to bring them to life.

Peter Lineham, a Massey University lecturer, is convenor of the working party on religion. 'With 600 entries per volume, it became clear that, no matter how good they were, we wouldn't get more than 30 people in,' he says. Before getting down to some serious 'horse trading' with Orange, Lineham meets colleagues to debate who should be put forward.

'It's like the religious wars all over again,' he says. 'Some groups are very keen. The Baha'i, for instance, and the Jewish community. One of its octogenarians set about writing, apparently convinced that every Jewish person in the country was worth an entry.

'We've just pulled off an interesting case for volume five though,' he announces with glee. 'Sidney Koreneff. A female French resistance fighter who later became an Anglican priest.' I have to admit, it doesn't get much better than that.

The joy of discovery — of lives 'rescued' from the rubble of neglect, or simply raised up for a new generation to appreciate — permeates the pages of the dictionary. Even the descriptive tags beneath the names have a certain allure: 'Pedlar, importer, viticulturist', 'Furnisher, singing teacher, composer, astronomer', 'Boatbuilder, rugby player, tourist guide', 'Woman of mana, suffragist', 'Shearer, lay reader, wrestler'.

Begin this last entry and you enter the world of Ihakara Te Tuku ('Ike') Robin, Hawke's Bay shearing contractor and, during the 1920s, a legend on the wrestling mat. Born in 1886, Robin was blessed with a marvellous physique — in his 20s he stood over 1.8 metres tall and weighed 108 kilograms — and had the mental and physical agility to make him a superb sportsman. In one Napier sports day he took part in the shot put, hammer throw, caber toss, high jump, tug of war and two types of wrestling, winning many of the events and collecting £26 in prize money.

He was a 300-a-day shearer who eventually employed 100 men in his contract gangs, and offered work and board to homeless Maori. His wife, Mei, ran gangs of her own, working the coastal stations of central Hawke's Bay and others as far inland as Taihape.

In 1926, Robin took only three rounds to defeat the Australian heavyweight champion, Clarence Weber, and became so well known in this country that a patented wire-strainer for fencing was named the 'Ike Grip'.

A deeply religious man, Robin served as a lay reader in the Anglican church for nearly six decades and was a friend and advisor to the first two Maori bishops. He met royalty on behalf of Hawke's Bay Maori and once entertained the Trapp Family Singers. An enthusiastic preacher, he once became so absorbed in his message that he failed to notice the congregation had departed, leaving only his dog to hear him.

A singular zest and appetite for life was also the hallmark of Rangi Kuini Wikitoria Topeora, an important figure in Maoridom during the first half of the nineteenth century. One of only five women to sign the Treaty of Waitangi, Topeora gained prominence as an orator, singer and composer of waiata.

Four marriages and a string of other relationships suggest a woman whose passions matched her pride as a leader among the Ngati Toa. Nor did she shrink from violence or brute strength to settle matters. When she discovered that her husband was having a liaison with a slave on Kapiti Island, she had the woman killed and eaten. Another time, she competed against a Te Ati Awa woman for the right to marry a man by outrunning her and throwing a dogskin cloak over her male prize.

Initially a supporter of the Treaty, she later denounced Pakeha settlers in Otaki — and harvested rebuke from an old chief, who declared she was no better than a dog's daughter. The chief, who went on to compare the benefits of peace — pigs, potatoes, tobacco — with the discomforts of war, appears to have won the day, but it is the fiery Topeora who is remembered.

Though *The Dictionary of New Zealand Biography* is in the business of preserving, and even of rescuing 'lives', it has also, in rare instances, been known to radically alter them, and nowhere to greater effect than with Edmund Bohan. Put off a career in history by the academic in-fighting he witnessed while taking a degree in Christchurch, Bohan left for Britain, where he pursued his other love, singing. For 26 years he did the oratorio circuit, occasionally appearing in operas as guest principal and, thanks to a big repertoire, notching up some 600 concerts as principal tenor with a rising impresario.

Bohan's eventual return to New Zealand in 1987 coincided with the preparation for volume one of the dictionary. Bill Oliver, one of his former lecturers, was short of a writer for one of the early politicians, Edward Stafford, and suggested Bohan write 3000 words. 'I'd only been working on it a few days when I realised there was a colossal gap in nineteenth-century political history,' Bohan says. 'No one knew much about him. Sinclair had dismissed Stafford in a good but unfair sentence.'

I later look up the passage in Keith Sinclair's *A History of New Zealand* and laugh aloud. 'E.W. Stafford, a man with no obvious qualification except a conciliatory manner, was Premier on several occasions for a total of a dozen years, while giving always the impression of wishing to be elsewhere,' Sinclair had written.

Bohan ended his own dictionary piece on Stafford with an oblique return salvo. 'He was a pragmatic, down-to-earth, successful politician,' he wrote. 'For common sense and clear-sighted ability he must rank as one of the most effective of all.'

When Claudia Orange took the dictionary's helm for volume two, Bohan was invited to contribute pieces on a further five late Victorians and, with the help of a research grant, also wrote a full-length biography of Stafford, published in 1994. It was, says Orange, the first independent fruit of the dictionary project.

Other biographies followed, and now Bohan divides his time between (less frequent) singing engagements — 'mostly character roles, which befits an elderly tenor' — and writing.

Unable to leave the thing alone, I take a last look at volume four, chancing on Bernice and Doreen Lumley (1921–39). Dark-haired identical twins, they showed early promise in athletics, swimming, tennis and basketball. In 1938, Doreen represented New Zealand in track events at the British Empire Games, and the following year in Auckland competed against the unbeaten Australian gold medallist Decima Norman over 100 yards. In a spectacular race on uneven ground Doreen won, equalling the world record of eleven seconds. She was just seventeen. Bernice, who usually finished some three yards behind her sister, came fourth.

On 1 October 1939, the twins were killed in a fatal collision with a truck.

Their deaths shocked sportspeople across the nation, with more than 1000 paying their respects at the funeral.

I am surprised to discover that they went to school just up the road, less than a kilometre away. But then, it's that sort of dictionary. And New Zealand is that sort of place.

November 1998

Illustrations

Further Reading

The list below is intended as an introductory guide to useful sources. Many of the books include extensive bibliographies for more detailed study.

George Grey

Oceania, J. A. Froude, Longman, London, 1886

The Life and Times of Sir George Grey, KCB, W. L. Rees and L. Rees, H. Brett, Auckland, 1892

Sir George Grey, Pioneer of Empire in Southern Lands, G. C. Henderson, T. M. Dent, London, 1907

Sir George Grey KCB, 1812–1898: A Study in Colonial Government, J. Rutherford, Cassell, London, 1961

To Be a Hero, Edmund Bohan, Harper Collins, Auckland, 1998

Joan Wiffen

Valley of the Dragons: The Story of New Zealand's Dinosaur Woman, Joan Wiffen, Random Century, Auckland, 1991

Edmund Hillary

The Ascent of Everest, John Hunt, Hodder & Stoughton, London, 1953

High Adventure, Edmund Hillary, Hodder & Stoughton, London, 1955

High in the Thin Cold Air, Edmund Hillary and Desmond Doig, Hodder & Stoughton, London, 1963

Schoolhouse in the Clouds, Edmund Hillary, Hodder & Stoughton, London, 1964

A Yak for Christmas, Louise Hillary, Hodder & Stoughton, London, 1968

Edmund Hillary: The Life of a Legend, Pat Booth, Moa Beckett, Auckland, 1993

Jean Batten

Solo Flight, Jean Batten, Jackson & O'Sullivan, Sydney, 1934

My Life, Jean Batten, Harrap, 1938; reissued as *Alone in the Sky*, Airlife, Shrewsbury, 1979

Jean Batten: The Garbo of the Skies, Ian Mackersey, Macdonald, London, 1991

Felix von Luckner

Count Luckner, The Sea Devil, Lowell Thomas, Doubleday, Doran, New York, 1928

The Sea Devil's Fo'c'sle, Lowell Thomas, William Heinemann, London, 1930

Out of an Old Sea Chest, Felix von Luckner (trs Edward Fitzgerald), Methuen, London, 1958

The Sea Devil, Carl Rühen, Kangaroo Press, Kenthurst, 1988

Richard Pearse

The Riddle of Richard Pearse, Gordon Ogilvie, A. H. & A. W. Reed, Wellington, 1973

Suzanne Aubert

Never Let Go!: The Remarkable Story of Mother Aubert, Pat Rafter, A. H. & A. W. Reed, Wellington, 1972

The Story of Suzanne Aubert, Jessie Munro, Auckland University Press, Auckland, 1996

Herbert Guthrie-Smith

Birds of the Water, Wood & Waste, H. Guthrie-Smith, Whitcombe & Tombs, Christchurch, 1910

Mutton Birds and Other Birds, H. Guthrie-Smith, Whitcombe & Tombs, Christchurch, 1914

Tutira: The Story of a New Zealand Sheep Station, H. Guthrie-Smith, William Blackwood, Edinburgh, 1921

Bird Life on Island and Shore, H. Guthrie-Smith, William Blackwood, Edinburgh, 1925

Sorrows and Joys of a New Zealand Naturalist, H. Guthrie-Smith, A. H. & A. W. Reed, Dunedin, 1936

Guthrie-Smith of Tutira, A. E. Woodhouse, Whitcombe & Tombs, Christchurch, 1959

James K. Baxter

Jerusalem Sonnets, James K. Baxter, Bibliography Room, University of Otago, Dunedin, 1970

Autumn Testament, James K. Baxter, Price Milburn, Wellington, 1972

Jerusalem Daybook, James K. Baxter, Price Milburn, Wellington, 1972

Collected Poems, James K. Baxter, (ed. J. E. Weir), Oxford University Press, Wellington, 1980

James K. Baxter: A Portrait, W. H. Oliver, Port Nicholson Press, Wellington, 1983

The Life of James K. Baxter, Frank McKay, Oxford University Press, Auckland, 1990

Picture Credits

All references to the Alexander Turnbull Library, National Library of New Zealand Te Puna Matauranga o Aotearoa become ATL. Auckland War Memorial Museum becomes AWMM. Museum of Transport Technology & Social History becomes MOTAT. All unacknowledged images belong to the author.

George Grey
cover © Photographer: Edmund Wheeler & Son fl 1872–1914, ATL, PA2-1895
p.12 © ATL, 1/2-00508 7
p.23 © Auckland City Libraries (NZ)
p.30 © Fletcher Trust Collection
p.35 © Auckland Art Gallery, Toi o Tamaki
p.37 © ATL, 1/2-C-023299;F
p.38 © AWMM

Joan Wiffen
p.40 © News Media (Auckland)
p.42 © Michael Schneider
pp.44 & 50 *The Chain of Life in Geological Time*, Sir J. William Dawson, The Religious Tract Society, London, 1885
p.46 *Valley of the Dragons: the story of New Zealand's dinosaur woman*, Joan Wiffen, Random Century, 1991
p.49 © Paul Fisher
p.54 © Joan Wiffen

Edmund Hillary
p.58 © ATL, 1/2-020196; F
pp.64 & 67 © AWMM
p.77 © Royal Geographic Society, London

Jean Batten
pp.80, 89, 90, 93 © MOTAT
p.82 © ATL, New Zealand Free Lance Collection, C-1377-1/2
p.97 © ATL, G. Patterson, PAColl-0889-1
p.99 © *The Weekly News* (*New Zealand Herald*)
p.104 © The Herald and Weekly Times Photographic Collection
p.106 © Malcolm Shea

Felix von Luckner
p.108 © Bildarchiv Preussicher Kulturbesitz, photographer: F. Langhammer, 1925
pp.110, 113, 115, 130 © AWMM

pp.117 & 124 © Royal New Zealand Navy Museum
p.126 © News Media (Auckland)
p.127 © *New Zealand Herald*
p.128 © Air Logistics

Richard Pearse
p.132 © News Media (Auckland)
p.137 © Mr & Mrs Pearse, Timaru
p.138 © South Canterbury Museum, 1999/131.1
pp.144, 147, 149, 152 © MOTAT
p.157 © *Southland Daily News*

Suzanne Aubert
p.158 © ATL, PAColl-6181-22, taken by Joseph Zachariah (1867–1965)
pp.161, 164, 168, 170, 173, 175, 177, 178, 180, 185 © Sisters of Compassion, Island Bay
p.176 © ATL, Eph-A-Pantomime-1894-01-opp5

Herbert Guthrie-Smith
pp.186, 188, 190–91, 192, 194, *Tutira: The story of a New Zealand sheep station*, Herbert Guthrie-Smith, Godwit, Random House, 1999 (first published 1921)
pp.196, 199, 201, 203 © Gretchen Absalom
p.204 © Arno Gasteiger

James K. Baxter
p.206 © ATL, F-58011-1/2
p.209 © Gary Blackman
p.213 © Archives New Zealand/Te Whare Tohu Tuhituhinga O Aotearoa, Head Office, Wellington: National Publicity Studios Photographic Collection, ATL, F154591/4 (A16659)
p.215 © *Otago Daily Times*
p.217 © W. McKaskell, ATL, F 31258 1/2
p.226 © *New Zealand Herald*

The Dictionary of New Zealand Biography
p.230 (top) © The Dictionary of New Zealand Biography/Claudia Orange
p.230 (bottom) © The Dictionary of New Zealand Biography/Bill Oliver
p.233 © ATL, F-30871-1/2, Sister Anne Henry Collection
p.235 © ATL, MS-Papers-2754-7-1, Katerina Nehua Collection
p.236 © ATL, PA12-2130
p.238 © ATL, F-46733-1/2, PAColl-0785, New Zealand Free Lance Collection
p.243 © ATL, F-170330-1/2
p.248 © ATL, C-23402-1/2, PAColl-5671-37, Auckland Star Collection